MONOGRAPH PUBLISHING ON DEMAND
SPONSOR SERIES

A COMPARATIVE ECONOMIC HISTORY OF LATIN AMERICA 1500 - 1914

Volume 3: Brazil

By
LAURA RANDALL

Published for
INSTITUTE OF LATIN AMERICAN STUDIES
COLUMBIA UNIVERSITY
by
UNIVERSITY MICROFILMS
INTERNATIONAL
1977

Produced and distributed *on demand* by
University Microfilms International
Ann Arbor, Michigan 48106

Library of Congress Cataloging in Publication Data

Randall, Laura Regina Rosenbaum.
    A comparative economic history of Latin
America.

    (Monograph publishing on demand : sponsor series)
    Bibliography: v. 1, p.   ; v. 3, p.
    Includes indexes.
    CONTENTS: v. 1. Mexico.—v. 2. Argentina.—
v. 3. Brazil.—v. 4. Peru.
    1. Latin America—Economic conditions—Collected
works. 2. Comparative economics—Collected works.
I. Title.

HC121.R36 1977   330.9'8   77-81283
ISBN 0-8357-0273-1 (v. 3)

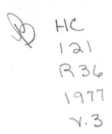
TABLE OF CONTENTS

LIST OF TABLES

LIST OF MAPS AND ILLUSTRATIONS

CHAPTER 8

BRAZILIAN COLONIAL ECONOMIC HISTORY

The African Background

The greatest African contribution to the economic development of the Americas was, of course, the labor of the millions
of slaves and their descendants, who performed all, most, or
a very large share of the physical work in the many colonies
and successor states of Atlantic America from Maryland to La
Plata, as well as most of the domestic services, and in Brazil, a large portion of the skilled craft labor. Also enor-
mously important was the large complex of plants brought from
Africa, many of which became staples of subsistence and commercial agriculture in tropical America.

What was there in the African background that made possible the greatest cycle of forced labor in all history? The
traditional white racist view was that Africans were a race
peculiarly fit for slavery in the American tropics, being
strong and docile, resistant to the tropical sun and diseases, used to heavy field labor and to slavery itself, and
capable of no higher station in life. The last allegation
can be dismissed out of hand; the rest are at best over-
simplfications. The Africans were on the whole taller than
many other peoples, including the Indians of tropical America,
but one cannot prove that they were stronger. Most slaves
lived out their lives without actually rebelling, but there
were so many instances of resistance, some in Jamaica, Haiti,
and Brazil on a very large scale, that there is no case for
believing that Africans were more docile than any other group
of forced laborers.

The dark melanin in the skin of Negroes inhibits the
damage that would otherwise come from long exposure to the
tropical sun. The normally ectomorphic physique of Negroes
(slim bodies, long limbs) is well suited for the release
through evaporation of excess body heat in the tropics. But
Mongoloid peoples whose physical peculiarities are adapta-
tions to cold climates have flourished in tropical East Asia
and America, and white peoples have successfully occupied
much of torrid Arabia and India. Resistance to disease was
very important. Modern research has made it clear that Old
World diseases were the chief factor in wiping out 90 per
cent, 95 per cent, and even 100 per cent of the Indians in
many parts of America, a catastrophe that created the demand
for the import of African slaves in the first place. Africans were not immune to diseases, but since they had come,

like the Europeans, from areas within the Old World disease
pool, colds and measles did not kill them as they killed so
many Indians; smallpox and typhus merely decimated them, while
they annihilated whole nations ōf Indians. Many Africans had
a hereditary blood condition called sickle cell anemia, which
provided some immunity to malaria, but which was so great a
disability at high altitudes that few Africans survived there.
They were presumably more resistant to many other tropical ill-
nesses than were immigrants from temperate Europe. These biologi-
cal conditions made large-scale African slavery possible in
America, but they are not the full explanation.

The question of whether Africans were used to heavy field
labor and to slavery, and were therefore culturally fitted for
the immense American slave trade and plantation system, has
been argued with much heat. Over 95 per cent of the slaves
brought to America came from within 500 miles of the West
African coast running from Senegal 3,500 miles down to Angola.
(Most of the rest came from Mozambique to Brazil in the last
two centuries of slavery.) This is an immense area of more
than 1,750,000 square miles, including the rain forests and
wet savannahs of the Guinea Coast and the Congo, the huge dry
savannah belt of the Western Sudan north of it and a smaller
one in Angola south of it, and the beginnings of the deserts
north and south beyond them (but few mountains that would im-
press an American save for the Cameroon Range). Hundreds of
states and tribes were to be found in this area, including
most known types of human society, which makes generalizations
about the background of slavery difficult.

The total population of Africa in 1500 may have been anything from 10 to 60 million; opinion now inclines to the
higher half of the range. Probably almost half the Africans
then lived near the Guinea Coast from the Senegal River to
Mt. Cameroon or in the Western Sudan behind it, almost a quarter in the present territory of Nigeria alone. This great
West African area, "Guinea" to the slavers, although it is
less than 10 per cent of Africa, provided America with at
least three quarters of its slaves. This concentration of
population near the coast that was nearest to tropical
America was one of the conditions that made so large a slave
trade possible.

Most of the tribes were small, especially south from
Mt. Cameroon to Angola, and lived by some combination of hunt-
ing, gathering, fishing, and horticulture; in many such
groups the women alone did the gardening. Most small groups
had no chiefs or other coercive governmental institutions,
little formal slavery within the group, and little opportunity
to capture and sell others into slavery. Clearly the members
of these tribes were not culturally predisposed to New World
slavery, whether in plantation agriculture so different from

their own mixed economy or in domestic service. Yet hundreds
of thousands were captured and sold across the sea, especially from Angola, where these small groups predominated.

On the Guinea Coast and in the Western Sudan most of the
population was concentrated in large ethnic groups such as
the Yoruba and the Ibos that might number over a million.
Some of these peoples were unified under elaborate monarchies, for example, the Bini and the Congo, and some of these
monarchies expanded into multiethnic empires, for example,
the Ashanti and the Dahomey. The common people in such
states were mostly peasants who practiced a horticulture inten-
sive and extensive enough to approach the agriculture of Europe
and the European-dominated New World, although they usually
used digging sticks and hoes instead of the plows and draft
animals of Eurasia. Most of the monarchies were absolute,
in theory at least. The kings were often like Pharoahs, divine, ritually isolated from their subjects and from the
ground, theoretical owners of all land and animals, possess-
ing large capitals, palaces, bureaucracies, harems, and ritual
obligations, frequently engaged in violent politics and war.
A king who was Muslim, as most were in the Sudan, gave up
divine claims, but little else.

Most of these monarchs held many slaves: household
servants, harem servants, officials, soldiers, craftsmen,
and peasants. So did most of their aristocracies. Slaves
might have been born in bondage, enslaved for debts or crimes,
bought, or captured in war. Although very numerous, slaves
were minorities in all states save a few Saharan oases, where
all the peasants were slaves. And of course kings and private
slaveowners could usually sell slaves abroad, perhaps not
fellow countrymen but certainly prisoners of war. The Sudanese had sold slaves across the Sahara to the Mediterranean
area and beyond since Pharonic times. When the Portuguese
reached the Guinea Coast in the fifteenth century, most of
the kings of Guinea were quick to take the larger profits
that came from direct trade with this Mediterranean market
instead of sharing the proceeds with Sudanese and Arab-Berber
middlemen to the north of them, as had been necessary before.
Then came the apparently insatiable demand for slaves in
America, for 350 years and more. Supply expanded rapidly to
meet demand.

The result was a most turbulent and feverish period in
the economies and societies of West Africa. The slave
trade brought great wealth to the African courts and merchant
groups that managed to stay ahead of the game, and paid for
much of the great cultural outburst in sculpture, costume,
music, and the dance from the sixteenth to the nineteenth centuries. On the other hand, millions of Africans were killed
or exported in the course of slaving wars and operations,

whole villages and districts were depopulated, kingdoms were
destroyed, and many small peoples were dispersed. We have no
precise knowledge of how many slaves actually reached America,
perhaps 10 or 12 million. It is even harder to tell how many
more millions were originally torn from their African homes.
The widely quoted figure that slavery cost Africa 40 million
people is probably an overestimate. Some scholars think the
total population of West Africa remained roughly constant while
slaving losses canceled natural increases; others think it
declined significantly. The total wealth of West Africa
probably increased and certainly became more concentrated.

Native African slavery and the slave trade across the
Sahara were ghastly enough, but it is hard not to believe
that the much larger scale of the Atlantic slave trade, the
commercial impersonality of the great American plantations,
and the extreme racism of the whites in America were not, in
sum, even worse. Some highly placed Africans objected. Two
eighteenth-century kings of the Ashanti legislated against the
overseas slave trade, ineffectively. They and several other
kings refrained from it, until pressed by the necessity to
secure guns by selling slaves. The all-important payment
made by European slavers to African slavers was not the large
quantity of trinkets and rum, but the relatively small number
of guns without which any African state near the Atlantic
Coast ran the grave risk of being conquered by its neighbors
and having its population, peasant and king alike, sold into
American slavery. The despotic structure of most large African states, the familiar and accepted institutions of slavery
at home and slave trade with foreigners, and the willingness
of most African elites, motivated by greed and fear, to take
advantage of the new wealth and weapons offered by the Europe-
ans--all of these factors, rather than any alleged predis-
position of ordinary Africans to be slaves, helped make the
great American slave trade possible.

It was, instead, the Europeans who were culturally predisposed to regard Negroes as natural slaves. The belief was
fully developed by 1500, fed by age-old fears of the night,
of dark beasts, and of black-skinned devils, and by knowledge
that most Negroes who reached the Mediterranean world had been
brought as slaves. This racism was later much exacerbated
by contempt for the wretched slaves, fear of their revenge,
the will to believe that profitable business must be righteous,
and the twisted sexual component of race relations. The slave
trade really was a trade; over 95 per cent of the slaves were
bought from African slavers, not captured directly by European
raiders. Slave merchants believed they could pick the best
slaves for each servile task. It was widely reported that
Muslim Hausa made the best gang leaders, that Ewe women were
best in bed, and that the Yoruba made the best field hands.

This was probably about as reliable as modern stereotypes about Italians and Jews, but it encouraged the importation of such groups, and thereby made possible the predominant Yoruba influence in so much of Negro religion and culture in the West Indies and Brazil.

Slave owners demanded field hands, domestic servants, and mistresses. If many African hunters could not learn field work and died, if many African warriors would not serve and were killed, most slaves were in fact successfully broken in. The slave system thus tended to destroy or at least simplify the many skills and cultures that the slaves brought with them. A chained hunter could not practice or transmit his art. A skilled gardener of many crops might be forced to slave at sugar alone. Few whites had any respect for the elite arts of Africa, so they could never be established in most parts of America, while in other parts they survived in simplified form, patronized no longer by kings but by slaves. Only in Brazil were the whites often so lacking in skilled crafts that African modes of blacksmithing, for instance, could survive on a large scale for centuries. Likewise only in Brazil were there a few cases in which illiterate slave owners allowed Muslim slaves to keep plantation accounts and correspond with other plantation secretaries in Arabic. Some African religion and arts survived the acid bath of slavery to flourish again, in much evolved forms, in parts of the larger West Indian islands, the Guyanas, and Brazil. But most African institutions and techniques, including economic institutions and techniques, were knowingly rejected or incomprehendingly suppressed by the whites. Debates as to whether the bronzecasters of Benin were more skillful than Benvenuto Cellini, or whether the Iberian peasants were, on the average, at a higher level than peasants in Guinea, are unusually sterile. Whatever the answer, very few Africans were allowed to contribute all that they were capable of to the development of America.

There is one major exception to this dismal story. Enough slaves were allowed to bring African plants with them, and to cultivate them in America, so that an impressive list of new crops were naturalized, some to become mainstays of agriculture in tropical America. Thousands of years before Columbus, West Africans had domesticated several kinds of millet and sorghum, several local varieties of beans and peas, the Guinea yam, okra, tamarind, the kola nut, the oil palm, and the watermelon. In addition, various African peoples had acquired a number of cultivated plants from Southeast Asia and Indonesia in the first millennium A.D., and these were first brought to America by Africans rather than directly from their oriental homelands: other kinds of peas and beans, the mango, the cucumber, the eggplant, the taro yam, the true yam, breadfruit, the banana, the coconut, and varieties of both dry and

wet rice that were better suited to the American tropics than
those grown in Europe. Naturally all of these plants were
"introduced" many times by many ships to many places. Better
cucumbers were later brought from Europe, better mangoes and
bananas from Asia. Some wild coconuts may have reached Paci-
fic America even before Columbus. But all of these plants
reached America from Africa, and were first cultivated and
popularized there by Africans. The introduction of a major
complex of plants, which hundreds of millions of people have
used for food, refreshment, or industry, is a major event
in economic history.

It should be added that coffee and the Old World cotton
now in universal use, gossypium herbaceum, were originally
domesticated in Africa, although they reached America through
Asian and European hands. Cane sugar came from Southeast Asia,
but it reached Europe and then America through Africa. These
African contributions to the economic development of America
have been balanced by the introduction of a very important
complex of American food plants, notably maize, manioc, and
the sweet potato, into Africa.

In sum, the Americas as we know them could not have
developed without the continuing contributions of Africa.
There is no escape from the paradox that the long history of
Negro slavery in the Americas was as great an evil as any in
history, and that at the same time this enormous transfer of
African resources across the Atlantic was crucial for the
building of much of the New World.

Colonial Economic Policy

Perhaps the single most important fact in determining
Portuguese Brazilian policy and Brazilian economic growth was
Portugal's possession of the Spice Islands and of Goa. Immensely profitable, they absorbed the major share of Portuguese attention, expenditure, and manpower. The small
population of Portugal when Brazil was discovered in 1500,
one million people, limited the amount of effective control
that the state could exercise over the colony. Limits on manpower and wealth led the state to delegate colonizing activity to individuals. The Portuguese government's involvement
in Brazil was less than that of Spain in her Latin American
colonies.

The prosperity of Brazil, and the Portuguese government's interest in the colony, largely depended on the commodities Brazil could export. In chronological order, dyewood, sugar, gold and diamonds dominated Brazilian exports
and Brazilian economic life. The inputs they required,
whether of food, raw materials, labor or other services,

determined Brazilian economic structure and level of income, during the time when the export of these commodities was profitable. The organization of the export trade depended on the terms governing colonization and trade set by the Portuguese crown. The first settlement arrangements were contracts with dyewood merchants; later arrangements were colonization contracts for large areas with persons called donatários. In general, the state maintained control of, and property rights in, Brazil. The direct costs were paid by Portuguese citizens, who obtained some of the profits of settlement. The first terms under which crown authority was delegated were those governing the dyewood trade in Santa Cruz (Holy Cross) as Brazil was then called. An expedition sent to explore Santa Cruz in 1501 returned to Portugal with brazilwood. The king, Dom Manuel, declared that brazilwood was from that time on a monopoly of the crown, and rented the newly discovered lands to a merchant, D. Fernão de Loronha. The contract was for three years, and could be renewed. At the request of D. Loronha, imports of competing dyewood from Asia were suppressed. In return, D. Loronha was required to send three ships a year to Santa Cruz, to explore 300 leagues of coast and to pay one fifth the value of the dyewood to the Portuguese crown. He was also required to establish fortifications for the defense of the new territory.[1] After the first few years, D. Loronha paid 4,000 cruzados, worth 1,000 contos* of reis (1937 prices); equals $61,893 U.S. 1937 prices.

During the reign of Dom João the income from brazilwood was equal to approximately 5 per cent of the government's income, which did not cover the expenditures on the defense of

------

*Note: The unit of account in Brazil for the period under study was the real (plural reis). Coins were equivalent to a given number of reis; this number varied over time. The cruzado caried from 400 to 875 reis; the moêda varied from 1,000 to 4,800 reis; the cruzado nôvo was set at 480 reis, and the escudo at 1,600 reis. The weight and fineness of gold per reis varied over time, while the value of gold itself also changed. Estimates of the purchasing power of these coins is given in Roberto Simonsen, História Econômica do Brasil, pp. 68-73. In recent times, the standard currency of Brazil, until 1942, was the milreis. One milreis was equal to 1,000 reis. A conto of reis was equal to 1,000 milreis. Brazilian currency was written as follows:

1:000$000	1 conto of reis
1$000	1 milreis
$100	100 reis

In 1942 the milreis was renamed the cruzeiro.

the new territory. Although direct exploitation was not profitable for the crown, it was profitable to the holders of the
dyewood contracts. In 1602 a shipment of 10,000 quintales of
dyewood yielded 40 contos. Expenses were the cost of dyewood
in Brazil, 10 contos; transport, 3 contos; payment to the royal
treasury, 21 contos; which left 6 contos profit--which was equal
to 15 per cent of sales, and also equal to $84,814 U.S. (1937
prices; a conto in 1937 was worth $61.983 U.S. For the Brazil-
ian exchange rate over time, see Table 9-4).

The preoccupation with the profitability of the dyewood
trade led a Jesuit to denounce it: "shameful is the cupidity
of man, that preoccupied with trade, he substitutes a block of
wood for the Holy Cross, dye for the true blood of Christ."[3]
The point is doubly forceful in Portuguese, for even the name
of the country (Holy Cross) had been changed to dyewood (Brazil).

Some notion of the relative attractiveness of investment
in Brazil and in India is that a boat of 120 toneladas capacity
cost over 1,500 contos of reis. A cargo of brazilwood brought
over 1,000 contos, while a cargo of spices was worth seven times
as much--about 10,000 contos of reis. A somewhat enthusiastic
observer estimated the dyewood trade at 20,000 quintals yearly
exported to Europe at a value of 2 1/2 ducados a quintal, and
4,000 ducados paid by D. Loronha to the crown each year. The
1937 value of these estimates is 13,500 contos of reis export
value and a payment to the crown of 1,100 contos. Simonsen
estimates that from 1500 to 1532, the dyewood trade yielded
120,000 contos, of which the crown received 30,000; to obtain
this amount, from 3 to 5 shipments a year were required.[4]

Although the dyewood receipts justified Portuguese interest in Brazil, the Portuguese could not maintain control
of Brazil if they maintained no more than logging camps and
an occasional fort. The Spanish were believed likely to
violate the Treaty of Tordesillas (which had been signed in
1494), and to encroach on Portuguese territory. The French
king, Francis I, wished to prevent the establishment of a
Spanish and Portuguese monopoly in America, and declared that
he "had never seen a clause in the last will of Adam conceding
such exclusive control to Kings Manuel and Charles." French
ships on the Brazilian coast cut brazilwood and attacked
Portuguese shipping. The Portuguese fleet attacked the French
and established a small garrison in Pernambuco in 1521; it was
destroyed by the French in 1530. In order to repel the French
and prevent the Spanish from entering Brazil, permanent settlement was required. The attractiveness of a settlement scheme
was increased by the worsening prospects in India, where the
heavy toll in human life to maintain Portuguese domination
was increasingly unacceptable: a sharp increase in Europe in

the supply of cloves and pepper resulted in a fall in their
price. By 1530, the India spice trade could not meet the increasing deficits of the Portuguese court; Portugal desperately
needed to develop an additional source of income. For these
reasons, therefore, Portuguese activity in Brazil increased.

In 1530 an expedition was sent under the command of Martim Affonso da Souza, who explored 3,000 miles of Brazil's
coast from Maranhão to Rio Grande do Sul. He seized French
ships and the fort at Pernambuco. In 1532, he founded the
first permanent settlement in Brazil at São Vicente, near
modern Santos, on the coast, while inland he established
Piratininga, near modern São Paulo (see map, p. 10).[5] In
1533 the system of captaincies was established to promote
the settlement of Brazil. A captaincy was a grant of land
from 25 to more than 60 leagues along the coast extending inland to 370° leagues west of the Cape Verde Islands (the line
set by the Treaty of Tordesillas). The grant carried with it
economic and political privileges and responsibilities. Under
this system, land was granted to a concessionaire, known as
the donatário, who received (1) approximately 20 per cent of
the land of the captaincy; (2) a monopoly and licensing
privileges over saltworks, water mills, and any other mills
that would be constructed on their lands; (3) unlimited enslavement of Indians and authorization for the sale of a
specified quota in the Lisbon market, usually set at 39 per
year; (4) 50 per cent of the value of brazilwood and fish;
(5) a tithe on the tithes of incomes and privileges pertain-
ing to the crown; (6) the right to levy tolls on river ship-
ing; (7) taxes on town officials, who owed allegiance to the
donatário; (8) a tax of 500 reis on town notaries; and (9) the
exercise of civilian commercial jurisdiction within specified
limits.

In return for these privileges, the donatário was to
enlist settlers, promote farming and trade by providing cattle, seeds, and tools, defend the settlers, and promote the
Catholic faith. The donatário was to provide his own funds,
without expectation of direct financial aid from the crown.
The settlers in the captaincy were (1) required to serve
with the donatário in time of war; (2) required to pay the
town the taxes and tribute that were paid in the kingdom of
Portugal, according to law. The king promised that in the
captaincy the excise, soap, and salt taxes would not be collected, nor would any be levied that were not listed in the
book registering duties paid to the king; (3) granted the
right to beg and receive sesmarias, which were grants of land,
without greater burden than the tithe due to the Grand Master
of Christ; and (4) granted payment of the church by the king.
The crown reserved for itself one tenth of the harvest and
of fish, the monopoly of the brazilwood, spice, and drug

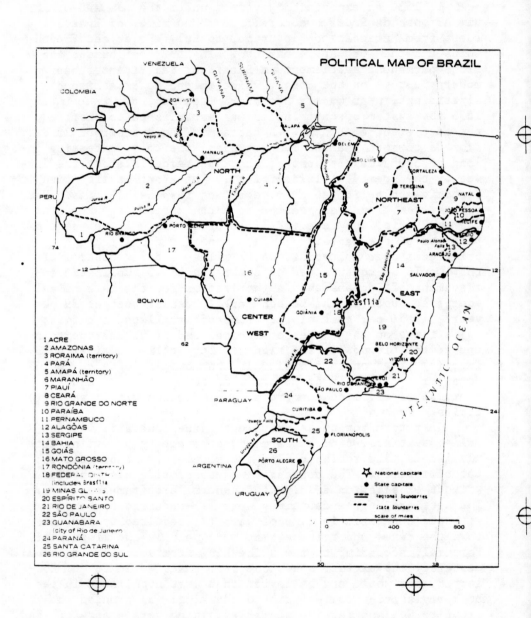

POLITICAL MAP OF BRAZIL

1 ACRE
2 AMAZONAS
3 RORAIMA (territory)
4 PARÁ
5 AMAPÁ (territory)
6 MARANHÃO
7 PIAUÍ
8 CEARÁ
9 RIO GRANDE DO NORTE
10 PARAÍBA
11 PERNAMBUCO
12 ALAGÔAS
13 SERGIPE
14 BAHIA
15 GOIÁS
16 MATO GROSSO
17 RONDÔNIA (territory)
18 FEDERAL DISTRICT
   (includes Brasília)
19 MINAS GERAIS
20 ESPÍRITO SANTO
21 RIO DE JANEIRO
22 SÃO PAULO
23 GUANABARA
   (city of Rio de Janeiro)
24 PARANÁ
25 SANTA CATARINA
26 RIO GRANDE DO SUL

☆ National capital
● State capitals
═══ Regional boundaries
--- State boundaries
scale of miles
0   400   800

trades, and one fifth of precious metals and stones.[6] Alfredo
Pimenta wrote that the king had thought of granting land only
for one life, but that this would not attract men and capital.
Land grants therefore were hereditary. The king had sovereignty over the land, but the donatários had direct ownership and
use rights.

Anyone who wanted to could go to Brazil. Once there, anyone who wished, either colonist or donatário, could send any
product from Brazil to any city in the Portuguese Empire or
to foreign markets (with the exception of articles whose trade
the crown kept for itself) without being subject to any tax
except the excise tax. Portuguese ships were not taxed in Brazil; foreign ships in Brazil, however, were taxed, while
ships in the ports of captaincies could not be loaded or leave
without permission of the donatário. Trade between captaincies was free of any tax.

The difference between the Portuguese system of settlement and that of the Spanish crown is striking. Any Portuguese could go to Brazil; only Spanish Catholics from Castile
could go to Spanish America. The Portuguese colonizers could
openly enslave Indians, while Spanish encomenderos, at least
in theory, were to educate them in the Christian faith, and
could not own or enslave any save hostile Indians. The Portuguese granted land outright, and provided for its subdivi-
sion in grants to colonists. The Spanish crown granted control over income from specified areas, but not the land itself, nor did it provide for the outright grant of land to
small holders. The Spaniards attempted to regulate trade,
and subjected it to heavy taxes; the Portuguese trade policy
was more liberal than that achieved in the Spanish Empire before independence. If easy access to trade, and the possibility of wide distribution of landownership alone sufficed
to guarantee successful development, as contrasted to a more
tightly controlled system with a heavy concentration of landownership, then Brazil should have been a more successful
colony than was Argentina, Mexico, or Peru.

The profitability of a colony, in the short run, depends
upon its ability to provide products desired by the colonizing nation. This requires both a favorable resource endowment and effective physical and administrative control of
the colony and of transportation routes between the colony and
the mother country. Brazil, if it did not yet provide gold
and silver, did provide dyewood, the demand for which continued
to be strong as European textile production increased.

Production of dyewood in quantities large enough to ensure the donatário a profit was hampered by the difficulty
both of establishing physical control of land held by Indians
and of obtaining an adequate labor supply. The donatário
Duarte Coelho complained that "we are obliged to conquer by

inches the land Your Majesty granted us by leagues." Once
land was wrested from the Indians, the donatários could not
obtain large numbers of settlers who obeyed them. The Inquisition had been established in Portugal in 1536; as a result,
many Jews, nonconformists, and dissenters left Portugal for
Brazil, where they lived as they pleased, not as the donatários
told them to. Indians were difficult to enslave; Negro labor
had not yet been introduced.

Even where an adequate labor supply was obtained, the
donatários were faced with continuing French attacks. Portugal
did not control either the whole coast of Brazil or the Atlantic. The individual donatários were unlikely to be able to protect that which Portugal could not: divided responsibility for
the defense of Brazil was an invitation to attack.

The heavy initial outlay, and the time required to establish control of a colony, would make it unlikely that a
colony could prove profitable in less than a generation. Nonetheless, two of the twelve original captaincies returned
profits before 1549--those granted in Pernambuco to Duarte
Coelho Pereira and in São Vicente to Martim Affonso de Souza.
At that time, there were 16 towns and villages which exported
brazilwood, cotton, sugar, tobacco, and other local products
to Portugal. A number of the towns were fortified and possessed shipbuilding and ship repair yards.[7] In order to protect and develop Portuguese colonization of Brazil, the king
altered the system of donatários in 1544, when he appointed
Tomé de Sousa governor general. The governor general had the
responsibility of defending Brazil, and also took over many
of the political and judicial powers of the donatários. Further, Bahia was named the capital of the newly united Brazil.
These two measures mark the creation of a single, united
colony. The Portuguese hoped to establish a unified, defensi-
ble coastal colony, rather than broadly scattered, vulnerable
settlements, and in this aim was successful.

Of the twelve captaincies, four were never settled,
four were settled briefly, and only four produced permanent
settlements.[8] Between 1560 and 1570, there were eight captaincies, with sixty sugar mills which produced roughly
3,000 arrobas (in Brazil, one arroba equaled 32.38 pounds) of
sugar yearly. There were about 17,000 people of Portuguese
origin, and 13,000 free Indians and slaves of African origin.
By 1583 the population under Portuguese control had grown
to 57,000: 25,000 whites, 18,000 "civilized Indians," and
14,000 Negro slaves. The four captaincies organized to search
for precious metals failed; those organized for settlement
succeeded.

In calculating the profits of the donatário system as
a whole, however, both the failures and the successes must be

included. The probable minimum expense of the exploration
colonies was (in 1937 prices) 38,400 contos of reis for 12
ships and half again as much for armaments. The settlement
colonies had to finance not only ships for colonization and
arms, but also seeds, tools, loans to colonists, ships for
export products, and working capital to finance the shipment
of exports. Simonsen estimates the 1937 cost of investment
in Brazil at 457,192 contos of which 283,200 was spent in
the captaincies, 121,600 was spent by Portuguese shipowners
for 38 ships used in the transatlantic trade, and 52,392
represented the value of export merchandise transported in
one year. Of this sum 41,418 represented the value in Brazil of sugar, 7,434 of brazilwood, and 3,540 of other merchandise. The value in Brazil of exports was about 19 per
cent of the fixed capital invested by the donatários in the
captaincies. If it is assumed that the population could not
exist at a level of consumption below $30 per capita in 1950
dollars, then 57,000 people times $30 equals $1,710,000 as
the minimum estimate of gross domestic product. If it is believed that proceeds from exports were concentrated in the
hands of the donatários, and represented income in addition
to (rather than part of) the $30, the estimate of gross
domestic product becomes $1,710,000 (U.S. 1950) plus 52,392
contos of 1937 reis ($6,184,801 U.S., 1950 prices). The fi-
gures imply a capital output ratio in dyewood of at least 5
to 1.

The profitability of the Brazilian export trade depended
not only on the cost of products in Brazil and the provision
of ships, but also on the price they sold for in Portugal.
Sugar was purchased in Brazil at 230,100 reis per arroba
(1937) and sold at 654,900 per arroba; brazilwood was purchased at 247,800 reis per quintal and sold at 1,416,000 reis
per quintal; other articles doubled in value. The total increase in value of products purchased in Brazil and sold in
Portugal was an estimated 118,590 contos (1937 prices) which
represented 68 per cent of the capital invested by Portuguese
merchants in ships and the purchase price in Brazil at the
ports. From this amount, taxes and other expenses must be
deducted to obtain profits of the export trade on invested
capital. If this came to no more than 18 per cent of capital, and no profits were obtained on the imports of Portuguese merchandise to Brazil, then it would have required two
voyages for shipowners to recoup their capital, after which
depreciation of ships and purchase of products would cost
about 64,552 contos against an increase in value of 118,590
contos. This left 54,038 contos from which to deduct taxes
and other expenses, which, even in the absence of profits
on imports, implies that once the initial capital had been
recouped, a profit of 75 per cent on current expenses was

possible. However, merchants selling Brazilian products in
Portugal sold Portuguese products to Brazil. If the profits
on imports were anywhere near as lucrative as those on exports, shipowners could have recouped the cost of their investment and possibly have earned a profit on one round-trip
voyage and doubled their capital in two or three round-trip
ventures. Against the high profits, the merchant had to
calculate the considerable risk of loss due to piracy and bad
weather.

Private trade clearly was highly profitable. Although
only two of the twelve captaincies had proved profitable to
the donatários by 1549, the continuing use of this form of
settlement implies that at least in the long run, the system
was profitable and stable. An indirect indication of this
is that when the crown abolished the captaincy of Bahia in
1548, in order to create Bahia as the capital of Brazil, the
heirs of the donatário of Bahia were granted a yearly pension
on the revenues of the king of 1,000 cruzados (173 contos in
1937 prices).*

The profitability of Brazil to the Portuguese crown, before large-scale production of sugar at the end of the sixteenth century, has been estimated at 6,200 contos (1937
prices) income from brazilwood, 4,140 from tithes on sugar,
and 600 from other Brazilian sources. Since the founding of
the city of São Salvador alone cost four times as much, and
the crown provided bureaucrats, Jesuits, and defense for the
colony, the colonization of Brazil was clearly a deficit for
the royal treasury.

Finally, it is possible that the nation of Portugal received benefits in addition to the revenues obtained by the
crown. Annual exports from Brazil were valued at 115,000
contos (1937). During the same period, Spain received more
than 1,000,000 contos in precious metals alone from its American colonies.

During the early period of settlement, although Portugal
had the freer, and presumably more favorable, development
policy, the Spanish colonies were palpably more profitable
because of their overwhelming advantage in silver and gold
production. The immediate (but not long-run) profitability
of colonization for the crown depended not on policy, but on
resource endowment. It has been suggested that the initial
lack of gold and silver assured that such profits as were
available went to Portugal rather than another nation. However,

---

*Later, new captaincies were created in the crown's name,
while six were granted to individuals. The reversion of captaincies to the crown, owing to lack of legitimate heirs, or
by confiscation, or by purchase became decisive only in the
eighteenth century.

Portugal was taken over by Spain from 1580 to 1640. The Spanish permitted Portugal to administer its colonies and were lax in blocking Brazilian occupation of the frontier beyond the line of the Treaty of Tordesillas. However, Spain changed the policy that Portugal administered by demanding a monopoly of trade with Brazil. This struck directly at Dutch trading interests, and to a lesser extent at English and French traders. As the Spanish were largely ineffective in their attempts to defend and administer Brazil, the newly outlawed trade was replaced by smuggling, piracy, and plunder. If gold and silver had been known to exist in Brazil, it seems likely that one of the three nations that made desultory attempts to establish a beachhead would have taken the decisive steps necessary to wrest Brazil from Portugal. The prospects of Brazilian profits suggested that such action was not worth the bother. Limited attempts to take over Brazil were made by several nations: (1) The English had traded along the coast during the early sixteenth century. After legal trade was cut off, Cavendish burned Santos in 1591, and Lancaster pillaged Pernambuco. The English, describing part of Brazil as "a country that hath yet her maidenhead, never sacked, turned nor wrought," tried to establish a settlement at the mouth of the Amazon in 1630. This was the last English attempt to occupy Brazilian soil. (2) The French had raided Portuguese shipping and trading posts, made alliances with the Indians, and established their own posts in Bahia and Pernambuco in the early sixteenth century. The French unsuccessfully tried to colonize Rio de Janeiro and Recife; they succeeded, however, in occupying northern Maranhão until 1615. (3) The Dutch had provided shipping between Brazil and Portugal, and were motivated to attack both because of Spanish exclusion of the Dutch from the Brazil trade, and because of the war between Spain and Holland (1572-1609 and 1621-1648). The Dutch attacked Bahia in 1604 and established the Dutch West India Company in 1624, with the aim of supplanting the Portuguese in Brazil. By 1630 they held 1,200 miles of the Brazilian coast, and improved the colony. The West India Company paid annual dividends of 25 per cent and more. Despite the prosperity that accompanied the Dutch administration, religious and political antagonism, along with resentment against the Protestant Dutch making profits from Portuguese Catholic Brazil, led to the outbreak of revolts against the Dutch in 1641. Indirect but decisive aid was foreshadowed by the signing of a treaty of peace and commerce with the English in 1642, which supplemented Portugal's inadequate navy. Many Dutch ships were sunk in the first Anglo-Dutch War (1651-1653), which made it difficult for Holland to maintain an Atlantic empire. In 1654 the Dutch left Brazil for the West Indies, where they grew crops in competition with those produced in Brazil.

The Sugar Industry

The Spanish period of Brazilian history (1580-1640) was marked by the increased importance of sugar cultivation, which rapidly outstripped dyewood and other local products exports. The characteristics of the sugar industry differed sharply from those of the dyewood export trade, and radically changed the organization and structure of colonial Brazil.

Sugar production, as contrasted to the gathering of dyewood, required a large investment of capital for the purchase of land, a sugar mill, slaves, and improved variety of sugar cane. The government promoted the production of sugar cane by exemption of sugar mills from taxes for ten years in the captaincy of São Salvador, and privileges of nobility and inpenharabilidade were extended to millowners.[9] The production of Brazilian sugar increased, sugar prices fell, which threatened to make production on the island of Madeira unprofitable, so that Portugal established a 20 per cent tax on Brazilian sugar in order to protect the Madeiran product. Nonetheless, the largest share of government effort went to protect the sugar industry: the governor of Bahia established a press for the colonists, who were enabled to earn enough to establish their own mills. Although in the Portuguese islands sugar mills of small-hand varieties had been used, in Brazil, water and animal power mills were used instead because the expense of Brazilian colonization required large-scale production for the colonization effort to be profitable. The first mills established were the medium-sized mills which produced 3,000 arrobas yearly; they were replaced early in the seventeenth century by mills of up to 10,000 arrobas capacity. The mills were built with capital borrowed from Portuguese merchants; this capital was needed to finance not only the production of sugar but also the production or purchase of food, animals, and equipment that the sugar plantation culture required. Thus the Brazilian historians Pôrto Seguro and Rodolfo Garcia wrote that "the sugar mill represented a veritable town, requiring the utilization not only of many men, but also required the cultivation of sugar cane, wood, pasturage, and food. In effect, the sugar mill . . . had to include one hundred colonists or slaves, in order to cultivate 1,200 tarefas of massapê (900 braças square) (and) in addition, pasture, gardens, casks, utensils, iron, copper, yokes of oxen, and other animals."[10]

In addition, the cane had to be transported. The high cost of transporting sugar overland, and the danger of attack from Indians en route, led to the establishment of mills in the coastal areas, along small rivers. The cultivation of sugar was so widespread, and its value so widely accepted, that for a time sugar served as money: many poor colonists

rented lands near sugar mills and were paid in sugar for the
cane they produced. The relatively large size and high cost
of sugar mills meant that many sugar planters could not afford
to own them. A sugar mill was worth at least 10,000 cruzados
($56,771 U.S., 1937 prices). The cost included 50 slaves,
15-20 yokes of oxen, carts, ships, tools and equipment, salaries to free laborers, food for the slaves, and other expenses
of sugar preparation. The inability of small holders to with-
stand poor harvests, the death of slaves, or a fall in the
price of sugar led to the concentration of sugar land and
sugar mills in relatively few hands: the largest mills were
valued at 80,000 cruzados. Thus the sugar-producing unit com-
prised the millowner and a group of suppliers, the peasants,
who corresponded to the French habitants and the English
smallholder. A distinction is, however, at once found, for
in the English and French colonies the functions of planter
and of millowner were united in the same person. In Brazil,
the millowner only exceptionally was also a planter. Associated with each mill there were from five to ten peasants,
each of whom farmed land consisting at the most of 40 tarefas
(.372 acres). A large-scale establishment would, then, con-
sist of the peasants, each with 40 tarefas, or 15 acres, making
in all 150 acres, whence would be harvested 3,225 tons of
cane, the produce of which would be 160 tons of sugar. With
a water-driven mill taking 50 cartloads of 600 lb. each, or
13 tons per day, the season would extend over 250 days, or
from September to April. An establishment of only five peasants supplying an ox-driven mill would have a capacity about
equal to half that of a water-driven mill. The mean capacity
of the sugar mills would depend on the proportion of water and
of ox-driven mills, and with an equal number of each the
average output of a sugar mill would be about 100 tons of sugar
yearly.

The sugar-growing lands were divided from each other by
wide lanes so as to diminish the fire risk, and each peasant
owned on an average twenty slaves, or 0.75 slaves per acre.
Each tarefa afforded from 25 to 35 cartloads of 600 lb. each,
whence were obtained 30 arrobas of sugar, which was a whole
day's work for a mill served by six to eight oxen. A water-
driven mill could crush up to 40 or 50 cartloads, but the quality of the work was thought to be inferior.

The possible number of crops capable of being taken off
from one planting is mentioned as forty or fifty. but so many
were not advised, for though the second cutting was the sweet-
est, there was afterwards a fallingoff in the sugar content
of the cane. The cane might suffer from drought, and the
weeding was carefully done. A root-eating worm did great
damage, and a caries, or decay, of the stalk often made its
appearance. The bagasse might be used as fodder, but it was

much better to use it as fuel, as the ashes made a valuable
manure. The sugar made was of three qualities, white, muscovado, and panela. The proportion of each depended on the care
in the cultivation of the soil.

The peasants worked on shares and received either two
fifths or one third of the sugar. The bagasse, panela sugar
and molasses, belonged to the mill owner. The proportion of
white and of muscovado sugar allotted to the peasant was subject to arrangement, and he could, if he wished, take payment
in money or in kind.

All sugar made in the first boiling seems to have been
clayed (by covering the upper surface of the impure magma of
crystals and molasses, contained in an earthenware cone, with
a layer of wet clay, whence the water percolated slowly
through the material, displacing the molasses). . . . The
clayed loaves were separated into two portions, the upper part
forming the white sugar and the lower, or teat of the cone, to
which molasses still adhered, was called muscovado . The drain-
ings were boiled into a low-grade sugar called panela."11

The different qualities of sugar commanded different
prices; in the seventeenth century, the ratio was white sugar
3, muscovado 2, and panela and raw sugar 1.12 This information is useful in estimating the profits of sugar production.
The price of sugar in foreign markets, if the millowner owned
the ships in which sugar was transported and could earn the
foreign price, times the quantity sold, would indicate the
gross receipts earned by a sugar producer. Sugar prices from
1521 to 1702 are shown in Table 8-1.

In 1642 a shipment of sugar from Brazil frequently cited
in analyzing the sugar industry was as follows: 84 cwt. of
white sugar and 60 cwt. of muscovado. The value of these
amounts of sugar at retail prices in London would have been
about Ł1,050; their declared value in Brazil was Ł200/1/6.
Sugars purchased in Brazil sold at triple the price in Portuguese wholesale markets; the additional information implies
that the markup from wholesale to retail price was an additional 67 per cent of wholesale price. The wholesaler, however, had to pay the expenses for export taxes (Ł49/6/2),
scale and tare (Ł2/0/4), warehouse tax (Ł14/8), hooping and
nailing (Ł4/19/0), branding (Ł7/4), shipping (Ł4/8/0),
brokerage (Ł1/5/8) and billing (Ł14/8) for a total of
Ł63 9s. 0d. Sugar purchased for Ł200 could be sold at wholesale for an estimated Ł600-667, which, minus Ł64, left Ł536-
603; subtracting purchase price in Brazil left Ł336-403. If
shipping charges included allotment for risk and depreciation,
then this sum represents profits on sale of sugar.

An alternate estimate of profits that could be obtained
on trade with Amsterdam, rather than London, in 1620 was
drawn up by a founder of the Dutch West India Company. He

assumed that Brazil produced 15,000 tons of sugar per year, divided equally between white, muscovado, and panela sugar. His estimates of the value of trade in Brazil sugar, and the profit rates implicit in his figures are presented in Table 8-2. Total receipts were Ŀ870,833, from which total costs were Ŀ386,833, leaving a net profit of Ŀ484,000, and an average profit rate of 131 per cent. It is clear that the lower the quality of sugar, the higher the wholesaler's profit. However, Antonil, writing at the beginning of the eighteenth century, suggested that 70 per cent of the sugar produced was white, and the remainder muscovado. If this is correct, the profits realized would be slightly lower than the 131 per cent suggested here:[13] using the prices shown in Table 8-2, a profit of 129 per cent is estimated. The profits on total trade with Brazil are higher, once earnings on Brazilian imports are included. The Dutch estimated in 1620 that an additional Ŀ250,000 was earned on goods sent in on barter and on refining half of the sugar imported.[14] Since the Dutch West India Company farmed out the right to trade in sugar to private traders, and they controlled only half of the sugar-producing area in Brazil, profits were less than those anticipated in 1620. In 1644 gross revenue was Ŀ245,430; net revenue was Ŀ125,223. Both figures exclude rent and tax income, and sums due in payment of debts.[15]

Profit on the wholesale export of sugar to the Amsterdam market was at least 130 per cent in 1620; it was at least 167 per cent twenty years later on exports to London, where sugar supplies were shorter and prices correspondingly higher. Profits on the production of sugar at the end of the sixteenth century have recently been estimated by Furtado, who assumes relatively high personal consumption expenditures were financed out of sugar profits. He believes "that the sugar industry was profitable enough to self-finance a doubling of productive capacity every two years, which was apparently the rate of growth during the most thriving phases."[16] The profit rate, before deducting half of profits for expenditure on imports of consumer goods, was 67 per cent; that is, a profit of Ŀ1.2 million was earned on an initial outlay of Ŀ1.8 million for sugar mills.* If slaves were able to build some of the mill buildings, then, Furtado believes, cash expenditure of no more than Ŀ1.2 million was needed to replace the sugar mills.

Simonsen's figures indicate that just over 1/7 of fixed capital invested in donatários was represented by receipts in

---

*Celso Furtado, The Economic Growth of Brazil, lists slaves and oxen in addition to mills; some earlier authors indicate that they were considered part of the value of the mills.

Brazil for sugar, excluding the cost of shipping. According to Furtado, however, sugar working produced Ł1,500,000 in Brazil against Ł2,250,000 fixed investment. The 120 mills produced 100 tons yearly, giving 12,000 tons in 1600. Under the Dutch, Brazil exported an estimated 20,000 tons yearly, but following the destructive war between the Dutch and Portuguese, production had fallen by 1635 to an estimated maximum of 15,000 tons.[17] By the 1640s this had risen to about 24,000 tons per year,[18] with an additional amount in Portuguese-controlled Brazil.

The revenue in Brazil for 15,000 tons has been indicated as at least Ł320,833. If we accept Furtado's estimate of Ł1.8 million invested in sugar mills, then sugar receipts were one sixth to one quarter of fixed capital costs, which reflects the higher cost of the larger sugar mills. Furtado attacks Simonsen for being too conservative, as Simonsen rejected estimates of 35,000 tons of sugar produced and exported in 1600, and 80,000 tons in 1650.[19] If these amounts were accepted, they would yield the income estimated by Furtado. Only by assuming that all sugar milled was exported, that only the most profitable varieties were sold, and the largest possible value for a "chest" of sugar exported is accepted, can Furtado's figures be reached.*

If the prices indicated in this chapter are correct, then Furtado must believe that the volume of sugar exported was four to five times greater than that indicated in most seventeenth-century accounts. Furtado used his sugar receipts estimates to generate a per capita income figure for seventeenth-century Brazil of some $350 U.S. He obtained this by including as people only 30,000 freeborn whites. But the total population within the Portuguese-controlled part of Brazil was estimated at 100,000 in 1600.[20] Even if Furtado's figure were accepted, per capita income—including all people, not just legally free persons—would be $105 U.S. The justification for omitting slaves and Indians from the income per capita estimate is the belief that they could not have

------

*The weight of a chest of sugar is difficult to determine. The weight of sugar chests is given in arrobas. An arroba was equal to 25 to 32 arratels, according to region. An arratel was equal to 12 to 16 ounces, according to region. (C. R. Boxer, The Golden Age of Brazil, p. 356). Chests of sugar seem to have been smaller at the beginning of the colonial period than at the end of it, not only because the size of ships increased, but also because the sugar traders increased the size of chests in order to reduce the share of tax per pound of sugar. This occurred because the tax was levied per chest of sugar. In the early eighteenth century, the crown set the standard chest weight at 35 arrobas.

received more than subsistence income. A revised estimate of
sugar income, accepting Simonsen's estimate of 25,000 tons
of sugar, is Ł534,000 annually, in 1620.* At that time, there
were roughly 128,000 people, of whom about 44,700 were white.
Assuming that 83,300 Negroes and Indians had a subsistence
income of $30, their total income was $2,499,000.

The above estimate of sugar receipts is perhaps one third
of Furtado's, and is divided by total population, yielding a
per capita income of $40; per capita income for whites was
about $59. The average white income compares favorably with
that obtainable in Spain or Portugal at the time, while the
average income for the colony is consistent with current estimates of the income of raw material producing colonies at
early stages of development. Moreover, some estimate of the
extreme wealth obtained, as a maximum from the mills, can be
found by dividing sugar receipts by the number of sugar mills,
which yields $22,280 per mill.

During the sugar boom, trade was, in part, an engine of
growth for the Brazilian economy. As in the case of Mexico,
sums earned from trade and spent in Europe or remitted to
Europe in payment of taxes did not add to Brazilian income.
Sums earned from trade and spent in Brazil were available for
spending and investment in Brazil; a considerable fraction
of sugar earning could be expected to be spent on inputs to
the sugar industry: animals, slaves, machines, and land, as
well as food crops. The demand for these inputs could be
expected to fluctuate with the demand for Brazilian sugar.
As long as Brazil produced a large share of the world's sugar,
and the Dutch marketing agents and French cooks continued to
popularize the use of pastries, candies, preserves, choco-
late, and other sugar-using products, such as tea and coffee,
the demand for sugar expanded at a rate that offset the expanded supply, so that sugar prices were stable during the
first half of the seventeenth century. An estimate of the
income growth of Brazil under Dutch management (1630-1654) is
made by using the figures supplied by Charles Boxer, in The
Dutch in Brazil.

In the early 1620s optimists estimated that if Brazil
were taken by the Dutch, its more than 350 sugar mills, and
60 to 70 thousand people would yield a revenue of Ł727,200
per year, of which Ł436,320 would be provided by the sugar
trade. It was thought that the costs of conquest and defense
would not exceed Ł227,250, leaving a handsome profit of

---

*Income from the transportation and distribution of
sugar from Brazil to Europe is not included in this estimate
since income from these sources was largely controlled by
Dutch merchants. C. R. Boxer, The Dutch in Brazil, pp. 21,
32.

£499,950. With these profits in view, the Dutch West India
Company was able to raise £646,127 in paid up capital by 1623.[21]
At the expiration of the truce with Spain in April 1621, the
Dutch had secured one half to two thirds of the carrying trade
between Brazil and Europe, by operating under the names and
flag of Portuguese merchants. The volume of this trade is
given as some 50,000 chests of sugar, which implies a maximum
production of 25,000 tons if an average chest held 500 lb. of
sugar, 32,500 tons if it contained 650 lbs. The inability of
the Dutch to capture and hold Bahia led them to concentrate
their attack on Pernambuco, which gave them control of the
three surrounding captaincies. These contained 137 mills
with an annual production of 11,375 tons. The tax on sugar exports yielded £8,895.

Although the Dutch West India Company had captured
£3,363,300 in booty and ships between 1623 and 1636, its
expenses, excluding occupation costs, were £4,090,500, leaving a debt of at least £727,200.[22] In order to make the company profitable, the office of governor general was created
in 1636, and was filled with distinction by Johan Maurits from
its creation until 1644. Although Maurits' reforms made the
Dutch West India Company profitable by 1644, a fair evaluation of the progress of Brazil under the Dutch West India
Company must take into account income earned by private
traders that was not earned by the company itself. "Fortunes
were made by merchants who imported European provisions and
manufactured goods which they sold or exchanged for sugar; but
these fortunes were made by private traders for the most part,
although some of the company's employees continued to amass
wealth 'on the side.'"[23] Advocates of a monopolistic trading
system run by the Dutch West India Company with Brazil argued
that since the company had met the costs of conquering Brazil,
it should have the exclusive right to the profits to be derived from this area. The free-trade party argued that

> the Company could not in any event supply all the im-
> ports required for north-east Brazil, or buy up all the
> sugar for export, since it had not got sufficient work-
> ing capital. If the limited free-trade system were
> continued, the Company would soon derive much more profit
> from the fees, dues, taxes, tolls &c., which it exacted,
> than it could ever hope to gain by trading on its own ac-
> count with insufficient resources. Netherlands Brazil
> would only attain lasting prosperity if it were ade-
> quately colonized; and colonists would never emigrate to
> a region where they could not trade freely but were at
> the mercy of a harsh and all-embracing monopoly. Pend-
> ing adequate colonization by Dutch and Germans, the
> existence of the sugar industry depended on the

co-operation of the Portuguese _moradores_ [inhabitants].
This could only be secured by honouring the terms on
which they had surrendered, allowing them to sell their
sugars to whom they chose and at prices mutually agreed
on, and not at those imposed by a monopolistic company.[24]

Estimates of the sugar production involved varied from
2,000 to 14,000 chests;[25] after a year of argument, a compromise agreement was reached on April 29, 1638.

The trade with Brazil in Negro slaves, dyewoods, and
munitions should be reserved to the Company, but otherwise free-trade would be allowed under license to all
inhabitants of the United Provinces who were shareholders in the West India Company. The _moradores_ of
the conquered captaincies would also be allowed to
trade on equal footing with those subjects of the United
Provinces, although they were not shareholders in the
Company, since it was realized that they had sunk all
their capital in their sugar-mills and had nothing left
to invest. On the other hand, the directors of the
Company and its employees (as distinct from shareholders) were strictly forbidden to participate directly
or indirectly in this private trade. All imports to and
exports from Brazil by private traders had to be declared, inspected, weighed, and registered in the presence of the Company's representatives, for the payment
of customs dues, freight, wharfage, &c. An _ad valorem_
duty of 10 per cent. was levied on all imports by private merchants to the colony, and they likewise had to
pay 20 per cent. on all Brazilian products exported, with
an additional tax of half a stiver on each pound of sugar.
Taxes, freight, and anchorage dues, &c., could be paid
either in cash or in sugar, in the latter event at the
Recife market-rate. Elaborate arrangements were drawn
up to check smuggling, and offenders were threatened
with dire penalties, but these proved largely ineffec-
tual in practice. Most of the Company's personnel were
easily suborned, and the skippers and crews of the ships
proved themselves adepts at the game of defrauding the
customs. Nevertheless, the edict of 29 April 1638 was
a beneficient move, and gave a great impetus to the
general trade with Netherlands Brazil by ending the uncertainty as to the Company's ultimate intentions.[26]

Although Maurits encouraged planters to grow food so
that the colony would not be dependent on imports to feed
itself, for the most part they preferred to raise the cash
crop: sugar. From 1636 to 1644, sugar production was estimated

at 218,220 chests valued at £2,545,200.* However, as shown
in Table 8-3, two thirds of this amount was exported by private traders.

Although the company also profited from its monopoly of
the dyewood trade, and from taxes on building timber, tobacco, and hides, it was far less lucrative than its sister
East India Company. "In July 1645 the West India Company's
shares of 100 florins were quoted at 46 florins, partly because the Company had only paid out two or three dividends
in the whole course of its existence. The 100-florin shares
of the East India Company, which was now paying substantial
dividends with fair regularity, were quoted at 460 florins."
This in part reflected the fact that the East Indies were
largely self-supporting in provisions, while the Dutch in
Brazil depended on imports.[27] The expenses of the Dutch
West India Company were correspondingly higher. The Dutch
West India Company, in its anxiety to reduce expenses, reduced the garrison in Dutch Brazil in 1641-1642. The withdrawal of the Dutch garrisons led to Portuguese attacks,
which were supplemented by naval support masterminded by Padre
Vieira. A chartered company for the Brazil trade was organized with the aid of Jewish capital in 1649. The company
provided convoys for all shipping engaged in the Brazil trade,
sharply reducing the effectiveness of Dutch privateers who
had seized 220 Portuguese ships going to and coming from
Brazil between the beginning of 1647 and the end of 1648.
The company obtained a monopoly of the chief imports from
Portugal: codfish, wine, flour, and olive oil. Its capital
was exempt from confiscation by the Inquisition. The benefits granted were of immediate benefit to Portugal, as the
cooperation of the Brazil Company's armada was an essential
complement to the land attacks in Pernambuco,[28] which culminated in the expulsion of the Dutch from Brazil in 1654.
"The final treaty with Portugal was made in 1662, the West
India Company receiving an indemnity of 8,000,000 gulden
(£733,333), to be spread over sixteen years, and certain
commercial privileges. In 1674 the Dutch West India Company passed out of existence, their loss on liquidation
amounting to 28,000,000 gulden (£2,566,667)."[29]

In tracing the growth of Brazil under the Dutch, it is
necessary to distinguish between income figures for all of
Brazil in the 1620s, and for Dutch-held Brazil in the 1640s.
Income from sugar was estimated at £494,000 to £607,916 in
1620. The average annual sugar income of Dutch Brazil
alone under Maurits was £317,263. Annual sugar production
estimates during this time range from 12,679 to 23,651 tons

_____

*Boxer, op. cit., p. 114. This looks like the rounded
value, for sum from table = £2,538,108.

per year. "The figures last quoted are probably nearest the
truth, and they indicate the dominating position held by
Brazil in the European trade before the establishment of the
French and English sugar colonies."30 Since sugar prices
were roughly stable, gross income grew correspondingly, from
Ł494,000-to- 608,000 to Ł790,000-to-972,000. As total population in Brazil grew from 100,000 in 1600 to 184,000 in
1660, the per capita income of Brazil grew from $40 in 1620
to $43 in 1645. The per capita income of the white popula-
tion increased from $59 to $63.* Gross national product grew
approximately 2.5 per cent per annum; population increased
at a rate of 2.1 per cent; per capita income increased 0.3
per cent per year. Most of Brazil's growth during the sugar
cycle took the form of expansion of production at existing
levels of technology and income.

The base of Brazilian prosperity during the "sugar
cycle" was diminished inl 1654, when the Dutch were expelled
from Northeast Brazil. When they left, they took with
them knowledge of sugar production techniques. They also
took with them large numbers of Portuguese Jews, who feared
that they would be more harshly treated by the Brazilians
and Portuguese than they would be by the Dutch. The Portuguese Jews resident in Brazil had been heavily involved in
marketing Brazilian sugar. The loss of the Dutch and of
the Portuguese Jews therefore deprived Brazil of funds which
they had invested in Brazil, tools, slaves, and equipment
that they had used there, the technical knowledge they had
brought to the Brazilian economy, and the trade connections
and control of shipping that were invaluable in marketing
Brazilian products. When the Dutch reestablished themselves
in the West Indies, they had the advantage of a location
closer to European markets, and control of shipping and marketing facilities. As Dutch sugar production soared, sugar
prices fell (see Tables 8-1 and 8-4) by 35 per cent between
1643 and 1652, and continued to decline until the early
1690s, when they were 51 per cent of the 1643-1652 level.
Tbe fall in prices was not offset by an increase in the
quantity of Brazilian sugar produced: by the beginning of
the eighteenth century, production had fallen to 16,670

---

*Note: The income estimate is based on the assumption
that the nonwhite population of 93,647 had a subsistence income equal to $30 U.S. and that the 62,952 whites had an in-
come of Ł790,000. The conversion rate in both this estimate
and that for 1620 is, following Furtado, one pound equals
five dollars. If an upward adjustment is made in the conversion ratio to compensate for price changes, the income figures for whites and per capita would probably increase for
both 1620 and 1644. There would be no change in the subsistence income estimates.

tons yearly, while production in Bahia fell to half its
highest level by 1749-1766, if Antonil's estimates are accepted. Deerr, however, while accepting Antonil's figures
for the number of sugar mills, estimates their production
at 21,055 tons, as he believes that the capacity of sugar
chests was greater.31 Nonetheless, Bahian production was
probably greater than that of any other area in Brazil: in
1711, Antonil estimated production as shown in Table 8-5.

In 1749 only 230 mills were operating in Pernambuco;
by 1761 Pernambuco production increased to 248 factories with
an annual production of 6,000 tons. Production also increased
in Parahyba, Serinhaem, Olinda, Igarassu, and Itamaraca, but
fell off in the other provinces. By 1798 Bahia export rose
to 8,900 tons, and that of Campos to 36,000 tons from 300 factories in operation. Production continued to increase during
the first quarter of the nineteenth century; São Paulo produced 1,800 tons from 458 mills in 1813; Bahia produced
16,000 tons in 603 factories in 1833, for an average of
from 26 to 30 tons per factory, well below the levels at-
tained during the height of the sugar boom in the seventeenth century.32

Although Brazil regained and passed the level of sugar
production that it had achieved during the "sugar cycle," sugar
never again regained its share of importance in Brazil,
despite increased per capita sugar consumption in England,
both because of lower prices that sugar earned (see Tables
8-4 and 8-6) and because of more profitable activities that
were developed in Brazil. Nonetheless, it would be an error
to believe that the decline in sugar production meant that
sugar production meant that sugar no longer provided a large
share of Brazilian economic activity. It has been suggested
that sugar provided more than half of Brazilian economic activity until the middle of the eighteenth century.33

Sugar cultivation was not carried out by Portuguese settlers. Their attempts to force Indians to work at sugar
cultivation failed; an alternate source of labor had to be
found. The Portuguese-controlled sections of the Coast of
Africa, above all, Angola, provided the needed labor in the
form of slaves. Slavery and serfdom were known on the African coast before the Europeans landed. Many Africans were
literate Muslims; most were members of highly skilled iron
age cultures. Europe had had long contact with Negro peoples,
who, therefore, were not thought of as romantic "noble
savages," in need of special protection. This protection, at
least in theory and in law, was given to the American Indians.
It was not given to Negro slaves.34 Above all, Negroes were
more immune to Old World diseases than were Indians.

In order to obtain slaves, desirable exports to trade

for them were needed. The three most important goods which
were produced in Brazil that could be exchanged for slaves
were brandy, tobacco, and sugar.[35] Tobacco cultivation was
therefore adopted with sugar cultivation, since tobacco was
needed to purchase the slaves who carried out sugar cultivation, and later worked in the mines.[36] At the same time, the
demand for tobacco increased in Europe.

As tobacco cultivation expanded, both the church and the
state condemned its use. The state, under the pretext that
land used for tobacco cultivation was needed to grow bread-
stuffs, prohibited its cultivation. However, it is claimed
that the motive behind this prohibition was the centralization of tobacco collection. In 1624 the sale of tobacco
became a state monopoly, the proceeds from which were to be
used to defray military expenses. One tax farmer bought
the monopoly privilege, and, in turn, sold it for various
subregions to others. On its arrival at the warehouse, tobacco paid a 15 per cent tax on its legally decreed value
of 100 reis per libra, and 3 per cent when it left the warehouse. In 1629 the Dutch West India Company shipped more
than 4,000 arrobas of tobacco from Brazil to Holland. Production was centered in Bahia, rather than in Dutch-held
Brazil, so that total production was probably much greater
than this amount. In 1642 the tobacco monopoly was abolished,
but taxes on tobacco were increased to double on entrance,
30 reis per libra, and from 3 to 10 per cent on exit. Tobacco manufacture was free. Retail sales were licensed, and
subject to payment of the sisa.[37]

The tobacco monopoly, which was sold in 1624 for 20,200
cruzados, yielded 32,000 in 1642 and 64,700 when it was reestablished in 1659. By 1716 it brought 1,400,000 cruzados.
Total tobacco receipts, including taxes on imports and exports, were more than 2,000,000 cruzados per year, one fifth
of total crown income.

Antonil, in 1711, described the economics of tobacco
marketing and tax receipts as follows: the receipts from the
rental of the tobacco tithe of 5 per cent yielded an annual
income of 12,000 cruzados in Bahia. Total charges on the
export of tobacco came to 65,200 crusados. The cost of shipping tobacco from Bahia to Lisbon was as shown on page 28.
A libra of tobacco in Lisbon was worth up to 24 tostões (6
florins); from this contract the king obtained 2,200 crusados. Tobacco sales in London reached 1,916,250 cruzados per
year. Exports from Bahia to the coast of Mina were 15,000
arrobas yearly.*

----

*André João Antonil (pen name for Andreoni), Cultura e
Opulência do Brasil, pp. 167-171. A cruzado nôvo equaled 480
reals. It was equal in value to 35$190 in 1937 prices. The
exchange rate was 6.1983 U.S. cents per milreis.

	Reis
A rôlo of tobacco, 8 arrobas per rôlo	8$000
A hide and charges for packing tobacco in it	1$300
Other charges in Brazil	774
Shipment to and charges in Lisbon	2$050
Total	12$124
25,000 rôlos from Bahia at 12$124	300:100$000
2,500 rôlos from Alagoas and Pernambuco at 16$620 for its better quality	41:550$000
	344:650$000

In 1674, in order to raise 500,000 cruzados for the crown, the tobacco monopoly was again reestablished. It was administered by a junta which doubled the tax paid on entrance to the warehouse to 1$600 reis per arroba of ordinary tobacco, and 800 reis on Maranhão and Pará tobacco, which was of inferior quality. The junta purchased tobacco at 4 to 5,000 reis per arroba. Of 30,000 arrobas a year, 24 were sold in powdered form (snuff) at 12 tostões a libra, the remaining 6,000, for smoking and chewing, at 6 tostões.[38] In 1711 it was estimated that the difference between the cost of importing tobacco and its final sales price was 1,260,000 crusados, which left ample margin to defray the manufacturing costs. Production of tobacco outside the state monopoly system was punished. Nonetheless, owing either to contraband sales or to overbidding for the tobacco contract, holders of the tobacco monopoly did not always earn a profit. From 1722 to 1724, the monopoly was purchased for 1,800,000 crusados, but yielded less than 1,100,000. In the middle of the eighteenth century the contract sold for 2,210,000 cruzados.[39] In 1803 the contract was rented for 1,160 contos a year, while the unfortunate circumstances of 1808 led to a fall in its rental price to 1,100 contos; at this time, the soap monopoly was also included in the contract, whose profits were estimated at 40 contos. At the end of the colonial period, the contract, including soap, rented for 1,440 contos. At this time tithes (as decimas) yielded only 774 contos, and the sisa 350. In no year did either the gold or the diamond mines give as much revenue to the crown.[40] Thus the tobacco trade, which was begun largely to obtain slaves for Brazil at the end of the colonial period, was itself a heavy user of slave labor and the most important source of crown revenue.

The Cattle Industry

We have referred to idle sugar mills and lands. Since the population continued to grow, it was necessarily engaged

either in local market or subsistence activities, or production of new export goods. A large share of activities for
the local market, which were undertaken when the profitability
of sugar production fell, had been developed to provide supplies for the sugar industry. The best-known activity of this
kind was cattle raising. When sugar production was large, cattle were needed to provide power for the sugar mills, to transport sugar, wood, and other merchandise, and to provide food.
Cattle had first been brought to Brazil in 1534.41 Simonsen
suggests that as many cattle as slaves were required by the
sugar industry.

The cattle industry had initially been located in the
sertão, in the areas inland from the sugar-producing litoral
of the Northeast. The inland location was necessary to protect sugar and crop land, as there was no barbed wire fencing
to ensure that the cattle would remain in breeding corrals;
for this reason, a Royal Decree was issued in 1710 which for-
bade cattle breeding within ten leagues of the coast.

A cattle fazenda required three leages of land, and water.
Brazilian Indians and mestizos adapted easily to working with
cattle, so that it was not hard to hire cowhands, although
labor continued to be scarce in other parts of the Brazilian
economy. After four or five years of work, the vaqueiro began
to be paid by giving him one calf of every four. The animals
thus received enabled the vaqueiros to begin cattle breeding
on their own. Since typical corrals held between 200 and
1,000 head, and land was relatively cheap, cattle breeding was
an activity that enabled men with small amounts of capital to
obtain economic independence. Thus, while large fazendas
contained many corrals and owned up to 20,000 head, economies
of scale did not preclude small-scale operations to the extent
they did in the sugar industry. There is evidence that men
migrated to the cattle regions from as far away as São Vicente
in order to achieve economic independence. The first who arrived took up the best lands for cattle breeding, closest to
the sugar mills. As increasing numbers of men bred cattle,
they established themselves on inferior lands, increasingly
far from the market. Their income was necessarily less than
that of the better-located cattle breeders. This alone would
have lowered the average income derived from cattle breeding.
As the price of sugar fell, and that of cattle in the North
also fell, the profitability of cattle breeding in the North
declined (see Table 8-7). Nonetheless, cattle breeding in
Brazil expanded in the South, from which cattle products were
exported to Europe, and in the Center, where cattle were used
to supply the newly developed mining industry.

According to Antonil, a rawhide in 1710 was worth one-half
the price of an ox. Rawhide cost 2$100 in Brazil Rs. 2$940
in Lisbon after curing; a cured half hide was worth 1$500 in

Brazil, and 1$980 after taxes in Lisbon. Imports to Portugal from Brazil of cured half hides were:

From Bahia, 50,000 at 1$980 reis	99:000$000
From Pernambuco, 40,000 at 1$750 reis	70:000$000
From Rio de Janeiro and other Southern Captaincies (Capitals), 20,000 at 1$640 reis	32:800$000
Total imports in reis	201:800$000 = $33,000, U.S. 1937 prices

Source: Roberto Simonsen, História Econômica do Brasil, p. 168.

Of the sums imported, royal taxes took more than 20 per cent of cured hides, and more than 30 per cent of the value of rawhide. The value of hides fell by roughly 50 per cent between 1702 and 1729.[42] Hides were cured by drying in the South, where salt deposits were lacking, and in the North were cured by salting. The large number of Argentine dried hides available led to relatively low prices for dried hides, higher prices for salted ones. Simonsen states that minimum weights were required for hides, and that more than 200,000 pieces of 31 to 32 libras were exported in 1759, and 288,069 in 1777; in the latter year, they were valued at ₤150,000. Average annual hide exports during the eighteenth century were valued at over ₤100,000.[43]

Horses and mules were raised in addition to bovines. Portugal needed horses to aid its armed forces in Angola, and required that ships leaving Brazil for Angola include horses as part of the cargo. Although horses were needed for cavalry, mules were needed for transport and power for the newly discovered mines in the late seventeenth and eighteenth centuries. The higher prices that were obtained for mules led Brazilians to raise mules instead of horses. In 1761 the crown attempted to limit mule breeding, but its attempts were futile.[44]

Gold and Diamonds

The place of sugar as a major export in the Brazilian economy was taken by gold and diamonds from 1695 to 1750. Just before the discovery of gold, the decline of the price of sugar and of tobacco in the last quarter of the seventeenth century led to an unfavorable balance of trade of Brazil with Portugal. Lisbon merchants refused to accept payment in sugar, and demanded payment in cash. The result was a severe shortage of coin in Brazil, which provoked a financial crisis. The Portuguese attempted to alleviate the coin shortage by increasing the nominal value of their money, and tried to stimulate the economy by promoting industrialization in Portugal, by founding Colonia do Sacramento in what is now Uruguay to facilitate smuggling with the Spanish American colonies, and by encouraging the search for gold, silver, and emerald mines in Brazil.[45]

Although small gold deposits had been known as early as 1572, the first really large deposits were not located until 1693-1695 in Minas Gerais. A number of Paulistas are credited with discovering the first major gold deposit. One of the more widely accepted stories is related by Antonil:

> Just a few years back, when Artur de Sá was governor of Rio de Janeiro, they began to discover the general mines of Cataguas. They say that the first discoverer was a mulatto who had worked in the mines of Paranaguá and Curitiba. He accompanied some Paulistas into the interior to capture Indians and when they arrived at Tripuí he went down the bank with a wooden bowl to dip out some water from the creek now known as Ouro Preto. After scooping out some water in the bowl and throwing it on the bank, he noticed that the water contained some small grains the color of steel, and he didn't know what they were. He showed the grains to his companions who were unable to identify or to appreciate what had been discovered. They only observed that it was some kind of ill-formed and unknown metal. Arriving later at Taubaté, they asked about the kind of metal they had brought. Without any further examination, they sold some grains to Miguel de Souza, an eighth (3.586 grams) for 160 réis. Neither the sellers knew what they sold, nor the buyer what he bought until it was decided to send a few grains to the governor of Rio de Janeiro, Artur de Sá. He ordered them examined and found they were very fine gold.[46]

The Portuguese not only failed to recognize gold when they say it, but also were unable to work it thoroughly when they found it, since they knew even less about underground mining techniques than did the Spaniards.[47] The news that large alluvial (riverbed, i.e., surface) deposits had been found was not met with unmixed rejoicing. The governor general of Bahia wrote in 1701 that

> there was a grave risk that Brazilian gold would ultimately be of no more use to Portugal than Mexican and Peruvian silver had been to Spain. Gold, on entering the Tagus, might leave the same river soon afterwards to pay for imports from England, France, Holland and

Italy, "so . . . these countries will have all the profit
and we will have all the work." The mining camps also
threatened the colonial government's authority, as they
were peopled by "vagabond and disorderly people, for the
most part base and immoral."[48]

Antonil's less-biased description indicates some of the
economic difficulties that followed:

Each year a crowd of Portuguese and of foreigners came
out in the (annual) fleets in order to go to the mines.
From the cities, towns, plantations and backlands of Brazil, come Whites, Coloured, and Blacks, together with many
Amerindians enslaved by the Paulistas. The mixture is of
all sorts and conditions of persons: men and women;
young and old; rich and poor; nobles and commoners; lay-
men, clergy, and Religious of different Orders, many of
which have neither house nor convent in Brazil.[49]

Thus, the cultivation of sugar and tobacco was often abandoned;
so many slaves were sent to work in the mines that there was a
shortage of field hands in Bahia, Pernambuco, and Rio de
Janeiro. The area around the mines suffered for lack of food
production; traditional Brazilian exports declined. Once arrived in the mining district, the new miners ignored civil and
secular authorities, obeying instead the common law of the
mining camps. They avoided or refused the payment of the royal
fifths tax on mining output, and succeeded in defying the
authority of the crown until the outbreak in 1709 of a civil
war in the mining camps between the Paulista pioneers and new-
comers of mainly European origin.[50] Both sides appealed to
Lisbon for help; the Paulistas lost the war and the crown sent
out the first governor of Minas Gerais the following year.
His aims were not the simple extension of mining activity;
rather, they were the establishment of crown authority, the
control of mining activity, and an increase in crown revenue.
The extension of mining activity largely fell to the Paulistas,
who prospected in new areas. The crown, however, implicitly
attempted to limit mining activity. In 1702 construction of
a new road to the mines was stopped "by order of the Crown,
whose advisers considered that the fewer the routes leading
to the mines, the easier it would be to supervise them." In
pursuance of this policy, the closure of the river São Francisco route was decreed by the crown in February 1701, despite
the fact that most of the essential supplies for the mining
camps came in by this way. Another restrictive measure proposed by Dom João de Lencastre in 1701 was that nobody should
be allowed to go to the mines without a passport signed by
the governor general at Bahia, or by the governors of Rio de

Janeiro and Pernambuco, and that these passports should only be granted to persons of credit and substance. This measure was in fact adopted by the crown but its enforcement proved to be impracticable, as did the enforcement of the other restrictions mentioned, because the wooded land made evasion easy, while the dependence of the mines on outside areas for vital supplies made evasion of the prohibitions necessary for survival. The crown also futilely attempted to limit the number of Negro slaves sold to the mines, in an effort to maintain an agricultural labor supply. Since the plantation owners themselves could earn more by transferring slaves from agriculture to mining, the law was a dead letter, from the time of its adoption in 1701 to its repeal in 1715. Equally useless was repeated legislation, beginning in 1698, which limited the number of goldsmiths and, in 1766, prohibited them from working in Brazil outside the Royal Mints and Smelting Houses.[51]

The distribution of mining rights, known as _datas_, was anything but orderly in the first years; the armed force of the claimant determined who, in fact, worked the deposit. The governor of Rio de Janeiro therefore promulgated a mining code for Minas Gerais in March 1700, which was enacted by the crown in 1702, and remained in force throughout the remainder of the colonial period.

> Under the provisions of this code, the first man who discovered gold in any place had the right to choose the site of the first two datas. ˙ The third was allotted to the Crown, and the fourth to the Crown's representative or _Guarda-Mór_. These were called _datas inteiras_ (complete allotments) and they each measured thirty square _braças_. All the other _datas_ were distributed by drawing lots, and they were demarcated in proportion to the number of working slaves that each miner employed, on the basis of two square _braças_ for each slave. The Crown's _data_ was immediately sold to the highest bidder to mine on his own account, the price being credited to the royal exchequer. Once the distribution of _datas_ was made, miners could buy, sell, exchange or amalgamate their holdings by mutual arrangement. . . . The distribution of the _datas_ was the responsibility of the superintendent, Guarda-Mór, and other crown officials appointed for the purpose, all of whom received a handsome rake-off for their pains. There were a few districts where _datas_ were not officially distributed, and where ownership of a gold digging (or washing) was established simply by prior possession. These were the so-called General Mines of the Ouro Preto district which soon gave their name to the whole region of the Serra do Espinhaço and beyond.[52]

The crown regulations did not succeed in controlling all mining activity nor in obtaining all the revenue for the crown that it was entitled to by law. Instead, smuggling was widespread. The crown therefore seized the opportunity of taxing not only gold, but also of taxing inputs to mining activities, so that its revenues did in fact increase. For example, in 1711 the crown placed an additional tax on African slaves who were allotted for reexport to the mines; those coming from Angola were taxed at a higher rate than those from Guinea. The governor general at Bahia complained that Sudanese slaves from Guinea were stronger than Bantu from Angola, who sold for lower prices. The tax was therefor disproportionate; the governor general therefore amended the law by imposing a flat rate of four and a half milreis per head on all imported Negroes irrespective of origin "so as to avoid the deals and deceits which usually occur in such valuations."[53] The problem of taxation was not, however, essentially one of fairness of the tax, but one of collecting any tax at all. Just as the tax on tobacco had led to tobacco smuggling, so the tax on gold led to gold smuggling. Government revenue came not so much from de facto modification of tax law as from a clear show of force. Crown revenue from gold mines and their suppliers was obtained by confiscating contraband goods. For example, Manuel de Borba Gato, a crown official, "confiscated many of the convoys of goods coming from Bahia, remitting the proceeds in gold to the royal treasury at Rio de Janeiro, as also the proceeds from the sale of Crown mining allotments. The total yield from these sources amounted to more than eight arrobas in the time of Borba, who sent them through a certain João Martins. And this was the first gold that the King received from these mines." Confiscations were often the most important tax source from the mining regions during the eighteenth century. Yet even when the crown controlled secular offenders, they were unable to cope with clerical smugglers, who remained outside crown jurisdiction.[54] Some notion of the probable size of contraband is given by the fact that the highest total tax collections in the mining district, based on separate tax items collected, came to about 300 pounds of gold. Yet in order to avoid the payment of the royal fifth, the gold miners agreed in 1713 to pay 440 kg.-- virtually 1,000 lb.--of gold a year in commutation of this tax.[55] This coincides remarkably with Antonil's estimate that less than one third of the gold mined was actually declared.[56] If a full 20 per cent had been paid on the gold, then the 700 lb. tax difference times 5 would give a contraband volume estimate of some 3,500 lb. This is probably a minimum estimate of smuggling. An alternate method contrasts total tax collections in Minas Gerais of 10,500

drams of gold, equal to 37.3 kg. of gold to 14,500 kg. of
gold recorded as arriving that year in Lisbon. Even if previous year's hoards are included in the shipment, the disparity between tax collections and recorded shipments gives
an indication of the reason for the crown's vast dismay. It
seems likely that a large share of this gold was sent to
London in payment for British goods. Brazilian economists
have argued that it was the remarkably large accumulation of
gold in British hands that provided England with cheap capital needed to finance its industrial revolution, and control international trade by becoming the world's leading
international banker. Yet bullion alone was not sufficient
to explain Britain's economic development; the ability to
provide goods and services with which wealth was created
and bullion earned was also necessary. This lesson was not,
however, immediately learned by the Portuguese. When diamonds were discovered in the 1720s, the reaction of the crown
was even more repressive than it had been of gold mining
and processing activities.

Diamonds, when discovered, were as unrecognized as had
been the first grains of gold. The gold miners and their
slaves thought that the raw diamonds were

> merely some kind of crystals. They were used as
> counters and scoring points in card games, and changed
> hands freely for many years. When someone . . . who
> had been in India finally recognized their real nature,
> the discovery was kept secret by this man and his
> cronies, who quietly secured all they could without
> arousing suspicion. In 1726, some of these stones came
> into the hands of Don Lourenço de Almeida, the governor
> of Minas Gerais. He likewise pretended that he did not
> know what they were, though in point of fact he identi-
> fied them at once, since he had become a connoisseur of
> these gems during his long residence at Goa, which was
> then a center of the diamond trade. Dom Lourenço also
> collected as many diamonds as he could from the unsus-
> pecting miners, but someone at Villa Rica soon gave
> the game away. Crowds of adventurers with their slaves
> turned from gold to diamond washing, penetrating to
> the remotest parts of the Serro do Frio.[57]

The crown was informed of the discovery in 1729, and it
reacted by attempting to tax and restrict diamond output in
order to increase crown revenue and maintain the market
price for diamonds. A capitation tax was placed on slaves
working in the diamond district; friars and free Negroes were
prohibited from staying there; everyone not engaged in searching for diamonds was to be expelled from the area, no matter

how long his prior residence. As a high minimum price for
datas and successive rises in the capitation tax had failed
to limit the production of diamonds,

> the Crown finally resolved to ban the mining of diamonds
> altogether for some years until prices recovered. This
> decision was implemented by an edict of the Count of
> Galveas in July, 1734, which likewise prohibited gold
> mining and washing in the Diamond District. Anyone,
> bond or free, henceforth found in the sites of former
> washings and mines would be summarily arrested, even if
> no diamonds were actually found on him. Slaves appre-
> hended in this way were to be flogged and sold; and
> free men were to be fined, imprisoned, and subsequently
> expelled from the District. No one living there was
> allowed to possess any mining instruments. Later orders
> increased the severity of the punishments inflicted on
> real or suspected diamond diggers, smugglers, and
> traders, nor was any appeal allowed from the judicial
> authority exercised by the Intendant.[58]

The vastly reduced production had the hoped-for effect
of raising diamond prices, and the crown therefore decided
to resume diamond production on a limited basis. A contract
for the mines was therefore signed in 1739, and put into operation in 1740, by João Fernandes de Oliveira in partnership
with Francisco Ferreira da Silva.

> This contract was for the four-year term, January 1, 1740
> -December 31, 1743. The search for diamonds was thereby
> limited to the bed of the river Jequitinhonha with its
> banks and immediate neighborhood. Not more than 600
> slaves were to be employed by the contractors in the
> actual mining, for each of whom an annual capitation tax
> of 230 milreis was paid to the Crown. Any of the con-
> tractors' slaves found washing or digging for diamonds
> outside the allotted area would be confiscated to the
> Crown, as would any slaves over and above the permitted
> 600 who were found in them. All diamonds mined by the
> slaves were kept in the Intendant's safe, and were only
> handed over to the contractor for remission to headquar-
> ters at Lisbon. Contractors were empowered to recover
> debts due to them by distraining the property or imprison-
> ing the persons of their debtors. The local Crown offi-
> cials, from the Intendant downwards, were ordered to af-
> ford the contractors all judicial and administrative
> facilities in the execution of their contracts. If the
> contractors suspected anyone of mining, buying, or sell-
> ing diamonds, they could inform the Intendant secretly

of their suspicions. He in his turn was authorized to
expel from the district any individual accused in this
way, nor could the accused appeal against this decision.[59]

The restrictions and contract system were hardly popular;
they were enforced by four companies of at least sixty men
each, who, unlike most Portuguese soldiers, maintained a "high
standard of dress and discipline."   The dragoons were
authorized to stop and search anyone for gold and diamond contraband, and were rewarded proportionately to the sums seized.
Illegal mining continued, both by free men and runaway slaves.
The official estimate of diamond production is necessary a
minimum estimate; 1,666,569 carats dug from 1740 to 1771, worth
15,515:403$662 of which 4,644:181$588 was paid to the crown.[60]
Continuing crown misgivings about the operation of the diamond
contract led to a tightening of the rules governing the diamond
trade by the Marquis of Pombal in 1753, and the abolition of
the contract system in favor of direct operation on behalf of
the crown in 1771. The crown monopoly, known as the Real
Extraccão, remained in existence until 1835. The bulk of the
Brazilian gold and diamonds were mined by 1760, after which
mining activity tapered off and Brazil reverted to agricultural production for export, the major crops being cotton and
sugar.
    During the mining boom, most of the work had been done
by slaves. The gold mines were visited by John Mawe at the
beginning of the nineteenth century; the conditions he
describes are typical of the mining operations for the past
hundred years.

> In the operation of getting gold, the heavy work is as-
> signed to the male negroes, and the lighter labor to the
> females. The cascalho [gravel], dug from these pits by
> the former, is carried away by the latter in gamellas,
> or bowls, to be washed. When a sufficient quantity has
> been procured, the men proceed to that process, . . .
> they did not, in the first instance, attempt to separate
> the gold from the black oxide of iron, but emptied their
> gamellas into a larger vessel, by rinsing them in the
> water which it contained. The substance deposited in this
> vessel was delivered out, in small portions of about a
> pound each, to the most skilful washers, as the operation
> of washing, or as it was termed, purifying it, required
> great niceness and dexterity. Some of the grains of gold
> were so fine as to float on the surface, and of course
> were liable to be washed away in these repeated changes
> of water; to prevent which the negroes bruised a few
> handfuls of herbs on a stone, and mixed the juice in small
> proportions with the water in their gamellas. Whether

this liquid did in reality tend to precipitate the
gold, I could not positively ascertain, but the negroes
certainly used it with the greatest confidence.

There is another mode of separating the gold from
the calcalho called canoe-washing, which is extremely
interesting. The canoes are made in the following manner: Two ten or twelve-inch planks, about twelve or
fifteen feet in length, are laid on the ground, forming
an inclined plane, sloping about one inch in twelve:
two other planks of similar dimensions are fixed in the
same direction at the lower end, forming a second inclined plane, with a fall of six inches from the former.
On their sides are boards placed edge-wise, and staked
down to the ground so as to form long shallow troughs,
the bottoms of which are covered with hides tanned with
the hair on, having the hairy side outwards, or, in
defect of these, with rough baize. Down these troughs
is conveyed the water containing the oxide of iron and
the lighter particles of gold; the latter substance pre-
cipitating in its course is entangled by the hair.
Every half hour the hides are taken up, and carried to
a tank near at hand, formed of four walls, say five feet
long, four broad, and four deep, and containing about
two feet depth of water. The hides are stretched over
this tank and well beaten, then dipped and beaten repeatedly, until all the gold is disentangled, after
which they are carried back and replaced in the troughs.
The tanks are locked up at nights, and well secured.
The sediment taken from them being light, is easily
washed away by the hand in the manner before described,
leaving only the black oxide of iron, called esmeril,
and the gold, which is so fine that mercury is used
to separate it.[61]

According to Boxer,

One of the few redeeming features in the life of slaves
in Minas Gerais--or elsewhere in Brazil for that matter
--was the possibility of their buying or being given
their freedom at some time, a contingency which was much
rarer in the French and English American colonies. Moreover, by the nature of their work in searching for placer
gold it was often relatively easy for them to secrete
gold dust and even smaller nuggets, apart from the fact
that some masters allowed their slaves to seek gold for
themselves after working a fixed number of hours for their
owners. In this way a fair number of slaves were able
to buy their freedom, and the hope of doing so was given
to many more. The story that the church of Santa

Efigenia was mainly built from the proceeds of the gold dust washed out of their hair by Negress devotees in the font may be apocryphal. but it is symptomatic of what could happen in Minas Gerais.62

At the beginning of the eighteenth century, diamonds were obtained by essentially the same method of washing the ore that was used in gold mining.63 By the end of the eighteenth century, this technique had been replaced by a system of troughs, sluices, and conduits. Mawe describes the diamond mining operations:

> On the heap of the cascalho, at equal distances, are placed three high chairs for the officers or overseers. In order to insure the vigilance of the overseers, these chairs are constructed without backs or any other support on which a person can recline. After they are seated, the Negroes enter the troughs. The Negroes employed in these works are the property of individuals, who let them to hire at the daily rate of three vintens of gold, equal to about eight-pence, Government supplying them with victuals. Every officer of the establishment is allowed the privilege of having a certain number of negroes employed. Each [Negro is] provided with a rake of a peculiar form and short handle, with which he rakes into the trough about fifty or eighty pounds weight of cascalho. The water being them let in upon it, the calcalho is spread abroad and continually raked up to the head of the trough, so as to be kept in constant motion. This operation is performed for the space of a quarter of an hour; the water then begins to run clearer, having washed the earthy particles away, the gravel-like matter is raked up to the end of the trough; after the current flows away quite clear, the largest stones are thrown out, and afterwards those of inferior size, then the whole is examined with great care for diamonds. The negroes are constantly attending to the cascalho from the very commencement of the washings, and frequently find diamonds before the last operation, When a negro finds one he immediately stands upright and claps his hands, then extends them, holding the gem between his forefinger and thumb; an overseer receives it from him, and deposits it in a gamella or bowl, suspended from the centre of the structure, half full of water. In this vessel all the diamonds found in the course of the day are placed, and at the close of the work are taken out and delivered to the principal officer, who, after they have been weighed, registers the particulars in a book kept for that purpose.

When a negro is so fortunate as to find a diamond of
the weight of an _octavo_ (17 1/2 carats), much ceremony
takes place; he is crowned with a wreath of flowers and
carried in procession to the administrator, who gives
him his freedom, by paying his owner for it. He also
receives a present of new clothes, and is permitted to
work on his own account. When a stone of eight or ten
carats is found, the negro receives two new shirts, a
complete new suit, with a hat and a handsome knife. For
smaller stones of trivial amount proportionate premiums
are given.64

There is no particular regulation respecting the dress
of the negroes: they work in the clothes most suitable
to the nature of their employment, generally in a waist-
coat and a pair of drawers, and not naked as some travel-
lers have stated. Their hours of labor are from a little
before sun-rise until sun-set, half an hour being allowed
for breakfast, and two hours at noon. While washing they
change their posture as often as they please, which is
very necessary, as the work requires them to place their
feet on the edges of the trough, and to stopp considerably.
This posture is particularly prejudicial to young growing
negroes, as it renders them in-kneed. Four or five times
during the day they all rest, when snuff, of which they
are very fond, is given to them.
The negroes are formed into working parties, called
troops, containing two hundred each, under the direction
of an administrator and inferior officers. Each troop
has a clergyman and a surgeon to attend it. With respect to the subsistence of the negroes, although the
present governor has in some degree improved it by allowing a daily portion of fresh beef, which was not allowed
by his predecessors, yet I am sorry to observe that it
is still poor and scanty: and in other respects they are
more hardly dealt with than those of any other establishment which I visited: notwithstanding this, the owners
are all anxious to get their negroes into the service,
doubtless from sinister motives.65

The sinister motives were, of course, smuggling (embez-
zlement) of diamonds outside the diamond district without paying the tax on diamonds due to the crown. At the same time,
owners tried to prevent Negroes stealing diamonds on their
own account. An eyewitness in 1735 wrote that

Ten whites are not enough to watch one Negro. For this
reason, the Negroes give very few large diamonds to
their masters, for they all prefer to give them to the

Negresses, who then sell them in the taverns to whites
who buy them secretly. The Negroes only give the small
diamonds to their owners, and this is one of the reasons
--and not the least of them--why it is not much use
employing Negroes in this work.66

After 1740 there was usually one white or mulatto overseer to supervise every eight Negro slaves:

But the latter still found means of cheating their em-
ployers, though only allowed to wear the equivalent of
a loincloth or G string when they were actually working.
   The slaves had to work in a stooping position facing
their overseer, so as to sift the cascalho in the
troughs and throw away the gravel while picking out the
diamonds. They frequently had to change places with
each other so as to prevent them from finding again some
diamonds they might have concealed in a heap of stones
or earth. Even so, they could sometimes identify the
exact spot where they had hidden a diamond, and return
under cover of night to secure it. The first thing that
old hands among the slaves taught the moleques or new
arrivals was how to steal diamonds. "For this purpose
they practice on them with beans, or grains of maize,
which they throw from a distance into the mouth, and in
this way they teach them to catch them in the mouth and
swallow them." They also practice sleight of hand and
other tricks which enabled them to hide a diamond between their fingers, or in the palm of the hand, and
convey it to the mouth unseen. By dint of practice,
they could even pick up a diamond with their toes, "concealing it between them for hours on end, and walking
with it in this way to the slave quarters." Another
favorite trick was to push the diamond up a nostril
when taking snuff, or when pretending to do so. The
slaves also let their nails grow long, so as to con-
ceal small diamonds behind them, and they had recourse
to many other ingenious methods, too complicated to
describe here. Swallowing the diamond seems to have
been their favorite device. When a slave was suspected
of this practice, he was locked in a strongroom and
given a violent purge of Malagueta pepper.
   When a Negro found a diamond which he saw no chance
of concealing, he stood upright, clapped his hands, and
then extended his arms upwards and sideways, holding the
gem between the forefinger and thumb.67

The Labor Supply

The condition of slaves in the gold and diamond mines
was not worse than that which had obtained earlier in dyewood
gathering and sugar production. The conditions of life of
slaves in Brazil, although far from enviable at any time, improved during the colonial period. The Portuguese colonists,
unaccustomed to the tropics, claimed that white men could not
survive heavy labor there; above all, their desire to rise in
the social scale made many colonists believe that poverty was
preferable to work. Negro slaves are first recorded working
in the sugar mills of São Vicente in 1535.[68] Official
authorization to bring slaves to Brazil was granted in 1549,
while in 1595 the Portuguese Gomes Reynal was granted the
right to introduce 38,250 slaves in nine years.[69] An estimate
of the need for Indian labor in the Northeast of Brazil is
that cattle raising required from ten to twelve people for
three leagues. The demand for Negroes in the Northeast is
that three leagues of sugar or tobacco cultivation required
from 800 to 1,000 slaves.[70] Thus, 52,053 slaves were imported
from Angola to Brazil between 1575 and 1591.[71] Mortality must
have been great, as only 14,000 Negroes were reported in Brazil in 1585, and 20,000 in 1600.[72] Slaves who worked in the
sugar fields in the seventeenth century "wore out" so that
they had an "effective life" of seven years.[73] Slaves working
in sugar mills and the mines in the late seventeenth and
early eighteenth centuries had an average life of ten or
more years. In the late eighteenth century "the average life
span was low, about fifteen years; a slave was productive at
the longest for only eighteen to thirty-six years, and most
of them died of pulmonary tuberculosis and dozens of intesti-
nal diseases."[74]

The conditions of the slave trade in colonial Brazil were
influenced by fifteenth-century Portuguese slave trade practices. Slaves were not counted as individuals, but by height
and volume in toneladas. The unit of measurement was the
peça de India, which was 1.75 metres, the ordinary height of
an adult Negro. Three peças equaled one tonelada, on the
assumption that other cargo occupying the same space would
weigh that much. In order to keep accounts, the height of
Negroes was added, then divided by the standard size, 5.25
metres, to obtain the toneladas. In practice, average
valuations were used. Two children from 4 to 8 years were
counted as one peça; three children from 8 to 15 years as
two peças. Adults from 16 to 34 years equaled one peça.
From 35 to 40 years, two Negroes equaled one peça, while
relatively few Negroes over 40 were bought as slaves.[76]

The slave voyage began when the Africans who were imported from Angola were baptized in lots before they left

their own shores. Shipowners often provided inadequate food
or water for the number of slaves on board; mortality ran
close to fifty per cent. "On their arrival in Brazil they
learn the doctrines of the Church and the duties of the religion into which they have entered. These bear the mark of the
royal crown upon their breasts, which denotes that they have
undergone the ceremony of baptism, and likewise that the
King's duty has been paid on them."[77] The Negroes were
"registered and marketed like any other merchandise, 'there
being no difference between Negroes and goods.'"[75]

The treatment of Negro slaves depended upon the work to
which they were assigned. The worst off were field slaves
who worked in the sugar plantations. Boxer, summarizing
various Portuguese chroniclers, writes that

> At harvest time and when the mills were grinding the
> cane, work on a plantation was sometimes continued
> round the clock, and otherwise lasted at least from dawn
> to dusk. In the winter or rainy season, the hours were
> not so long, and the more considerate planters did not
> compel their slaves to work until after the sun was high
> in the heavens and they had received a breakfast of
> "broth, or honey when there is some." On Sundays and
> the principal saints' days the slaves were supposed to
> be free to tend their own allotments after hearing mass.
> Some planters evaded this concession whenever they could,
> but others extended it to include Saturdays as well in
> the winter season when the mills were idle. Manioc and
> vegetables formed the slaves' staple diet, meat and fish
> being luxuries for them. All slaves were supposed to
> receive the rudiments of religious instruction from the
> local chaplain, to go to confession once a year, and to
> have all their newborn children baptized. On some plan-
> tations the slaves were allowed, or even encouraged, to
> indulge in their own African tribal dances and music on
> high-days and holidays, but such practices were frowned
> on by the stricter clergy and forbidden from time to
> time. The plantation factor (or foreman) had to inspect
> the slave quarters (senzala) daily, to ensure that they
> were kept clean and tidy, to hunt out malingerers, to
> see that slaves who were genuinely ill got medical
> treatment, and to send for the confessor if they were
> dangerously so.[79]

It was often said that three things were necessary for
slaves: (in Portuguese, the three Ps: Pao, Pão, and Panno),
cudgels to punish them with, and bread and cloth. Some notion of the barbarity with which the overseers (feitores) ran
the plantations is given by Antonil's instructions that the

overseers should by no means allow (others) or themselves to kick pregnant women in the belly, nor beat slaves with cudgels, since the overseers in their anger did not measure their blows and could mortally wound an able slave in the head, who was worth a lot of money, and lose it.[80]

Even Gilberto Freyre, who argues that Negro slaves in the big houses were better treated, and sometimes manumitted, by the masters they grew up with, goes into considerable detail about the sadistic treatment to which the men and the sexual abuse to which the women were subjected. It is, however, often suggested that the treatment of slaves by the Spanish and the British was even worse since the Portuguese manumitted their slaves or permitted them to use their earnings to buy their freedom more frequently than did the other European groups.[81]

The reaction of the Negroes to their enslavement was to rise in revolt and to flee to quilombos, which were communities of escaped Negroes. This was easiest in the years when the Brazilians were preoccupied with expelling the Dutch. The quilombos were located far from towns and highways, and produced enough crops and livestock to support themselves. In addition, their members ambushed passengers and goods on roads, and raided outlying farms and plantations to obtain new recruits and women.

> These Negroes reached such numbers that they became a plague everywhere in the captaincies. So bold and insolent did they become that they attacked not only to steal household property from the inhabitants but also to incite and carry off their slaves, some willingly and others by force; they would kill the overseers and many times the masters and ladies. Committing every form of aggression and always with cruelty, they had gained so much confidence in their forces that in a period of almost forty years the many expeditions sent with considerable authority by the Governors of Pernambuco to conquer them were never successful and many were dispersed.[82]

In the seventeenth century, several quilombos banded together to form the Republic of Palmares, which lasted from 1630 to 1697, when bandeirantes (men from São Paulo) hired by the government of Pernambuco succeeded in destroying it. While it lasted, Palmares showed an interesting kind of Brazilian political structure, including a king, a minister of justice, and legislative groups, and Bantu customs, which prevailed in daily life.[83]

The destruction of Palmares did not end all runaway slave communities or prevent Negro revolts in the eighteenth century.   Runaway slaves were dealt with by enlisting free Mulattoes, Negroes, Amerindians, and half-breeds

> into armed bands under the so-called capitães do mato ("bush-whacking" captains), who scoured the countryside in search of runaway Negro slaves. The capitães do mato in Minas Gerais were rewarded by gold payments for each Negro they apprehended, the rewards being calculated on a sliding scale in accordance with the distance and the length of time in which they had to operate away from their home base. .When caught, the Negroes were placed in the local jail and turned over to their masters after the latter had paid the stipulated reward.   The standing order or Regimento of 1722 enjoined the capitães do mato not to use unnecessary cruelty in the capture of runaway slaves, but this injunction was often disregarded.   Complaints were also made that the capitães do mato were likely to seize innocent Negro slaves who were going about their own or their masters' lawful business, and only surrender them on payment. They were also alleged to keep slaves whom they recaptured working for themselves for a long time, before informing the rightful owners of their apprehension.[84]

Negroes who resisted arrest were decapitated and their heads were exhibited by the capitães do mato in order to substantiate their claims for reward.   In March 1741, at the request of residents of Minas Gerais

> the crown ordained that all Negroes " who were found to be living voluntarily in quilombos should be branded with an F on the shoulder", a branding iron for this purpose to be kept by each town council. Those who were caught after deserting a second time, had an ear cut off, and death was the usual punishment for a third offense of this kind. Desertions still continued on a large scale, however, for many Negroes preferred to take the risk of being hunted down and killed to a life of toil under the lash. Indeed, it was alleged that they were proud of their branded F, regarding it as a badge of honor rather than of infamy.[85]

During the colonial period, Brazilian slavery cannot be said to have been more gentle or moderate than its American counterpart. Although there was a greater chance of manumission in Brazil than in the United States, Brazilian conditions in general were harsher than United States conditions.   Further, many Brazilian slave owners evidently believed "that it was more profitable to get everything possible out of adult slaves in a few years and then replace them"[86] with raw hands

than it was to raise a slave from childhood, and treat
him well, thus ensuring a longer and more productive
life.

The conditions surrounding the use of Indian labor were
somewhat different from those surrounding Negro labor. This
reflected the Indians' cultural level, their legal status, and
the attitude of the church towards them.

Unlike the Indians of Mexico or Peru, and somewhat like
those of Argentina, the Brazilian Indians had not formed themselves into vast political empires, the components parts of
which were economically linked by trade and tribute. The
Indians of Brazil were largely hunters and gatherers, or vil-
lage agricultural peoples who shifted their sites as slash-
and-burn agricultural techniques required. It was therefore
difficult to use them in activities for which they had little cultural or geographic precedent. Thus, it was more
likely that an Indian could be successfully employed in logging, cattle raising, or personal service than in plantation
labor.[87] At first the Indians supplied dyewood, food, and
labor service in exchange for tools and trinkets provided by
Portuguese traders and settlers. As the number of Portuguese
increased, their cumulative demands were harder to bear for
the Indians, whose desire for few or poor-quality Portuguese
goods appears to have been satisfied. The Indians therefore
demanded more and better goods for their help, playing one
Portuguese against the other. The increase in cost of Indian
labor raised the settlers' cost of living and lowered the
donatários' profit.[88]

Since the goods offered in barter were not sufficiently
attractive to attract many voluntary Indian laborers, the
Portuguese in Brazil acquired Indian slaves from their Indian
allies. These slaves had been captured in intertribal wars.
The Portuguese themselves enslaved Indians to obtain a labor
supply. The resulting Indian hostility and revolts, occurring
when the French were menacing the Brazilian coasts, led the
crown to adopt a new policy, ordering "that only those Indians
who had shown themselves hostile to the Portuguese were to be
assaulted, and, even then, only by the governor's army or by
the settlers acting with his license. The captives made in
what came to be called the "licit wars" might then legiti-
mately be enslaved."[89] The crown also called on the Society
of Jesus to Christianize the Indians, pacify them, and concentrate them near Portuguese settlements, where they would
be available both for labor and military aid in repelling
the French. The Society of Jesus accepted the commission,
but carried it out in a manner different from that envisaged
by the crown, and largely contrary to the desires of the settlers.[90]

The settlers, who called the Indians "cannibal heathen,"

wanted the Indians as slaves and military allies. The Jesuits,
who condemned Portuguese sin and wanted to save Indian souls,
wanted to isolate the Indians from the Portuguese, in order
to bring them up according to the precepts of Christian moral-
ity. The Jesuit Father Nobrega proposed a code for governing
Indians, according to which they would (1) be prohibited from
eating human flesh, and from making war without the license of
the governor; (2) be made to take only one wife; (3) dress
themselves, as they had enough cotton, at least after becoming
Christians; (4) remove sorcerers from them; (5) maintain justice among them and between the Indians and the Christians;
and (6) live quietly, without moving to other places, except
to be among Christians, who have enough land to supply them,
and with these, Fathers of the Company in order to be indoc-
trinated.[91] The Jesuits therefore established houses for the
instruction of the unbaptized in Christian doctrine, and col-
legios for the further education of Christians.[92] In order
to support these establishments, the Jesuits relied on aid
from the crown, alms, and revenues from the sale of their own
products. The first two, however, were difficult to obtain,
since the Jesuit Father Nobrega refused absolution of the
sacraments to the Portuguese who enslaved Indians unjustly
and lived in public concubinage.[93] The Portuguese, in protest, refused to give alms or hand over the revenues that the
crown had designated for delivery to the Jesuits.[94] Jesuit
income, therefore, was obtained from tithes paid by newly
converted Indians to the Jesuits, and from the results of
Indian labor for the Jesuit-directed community. Thus,

> the curate allowed no one to work for personal gain;
> he compelled everyone, without distinction of age or
> sex, to work for the community, and he himself saw to it
> that all were equally fed and dressed. For this purpose
> the curates placed in storehouses all the fruits of agri-
> culture and the products of industry, selling in the
> Portuguese towns their surpluses of cotton cloth, tobacco,
> skins, vegetables, yerba maté, and wood; they transported
> them in their own boats down the nearest river, and re-
> turning with implements and whatever else was needed.
> . . . They supplied everyone with abundant food and cloth-
> ing. They compelled the men to work only half a day, and
> did not drive them to produce more. They gave them many
> holidays, dances, plays, and tournaments. They forbade
> the women to sew; this occupation was restricted to the
> musicians, sacristans and acolytes. But they made them
> spin cotton; and the cloth they wove, after satisfying
> their own needs, they sold together with surplus cotton
> in the Portuguese towns. . . . For clothing, the Jesuits
> gave them each a cap, a shirt, stockings, and a poncho,

all made of cotton cloth--a thick, light-colored material. They made them shave their hair, and did not permit them to wear anything on their feet. The women also
went barefooted, and their only garment was a tipo or
sleeveless shirt of the same material described above,
girdled at the waist.[95]

Nonetheless, Marchant suggests that the Jesuits made the
Indians work more than they had before coming into contact with
the Portuguese, and that this, combined with the possible introduction of new techniques, increased the available surplus
of food products. This was extremely important, as the Indians
outside of the Jesuit area had refused to plant food crops in
1557, because "they saw no reason to add a growing crop to the
very land that the settlers threatened to take from them."[96]
It should be stressed that the problem of obyaining a labor
supply adequate to provide sufficient food, without oppressing
the Indians, vexed even the Jesuits. Nobrega,

very shortly after establishing his first casa in 1549,
. . . acquired a small number of slaves to produce food
for the two hundred or so natives of the casa. These
were Indians, victims, perhaps, of a licit war. Five
were to plant food, and some among the rest were to fish
and hunt. When after founding his first collegio between 1550 and 1551 he discovered how uncertain were the
alms of the settlers, he asked of the King some Guinea
slaves, and, with their labor, sustained his meninos.[97]

In some cases, however, the Jesuits oversaw the distribution
of labor of Indians to Portuguese. In the state of Maranhão
and Pará they refused to let Portuguese claimants of labor
obtain Indians without their guaranteeing in advance the payment of their respective salaries, according to the state law.
In most instances, they only distributed men, and not women
and children for labor. Exceptions were made for wet nurses,
and as punishment for disobedient Indian women, to serve high
colonial officials, or poor Portuguese women. The only exception to the rule that prior deposits had to be made for Indians' salaries was in the case of service of the crown.[98]
The Jesuits' efforts to protect the Indians failed at
first, and continued to fail, for both historical and medical
reasons. For example, in 1562 Mem de Sá, governor of Brazil,
proclaimed the Caaeté Indians outlaws and liable to enslavement as victims of a licit war. The excuse given was that
the Caaeté had murdered the first Bishop of Brazil in 1556.
In fact, however, the settlers had begun to enslave Indians
without the governor's permission, and permission was given
at least in part to maintain the semblance of legal control.

The Jesuit fathers correctly feared that declaration of a
licit war would lead not only to the enslavement of Caaeté in
distant areas, but also to slave raids within the Jesuit missions themselves. Between the raids and the flight of Indians, the population of the missions fell from 12,000 to
1,000. The governor, who had not intended quite so massive
a campaign, revoked his sentence against the Caaeté. The
Portuguese then reverted to paying Indians in goods to deliver
their fellows as slaves. The governor then ordered that Indians bartered into slavery were to be confiscated and sent
to live in the Jesuit missions. The governor's belated attempt to preserve the Indian population was entirely frustrated by two smallpox epidemics in 1562 and 1563. The first
epidemic killed some thirty thousand Negroes and Indians, but
few Portuguese--who were more immune. The second epidemic
killed between one fourth and three fifths of the survivors.
The Indian population in the area of Bahia had been initially
estimated at 80,000. By 1563 only nine to ten thousand Indians remained. The survivors, too weak to tend their farms,
sold themselves into slavery for food.[99] By the 1580s there
were virtually no free Indians left in the immediate vicinity
of Pernambuco, which had become the Brazilian center for
Negro slave trading, while some Indians remained in Bahia in
the Jesuit missions.[100]

> When the Portuguese wished either food or labor from the
> Indians, they went to the parishes. Under the supervi-
> sion of the Jesuits, an Indian principal would then
> agree with them as to the sort of wares to be exchanged
> and the sort of work to be done. Very often as many as
> one hundred natives a month would be working for the Por-
> tuguese. Usually, they went to work around the houses
> of the Portuguese, but occasionally they might help with
> the work on the fazendas as well. The Jesuits laid one
> restriction on the Indians' working for barter. As the
> number of Indians was small and as all their labor was
> needed to produce food for the parishes, no native was
> allowed to undertake outside work for barter until all
> his parish work was finished. The same care in finish-
> ing tasks was required of the natives when they went to
> work for the Portuguese. If a parish native left work
> unfinished, he was required to return and finish it. . . .
> In the case of a revolt of the Guinea slaves, the parish
> Indians went against them under Portuguese leadership,
> and then searched the countryside to find escaped slaves
> and to restore them to their owners. . . . In the south,
> the friendly Indians who were free, less wasted in num-
> bers by attack and disease, mixed much more on independ-
> ent terms among the Portuguese. In the absence of the

economic pressure of plantations, this second class
acted mainly as allies who helped the men of São Vicente
invade and open up the interior of the continent.101

The phrase "absence of the economic pressure of plantations" is a little misleading. It means that the São Paulo
area was less favored for purposes of sugar cultivation. The
result was poverty, and the search for alternate sources of
income. The Paulistas--Indians, half-breeds, and Portuguese
--therefore formed groups of men known as bandeiras, which
explored and opened up new territory, took Indians and sold
them as slaves, prospected for minerals, and, occasionally,
served as militiamen. They did not act as settlers; they
opened lands more rapidly than they could be filled with permanent settlers. Until export goods were found, it cost too
much to import Negroes: it has been estimated that there was
only one Negro for every 34 Indians in service during the
bandeirante era.102 Thus, the Paulistas took some 350,000
Indian prisoners in the sixteenth and seventeenth centuries.103
Royal edicts guaranteeing the freedom of the Indians (1570),
prohibiting their enslavement (1595), and restriction of slaving activities to "licit wars" were no more than a dead letter. "The encomiendas of Spanish America corresponded to the
'free services' (servicos forros) of the Portuguese, exacted
from Indians who were free by royal decision but maintained
in captivity, 'deposited' in the domiciles of the colonists.
The opposition of the Jesuits to this general tendency provoked a series of conflicts that culminated in their expulsion from the town of São Paulo in 1640."104 The bandeirantes'
raids on and destruction of Jesuit reductions at first provided them with a supply of Indians, but later forced the
bandeirantes to travel farther to obtain Indians. The decline
of the Brazilian sugar industry, and the greater availability
of Negroes after the reconquest of Angola in 1648, both
served to reduce the demand for Indian slaves. Thus the costs
of slaving increased as the anticipated price declined, so
that in the second half of the seventeenth century, bandeiras
increasingly hunted for minerals rather than slaves.105
     While it lasted, the Indian slave trade was as horrify-
ing as the African slave trade, and equally based on economic
considerations. For example,

Father Mansilla is not far from the truth when . . . he
writes that the life of the Paulistas in the second quarter of the seventeenth century can be summed up as a
constant "going and coming, and bringing and selling
Indians," and that in the entire town of São Paulo there
can be no more than one or two inhabitants who are not engaged in the traffic of human cattle, either going in

person or sending their sons and dependents to the sertão.

But even those who are left behind, restrained by
sickness or because of their sex, participate in their
own way in the sertão expeditions. They manage to have
someone go at their expense. It is a true partnership
of capital and labor, or rather, a contract, whereby
the wealthy supply the capital and the poor the heroism.
Even the religious orders cannot resist the temptation,
especially the Carmelite order. It organizes several
expeditions on the grounds that, in the view of the
monastery's limited means, its solution lies in the service of the Indians.

Armored and armed, the bandeirante needed

the chains, two or more braças long, with fifty or more
links or rings, and five, twelve or thirty neck collars.
Yoked one to another at the neck by padlocked shackles,
it is thus that the Indians, seized for captivity from
their villages and reductions, are dragged along weeks
and months on end until they reach the settlement.[106]

The crown did not effectively regulate the Indian slave
trade until 1757. In this year, regulations were passed under
Pombal, and the Jesuits' temporal power over the Indians was
suspended. In its place, the crown provided for concentrat-
ing Indians in communities under an administrator; at the
same time, it imposed the use of Portuguese, permitted the
Indians to be used as paid labor, and encouraged mixed mar-
riages, as a "solution through miscegenation" of the Indian
problem. This system remained in effect until its repeal in
1798; at the beginning of the nineteenth century, therefore,
colonists reverted to the old system of conducting offensive
wars against the Indians and enslaving the prisoners captured.[107] Decimation by slave raids and disease continued
throughout the nineteenth century.

Interregional and International Trade

The demand for Indian and Negro slaves depended upon
economic factors, as well as upon the desire to achieve social acceptance by owning slaves and avoiding physical labor.
In the beginning, before the Portuguese established military
dominance over the Indians, many Portuguese settlers must have
done their own work. The shift from free to slave labor depended not only upon the physical ability to obtain and hold
slaves, but also upon the financial ability to earn a profit
on slave labor. To a very large extent, this meant that

slavery was profitable when Brazil was able to produce goods
for export to European markets on favorable terms. The goods
produced and the regions producing them shifted markedly
throughout the colonial period (see Table 8-8). Thus, the
early captaincies specialized in the gathering and export of
dyewood and other forest products (1510-1580). The dominance
of logging came to an end because of the exhaustion of trees
near the coast, and the consequent increased difficulty of
logging operations, and because of the greater attractiveness
of producing sugar for export. While dyewood was found
throughout Brazil, sugar production was concentrated in one
region--the Northeast. The other regions therefore either maintained themselves on a combination of subsistence agriculture
and dyewood export, or attempted to share in the sugar wealth
by selling their regional exports to the Northeast. They
also traded with Peru, and Argentina, and looked for alternate
activities.

> By the early seventeenth century the captaincy of São
> Vicente had a modest export trade in salt meat, hides,
> fruit preserves and flour. It supplied both the coastal
> cities of Northern Brazil and Buenos Aires to the South.
> Trade with the latter was often conducted in roundabout
> fashion via Bahia, although one Paulista will mentions
> direct commerce with a merchant in Buenos Aires and Span-
> ish pesos and reales are known to have circulated on the
> plateau. In 1622 the Spanish crown, to which Portugal
> was then subject, suspended the Brazil-Plata trade.
> Since this was also a time when Dutch corsairs were
> threatening South Atlantic shipping, the main artery
> between Brazil and the Peruvian vice-royalty shifted to
> the overland route via Guiairá (modern Paraná) and Para-
> guay. This development virtually coincided with the
> thrust of the Paulista slave hunts into that region and
> suggests the possibility of some commercial basis for or
> corollary to the bandeiras activities. . .
> The Paulista plateau, however, was far from being a
> commercial emporium. Its economic base was essentially
> subsistence agriculture. The scarcity of coinage made
> payment in kind customary for exchange, wages, and local
> taxation. Cotton cloth, wax, hides, cattle, poultry,
> sugar, in fact any foodstuffs might serve as tender.
> Transactions or loans were frequently consummated without
> any documentation. Such phrases in the wills as "he owes
> me whatever he may declare as the truth" or "whatever he
> finds in his conscience" imply a pre-commercial regime of
> mutual trust and natural law.[108]

Jaime Cortesão has written that

São Paulo was a small city of vigorous, enterprising, active people, accustomed to the severest toil and exertion, but living with no comforts and the most modest resources. Other Brazilian cities, such as Bahia, Pernambuco, and Rio de Janeiro, whose economy was based on the cultivation and processing of sugar cane, were already enjoying more prosperous conditions of life. This same source of wealth, which required the large-scale importation of Negroes from Angola and Guinea, had made Brazil the clandestine intermediary for the traffic in slave labor which was likewise so necessary to the mining industry of Peru. And, if the silver of the Andes sharply intensified commerce and accumulation of wealth in Brazil, the Negro slave coming from Brazilian ports, or from Angola by way of these ports, had become more and more the instrument indispensable for the industrial activities of the Andean plateau. If we add to the Negro slaves the sugar, the fazendas, the rich furniture, and various food products, we can conclude that Portuguese and Spanish America were, from the economic standpoint, complementary regions. . . .

There are many documents and historical references from which one concludes that the Paulistas of that period entered Peru by two routes: the first, that of Asunción, whence one continued to Santa Fé; the other, a route leading directly across the sertão to the cities of La Plata and Potosí. The first was the normal route for those intending to remain in Peru for some time, while the second was used by those making a rapid foray to return immediately to São Paulo bringing Indians from the Siera and large or small cargoes of silver. Although this second route was much shorter, it was infinitely more difficult and risky, owing to the obstacles presented by the inhospitable plains of the Chaco and the Indians, particularly the Paiaguá and the Guaicuru. . . .

Once war was declared in the Peninsula between Portugal and Spain and Portuguese trade with the River Plata was forbidden by the Spanish government, there occurred the devaluation of Portuguese currency and, more important, an extreme shortage of the silver that came from Peru via Buenos Aires and via the sertão--two misfortunes having severe impact upon the economy of Brazil. Dom João IV made an effort to maintain peace in America and with it the lucrative traffic between the Brazilian ports and Buenos Aires. In 1642 he sent two orders on this subject to the governor of Brazil. Spain, ever fearful of Portuguese infiltration in her colonies, especially in Peru, was violently opposed to these designs.

A large number of royal orders attest that the Portuguese monarch then attempted personally and with enthus-
iasm to activate the search for gold and silver mines,
whether in the south or in Amazonia, such was the monetary imbalance created by the intransigency of Spain and
the depleted treasury of a country at war.[109]

The search for gold was successful in the 1690s, while
the discovery of diamonds soon followed. Moreover, the activities of the Peruvian silver mines began to decline (after 1630).
Although trade with Spanish South America was maintained, the
focus of Brazilian exports shifted increasingly from Peru to
Argentina to trade with Africa and the Far East. The goods
with which Brazilians traded were sugar and its products,
reexports of Portuguese goods, such as salt, oil, fine and
rough manufactured cloth, blouses, hoes, and other implements,
and consumer goods.[110] The gold and diamond discoveries led
to a direct increase in the quantity of slaves demanded and
the price that Brazilians were willing to pay for them. Brazil produced more goods that were desired on the African
Coast than did Portugal, and directly absorbed more slaves, so
that "In 1770, Martinho de Melo Castro, Portuguese secretary
of state, wrote that one could not 'without great sorrow see
how our Brazilian colonies have absorbed commerce and shipping
on the African coast, to the total exclusion of Portugal, and
what the Brazilians do not control, foreign nations do.'" In
addition, Brazilians also traded with India and with the
Dutch on the African coast, without using Portuguese middlemen.

In 1871, José da Silva Lisboa, late Viscount of Cairu,
observed that "African trade is of great importance here
(Bahia) and is directed to the supply of slaves, yet
nevertheless the profit that should accrue from it is
seldom realized. Its staples are tobacco, either waste
or second-grade leaf, and strong spirits. More than
fifty cargoes a year depart from Bahia in corvettes and
smacks; eight or ten corvettes go to Angola with European
goods, while the others go to the coast of Guinea to buy
slaves. The investment risked in entering this business
is small. A good smack of ten thousand cruzados and a
smack of twenty may be loaded upon capital borrowed at 18
per cent, and the investment is returned thirty days later
when the ship reaches its destination. A cargo may con-
sist of sixty slaves, confined to the hold for fear their
desperation may induce them to rebel or leap overboard.
If few die during the passage, the voyage is lucrative;
if many die, the merchant is wiped out because of the
exhorbitant interest he must pay for his capital. The

trade brings not only an abundance of slaves but also
much gold dust, each vessel carrying several arrobas
purchased furtively from the Negroes without the knowledge of the Dutch, who control this aspect of the commerce strictly. If the Dutch were to learn of the trade
in gold dust, they would demand satisfaction from the
petty African princes who head the little dynasties that
barter the gold. And as these princes are constrained
in all their trade by the Dutch, because of their fear
of the Dutch fortresses on the coast and the superiority
of the Dutch navy, they have much difficulty in exchang-
ing their gold. . . . The Dutch compelled the ships to
pay one quarter of the cargo of Brazilian tobacco as
tribute to the fortress of Mina."

The Brazilians improved upon the opportunity to buy British
and French goods from the coast of Mina; these were cheaper
than Portuguese goods. Slaves imported via Bahia were in
turn sold to mine owners.[111]

José Honório Rodrigues writes that thus

Brazil was the center of a three-way commerce and was
linked with Asia and Africa in trade in which Portugal
took no part. This Brazilian-Afro-Asian triangle was
established in the eighteenth century. It dissolved
following our independence. Imported into Brazil, in addition to carpets, pepper, and Oriental textiles of
cotton, silk, and damask, were slaves from Angola, Mina,
Bissau, and Cacheu, and wax from Angola. Exported from
Brazil were brandy, tobacco, flour, manioc, and dried
meat from Ceará. José da Silva Lisboa in a letter written in 1781 observed that "half of the best leaf" in
the tobacco harvest went to Portugal; "the rest, divided into rolls of three arrobas, goes to Africa to be
exchanged for slaves, and, a large part, to Asia, reduced to powder and as contraband, to the damage of
the royal contract; what remains is consumed in the
internal trade of the country."[112]

By 1796, Angola ranked third in the importation of products from Rio de Janeiro, after Porto and Lisbon, and Ben-
guela the sixth, following these three and Bahia and Pernambuco. Fourteen ships annually went to Angola and ten to Bene-
guela: sugar, brandy, rice, wheat flour, dry meat, tobacco,
bacon, manioc flour, beans, cotton, fish oil, coffee, hides,
sweets, lumber, gold, and leather were exported, in return
for Portuguese, Asian and African products, of which slaves
made up more than one quarter of Brazil's imports. Although

Portugal provided less than one third of Brazilian imports, Brazil accounted for three quarters of Portuguese international trade.[113]

Although internal trade within Brazil had a number of (national) justifications that will be discussed below, it was called into being to supply areas with inputs needed for the export trade: in this sense, internal trade was possible only when export markets were sufficiently strong to permit exporting regions in Brazil to demand food and transport supplies from nonexporting areas. Caio Prado has summarized this relationship as shown in Figure 4. The diagram indicates that Brazil behaved like a business firm, purchasing labor (slaves) and physical capital (manufactured goods) which it paid for with the receipts from the sale of its products, which had been produced using the imported inputs. These products were tropical commodities (sugar, dyewood, brazil nuts, etc.), gold, and diamonds. When money was scarce, the firm's (Brazil's) products were directly exchanged for the inputs (slaves, manufactured goods) necessary for their production.

At least to some extent, Portugal was enabled to enforce its mercantilistic legislation. Caio Prado Junior writes:

> Placed at the midpoint of this great current of tropical products, gold, and diamonds, Portugal was the compulsory intermediary between the colonial sources of supply and the markets. . . . Portugal's trade statistics for this period made this only too plain. Approximately two-thirds of the kingdom's exports to other countries was made up of the colony's products; and the figures we possess do not include the production of gold and diamonds, which, although very much reduced, still continued to contribute to the mother country's wealth.[114]

The effect of international trade on Brazil was different from its effect on Portugal. When international trade increased, the geographical area supplying the export industry sectors increased. Manufactured imports increased and Brazilian craft goods, which took the place of imports when none were available, declined. The net effect of this process on the size of the market for Brazilian goods depended on the physical location of the export sector. When sugar was the leading export, an increase in the quantity of sugar demanded led to an increase in the quantity demanded of land, food supplies from other areas of Brazil, and slaves from Brazil and from Africa. Because the sugar mills were located on the coast, the increase in the quantity demanded of cattle for transport, and other land transportation facilities was slight. (The demand for cattle, for food, and for power, did, of course

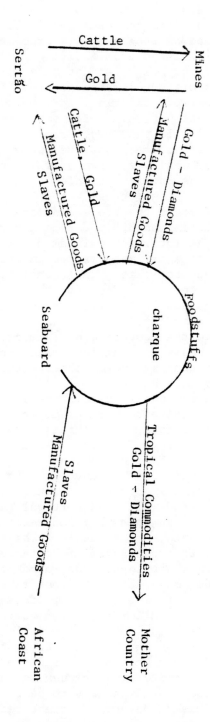

Figure 4: Brazilian Trade Patterns in the Eighteenth Century

increase.)

When gold and diamonds, which were found in the inland plateaus, were the leading export products, an increase in the quantity of gold and diamonds demanded led to an increase in the quantity demanded of food supplies from other areas of Brazil, slaves from Brazil and from Africa, and cattle for food and for transport purposes. At the same time, demand for inns and related transport supplies increased. The area along the transport routes between the mines and the coast began to fill in, the mining regions trading with both the Northeast and the South of Brazil. In this way, Brazil gradually became an inland nation composed of sections trading with each other rather than a series of enclaves, each of which traded with Portugal, Africa, and the Spanish colonies separately, and only to a limited degree among themselves. The international demand for gold and diamonds therefore did more to create a national market in Brazil than did the demand for sugar or dyewood. Similarly, the international demand for gold and diamonds created more of a national market in Brazil than did the international demand for cattle in Argentina, since cattle provided their own transport and food for their drovers. Both the nature and the location of Brazilian export activity led to the development of a national economy in the eighteenth century, which, despite the competition of imported goods, provided the economic basis of a national independence in the nineteenth century that was more cohesive than any of its Spanish-American counterparts.

Brazilian production and trade relations, however, were influenced by Portuguese commercial policy and treaty obligations. The determinants of Portuguese overseas economic policy were twofold. The first was current economic doctrine held by the Minister. The second was Portugal's inability to maintain independence from Spain without foreign military assistance. Portugal declared its independence from Spain in 1640. In 1642 Portugal and England signed a treaty according to which England recognized Portuguese independence and offered friendship. This implied but did not commit England to a guarantee of Portuguese independence. In return, England obtained, among other things, "free commerce subject to customary duties," "most favored nation" status, "a limited but effective extra-territorial jurisdiction under its own consul and immunity from Portuguese laws for English subjects."[115] In 1654 these privileges were extended; religious freedom was granted and English merchants were given "freedom of trade with Brazil and the west coast of Africa on terms of equality with Portuguese subjects, and provided that Portuguese customs duties to be paid by the English should never be raised above the current rate without the consent of two English merchants residing in Portugal and

chosen by the English consul."116   Because of the latter provision, English subjects "were for the future in a better situation than the Portuguese themselves."117   Finally, in 1661,
the treaties of 1642 and 1654 were reaffirmed as part of the
marriage contract between Charles of England and Catherine of
Bragança.   In addition,

> England received two million crowns dowry, Tangier,
> Bombay, a Portuguese guarantee of trade in the East In-
> dies against the Dutch, [and] the privilege of having
> resident merchants in Goa, Cochim, and Diu in the East,
> and in Bahia, Pernambuco, and Rio de Janeiro in Brazil.
> . . . In return, England was to aid the Portuguese in
> maintaining order in its East India possessions, and
> promised help if Lisbon or Oporto should ever be be-
> sieged, and pledged never to make a treaty with Spain
> which would interfere with the assistance guaranteed
> to Portugal.   England promised to aid Portugal to the
> extent of war with Spain, if this developed, and se-
> cretly promised to defend Portuguese possessions
> against all enemies.   Portugal also obtained two regi-
> ments of soldiers and ten ships.   As a result of the
> alliance, Spain recognized Portugal as an independent
> state in 1668, and England forced the Dutch to leave
> Portugal alone.118

The exchange may be summarized as follows: Portugal obtained a guarantee of national independence; England obtained
trading rights and privileges so extensive that it was granted
by law that which it obtained elsewhere by contraband trade
and piracy.   Portugal therefore gained national independence
at the cost of economic independence.   Yet this dependency was
not entirely unprofitable.

Portuguese trade with England and English possessions in
North America was extensive.   Until the middle of the seventeenth century, Brazilian sugar and tobacco had been traded
through Portugal in exchange for English woolens.   This
trade was disrupted by the Navigation Law of 1651, which provided that all exports and imports of England and its colonies
had to be carried in English or colonial ships in which the
ship's master and three fourths of the crew were English subjects.   The Navigation Act of 1661, however, had provided that
"goods imported in foreign ships of the country of origin must
pay the higher, alien tariff duties."   The tariff protection
on colonial sugar contributed to an expansion of production;
sugar prices fell, and although it cost about 30 per cent less
to produce Brazilian sugar than sugar in the English plantations, preferential treatment given the British product led
to a decrease in Portuguese sugar exports to England.   "By

1669 only 705 tons of white sugar, worth ₺38,480, were
brought from Portugal, not one tenth of what had been the
yearly importation before the rise of the English sugar plantations." By 1690 no more than 2,000 chests of sugar worth
₺40,000 was shipped to England annually; of this amount, one
quarter was reexported to other European ports.[119]
    Although pro-Portuguese sentiment was evidenced when the
Staple Act of 1663 was passed, requiring the colonies to buy
certain products not from foreign producers, but from England
after the payment of customs duties, the wine of Madeira and
the Azores was excluded from the provisions of the Act. The
decreasing sugar revenues combined with war expenditures led
Portugal to attempt to cut expenditures, in part by producing
at home goods that had previously been imported.[120] In 1686
the import of woolens of various kinds was prohibited, to be
fully enforced within two years. In 1690 a Regulation for
the Cloth Industry was published; soon after, Portuguese
nationalists could dress themselves in Portuguese cloth. The
Portuguese cloth industry developed at the time that the English cloth industry was being severely damaged by competition
of Irish and Spanish woolens and Indian silk. The English
could be expected to be especially sensitive to Portuguese
action on wool; it appeared, by 1700, that between Portuguese
protection of wool and English protection of sugar and tobacco, "that the active exchange which had gone on between the
two allies for over two hundred years was about to cease,
and this at the very time when the mines of Brazil were beginning to send a golden stream of riches across the seas to
Lisbon."[121] It had become clear that if French wines were ad-
mitted on a par with Portuguese wines, the French product
would outsell the Portuguese, and Portuguese demand for British woolens would decrease correspondingly. In order to
secure the wool trade with Portugal, the British were prepared to make concessions on wine, though not on sugar. The
British were especially anxious to secure the Portuguese
trade both because Portuguese goods, for the most part, did
not compete with British goods in world markets, and because
only one quarter of the value of all English manufactures exported to Portugal was paid for with the proceeds of Portuguese exports to England; the remaining three quarters was
paid for in money. In bullionist times, England felt that
"What trade can be more coveted by England?"[122] The Portuguese, for their part, not only desired to increase their wine
export to England, but also needed English military help in
the coming conflict with the Bourbons in Spain. Despite the
fact that the Portuguese attempted to persuade the English
to base their declaration of war on an issue that would not
involve Portugal, the Portuguese may well have thought commercial concessions necessary to help guarantee English

military support of Portuguese independence if war came. The
result was the famous Methuen Treaty of 1703, whereby Portugal
was forever to admit woolen cloths and the rest of the woolen
manufactures of the Britons free of duty; in return, England
was forever to "admit the Portuguese wine into England in such
a manner that even in war between England and France, or in
peace, no greater duties or customs or charges by whatever title should be imposed on Portuguese wine than is demanded of
French wine with one-third reduction." As Brazil grew, Brazil
absorbed English woolens, while England obtained Portuguese
wine and Brazilian gold.[123]

The Portuguese, by their alliance with the English,
obtained a number of benefits at the Treaty of Utrecht in 1713
that strengthened Brazil: France renounced its claims to the
North Bank of the Amazon and to any rights of navigation on
that river; England guaranteed this clause of the treaty. At
the same time, Spain ceded Colonia do Sacramento to the crown
of Portugal. England--whose contraband trade benefited by
Portuguese ownership of Colonia--again guaranteed the treaty
clause.[124] By 1713 Portuguese trade with England brought in
from ₤400,000 to ₤1,000,000 per year.[125] However, friction
developed between England and Portugal over increased English
activities on the East African Coast, and increased Portuguese
restrictions on foreigners in Brazil following the discovery
of gold and diamonds. Portuguese antagonism toward the English was effectively expressed by the Marquis of Pombal (José
de Carvalho e Mello), who was the head of the government from
1750 to 1777. According to Pombal

> In 1754 Portugal scarcely produced anything towards her
> own support. Two-thirds of her physical necessities
> were supplied by England. . . . The English came to Lis-
> bon to monopolize even the commerce of Brazil. The en-
> tire cargo on the vessels that were sent thither, and
> consequently the riches that were returned in exchange,
> belonged to them. . . . Gold and silver are fictitious
> riches . . . the more they are multiplied, the less is
> their real value. . . . The Negroes that work in the
> mines of Brazil must be clothed by England, by which the
> value of their produce becomes relative to the price of
> cloth. To work the mines, it is necessary to have a
> large capital expended on slaves. If this sum be twenty
> millions, the interest, which is one million, independent
> of the cost of extraction, must be the first money paid
> for this produce. Add to this the food and clothing for
> more than an hundred thousand persons, blacks and whites,
> which the mines carry to Brazil, which food is not to be
> had in the colony, but must be purchased from foreigners.
> Lastly, to supply the physical wants of the country,

which since the discovery of the mines had lost its arts
and manufactures, all the gold became the property of
other nations. What riches, great God! the possession
of which involves the ruin of the state'126

In order to become as wealthy as the English, Pombal
believed that Portugal needed to increase its control over
the economy, increase the technical skills available to the
economy, and increase and diversity the number of products
available to Portugal within the Portuguese Empire. In order
to obtain wealth as great as that of England, it was necessary
to follow English principles of action, and exclude England
from Portuguese trade, by violating the spirit, if not the
letter, of the Methuen Treaty. An early act, symbolic of
the new order, was "to allow Portuguese merchants to wear
swords as the nobility did, thus placing them on a level of
social equality with English colleagues and competitors."127
An increase in the power of the Portuguese crown in Brazil was achieved in a series of acts and treaties. Soon after
João V's death, a treaty with Spain was ratified whereby
Colonia do Sacramento was given to Spain in exchange for
part of Paraguay. Spain would thereby be able to cut down
on British smuggling through Colonia do Sacramento, while Portugal obtained the mission territory, administered by Jesuits.
The Indians in the missions were then open to enslavement by
raiders from São Paulo. Jesuit control was virtually extinguished in May 1757, when Pombal ordered the secularization
of civil power in Pará, extinguished the missions, and set
the Indians free. Pombal also attempted to abolish the color
bar against Indians by decrees which stated that Portuguese
who married Indians would be preferred for promotion, and for-
bade the use of insulting terms for the children of such mixed
marriages.128 These provisions, however, were not extended
to Negroes.129 In 1759 an edict exiled the Jesuits from Portugal and its possessions, and sequestered the Jesuits' houses
and goods.130
Whittling down the power of the English was a more complex matter. The special court privileges granted in 1647 and
1654 were abolished by the law of October 30, 1752, by which
the English judge conservator was forbidden to grand mandates
to impede the execution of writs or orders issued by the ordinary courts, under penalty of suspension for six months. A
series of Portuguese trading companies and chambers of commerce were created with authority which took precedence over
that of the English judge conservator. British commercial
privileges were struck down by acts paralleling the English
Navigation Acts.

By a decree dated June 7, 1755, the Portuguese trading
company of Grão Pará and Maranhão was established.

Every ship which sailed from Portugal to the Brazilian provinces of Grão Pará and Maranhão had to belong to the company and had to sail from Lisbon; no ship but that of the company could enter or leave any port of these provinces; no person who did not belong to the company could send, take, or introduce any goods whatever into them, although the company was prohibited by selling by retail in the colonies; and the exclusive right to import slaves was granted to the company. In 1759 another company was instituted on the same basis to trade with the provinces of Parahiba and Pernambuco. . . . The year following the establishment of the Company of Grão Pará, Pombal set up a Junta do Commercio. It had the power to regulate all affairs connected with commerce, to prevent and punish smuggling, and to grant or refuse license for opening retail shops. . . . This measure was directed especially against the English, because they carried on the principal commerce and engrossed much of the profit of the retail trade. . . . To curtail further the trade enjoyed by the English, the junta declared contraband a long list of articles. Tanned leather was prohibited entrance in 1758. New duties were added, such as an additional two per cent at Oporto to pay for the Porguguese frigates which accompanied the ships of the Alto Douro Wine Company on their voyage to Brazil. British merchants complained that the king granted royal letters of protection or moratoriums to his subjects who owed money to the English and prevented the latter from bringing suit for recovery. The Portuguese government often seized goods for the king's troops, or household, and even for convents and monasteries, from the English proprietor, who received no pay or payment only after an extended delay, while accounting houses and homes of the English were entered by common officers of the law without a proper order from the British conservator. Pombal thus conducted a vigorous campaign against English privileges and English commercial supremacy.

This was extended by limiting and regulating the scope of English trade in Portuguese wines.[131] Further, the Portuguese, in 1781, prohibited the import of cotton goods from England, and refused to admit woolen goods and printed linen from Ireland. Pombal coupled these protective acts with legislation fostering plantations of cotton, rice, indigo, coffee, and cacao, which were needed to take the place of declining mine activity. Despite the many difficulties involved in establishing new activities, production of these crops increased: cotton was of immediate importance in foreign trade. Rice served the domestic market as well as exports. Coffee and cacao cultivation spread within Brazil, eventually reaching locations best suited to their cultivation.[132]

The construction of warehouse facilities enabled the Portuguese to hold their crops off the market until they obtained a favorable price; by 1791 Portugal obtained a favorable balance of trade with England of nearly ₤252,000, "and English gold was shipped throughout Portugal to Brazil," a clear reversal of the trend whose cause is normally attributed to the treaty of Methuen, and an indication that Brazilian economic difficulties after 1791 had contemporary causes. Pombal, in a memorial written in 1775 which celebrated himself and his sovereign, wrote that "before 1750 it was rare to find a person who could write a legible letter, whereas now when a clerk is to be appointed numbers of excellently written letters are received." In addition, Portugal could now supply itself in textiles, carriages and many articles formerly imported; "observant foreigners did not fail to remark the millions spent in public and private building after the earthquake," and various aspects of culture flourished.[133] He clearly believed that he had laid the basis in skill and expenditure for an economically independent nation-state. Pombal's economic policy was continued by his successors as long as Portugal was militarily able to maintain its independence.

Administration

The success or failure of Portugal's policies in administering of Brazil depends on the criteria of colonial government adopted. The Portuguese government's aims shifted in emphasis from attempting to reap as much specie from Brazil as possible to attempting to develop a wide variety of Brazilian goods, as the basis of Portuguese economic autonomy. From the Brazilian's point of view, however, Portuguese policy needs to be judged not only on the above two criteria, but also on the criterion of whether Portuguese policy helped or hindered the formation of Brazil as a united and viable economic unit, with an internal market capable of supporting more than subsistence agricultural activities.

The crux of the dispute between Brazil and Portugal over the best method of administering the colony depended much less on international trade legislation than had similar disagreements between Spain and its colonies. Instead, major difficulties arose out of Portugal's attempts to regulate the internal economic activity of Brazil, above all, to control gold and diamond mining. The severity of the Portuguese administration of the diamond district is the most striking instance of behavior which eventually led Brazilians to seek either better treatment within the Portuguese Empire or independence from

Portugal. Additional conflict resulted from the preference
given to Peninsular Portuguese for advancement in civil service, monopolization of trade by Portuguese-born immigrants,
Portuguese denigration of Brazilians because of their Negro
blood, and high-handed methods of administration.

The content of Portuguese administrative policy has been
disparaged by Brazilian historians. For example, Caio Prado
Junior writes that "if we study the colony's administrative
legislation, we find a mass of enactments, subject to continual
modifications often of a contradictory nature, which appeared
to be entirely unconnected and to pile up with no guiding plan
whatsoever."134 ". . . application of the law was seldom uniform, but varied in accordance with the place and the time,
and was often ignored in practice, some reason always being
found should one prove necessary to justify this disobedience.
Hence, the relationship between what we find written down in
the legal documents and what we find in actual practice is
often vague, if not downright nonexistent."135 The Overseas
Council (Conselho Ultramarino) attempted to regulate in detail the life of the colony, so that many small administrative details had to be confirmed by the Council in Lisbon.
Although such centralization made the local administrator's
life a nightmare, it was imposed based on the probably sound
belief by the home government that its agents "were guilty of
negligence, incompetence, and even outright dishonesty." The
administration of finances was marked by its complexity and
venality, each of the various revenue sources having its own
Board to oversee its collection and to carry out judicial
functions arising from tax matters.136

The taxes collected resembled those imposed in the Spanish colonies. The main taxes were the tithe (paid in cash,
not in kind), customs duties, the duties leveled on all merchandise, slaves, provisions, and cattle entering Minas
Gerais, known as the entradas; and special taxes on mules
from the south, levied at Sorocaba in São Paulo. In addition,
there were the donativos, or voluntary contributions, the
tercos (thirds), and novos direitos (new duties) levied for
the services of law officials--scriveners, bailiffs, solici-
tors, and so on--and fees payable on nominations to public office, known as provisões and patentes. Apart from these
standard contributions, the crown also collected special
contributions to defray extraordinary expenses--the literary
subsidy created in 1772 in all the captaincies and in the
kingdom to raise money for the provision of public education,
and other "extraordinary subsidies" periodically raised to meet
emergencies. These were generally collected in the form of
special duties on cane spirits, animals slaughtered in the
public abattoirs, foodstuffs, and a capitation tax on slaves.137

Tax collection rights were auctioned to contractors,

usually for three-year periods. The population and the royal
treasury both suffered as a result of this practice. Moreover,
until the mid-eighteenth century,

> no central agency existed in Portugal with over-all
> responsibility for the collection and payment of Crown
> moneys. Throughout the kingdom and the empire each
> customs officer, tax receiver, paymaster, and treasurer
> was individually responsible for the receipt and disburse-
> ment of the funds he handled, subject only to checks by
> boards of audit in the colonies and by the parent Casa
> dos Contos in Lisbon. Owing to the resultant confusion
> and speculation, the king lost a substantial portion of
> his revenues, and whenever fiscal crises arose, par-
> ticularly during wartime and depressions, the Crown was
> obliged to cover deficits by devising new taxes, by
> calling upon its subjects to tax themselves through so-
> called voluntary contributions (donativos), and by al-
> lowing many of its obligations to remain unpaid.[138]

In the 1760s the treasury was reorganized, and staffed
with new personnel: accountants and bookkeepers familiar
with double entry bookkeeping, which system was then used in
keeping royal accounts, although there were few able to keep
accounts in this manner in Brazil. The administrative reforms
by themselves did not improve fiscal conditions in Brazil because of the heavy cost of the continuing war with Spain, including fighting over the Colonia do Sacramento.[139] These
war costs caused the viceroy to dip into the royal fifths,
which usually were remitted to Portugal (see Table 8-9). The
fall in remittances also reflected the general decline in
prosperity in Brazil as the mines ran out. Customs receipts
--an index of trading activity--fell one quarter from 1758-
to-1765 to 1768-to-1778.[140]

The viceroyalty's budget showed a heavy deficit during
the war years (1774-1777). Despite income obtained from the
sale of Jesuit properties, the government continued in debt,
while, at the same time it was owed 4,020 contos (millions)
of reis, more than one half of which had been due for more
than two decades. Fiscal problems continued to plague Brazil
through the colonial period. The viceroys, seeking a way out
of the financial impasse, attempted to promote economic development in order to create additional sources of taxable
wealth, and to stop evasion of taxes through contraband
trade.[141]

The increased production of sugar, fibers, dyestuffs,
cereals, and tobacco was encouraged.[142] Although in most
cases the success of these efforts depended on the natural
resources and climate of the area where promotion was

undertaken, in some instances removal of technical ignorance
was sufficient to stimulate new activity. For example, wheat
growing was handicapped "because there were no grist mills
and no one knew how to build them." Milling stones and a car-
penter who knew how to construct grist mills were sent to Brazil in 1772; by 1880 wheat farming began to increase, and wheat
was exported in the last colonial years.[143] Rice cultivation
also increased. Attempts to cultivate hemp failed, while indigo cultivation met with only temporary success.

One element hindering the promotion of these crops was
the lack of adequate marketing services. Most merchants
engaged in international trade were not independent, but were
commission agents. They

> were necessarily dependent on the instructions of their
> principals in Portugal who themselves were often mere
> intermediaries for British or other foreign interests.
> Because of such dependent relationships . . . local
> merchants could not ship "commodities other than those
> their superiors require . . .", and since the market for
> the small volumes of new products . . . was distinctly
> uncertain it is understandable that local merchants
> preferred to freight sugar, hides, and other tradi-
> tional goods for which there was an established demand
> rather than take a chance on the newer exotic commodi-
> ties whose quality was likely to be inferior to that
> available in the Peninsula from foreign sources.[144]

Contraband was a continuing problem during the seventeenth and eighteenth centuries in Brazil. Until 1591 there
was no bar to direct foreign trade with Brazil. Foreign
persons and ships properly cleared from a Portuguese port
could go to Brazilian ports in trade. They were permitted
to carry Brazilian produce to foreign destinations after stop-
ping at Lisbon for the necessary clearance.[145] When Spain obtained control of Portugal, a new policy was instituted. In
1591 "Philip II issued an alvará declaring that no unlicensed
foreign ships or persons would be permitted in any of Portugal's overseas possessions, excepting the Azores and the
Madeiras which were considered home islands. Even chartered
foreign ships were required to return from the conquests directly to Portugal without making any interim stops. Viola-
tors were threatened with dire penalties, and informers were
assured of a third of the value of the illicit goods they de-
nounced."[146] The policy continued in force until 1808; de-
tailed regulations were issued to prevent unlicensed foreign
ships from trading with Brazil.[147] The incentives to smuggling were great: legally imported goods paid 26 per cent ad
valorem on leaving Portugal and a further 10 per cent on

entering Brazil.[148] Export duties, commissions, freight and
other charges were heavy. A tobacco planter complained that
out of every 100 rolls of tobacco shipped to Lisbon, more
than 75 went to pay customs duties and freight costs. In 1756
the British Board of Trade estimated that of every Ŀ100 worth
of English goods sent to Brazil, Ŀ68 was paid in taxes.[149]

The short-run interests of the crown and its citizens
differed: the former wanted to earn the highest possible customs revenue; the latter wanted the largest quantity of goods
for the least price. High revenue through low taxes on heavy
trade was not considered. Further, heavy international trade
would have brought with it (large) dependence on foreign nations, as Portugal could not supply Brazil's economic needs.
Portugal therefore wanted to limit the Brazilian trade to
what Portugal could provide. To maintain that trade, Brazilian manufacture was discouraged. This happened both because
the Portuguese believed that the appropriate role of Brazil
was as a supplier of raw materials and a consumer of Portuguese manufactures, and because the Portuguese feared that
an increase in Brazilian manufactures would lead to a decline
in trade and customs receipts. The possibility that a Brazil
that was rich from manufactures would demand more goods from
Portugal, and pay taxes on them, apparently was not considered.

Just as Portugal desired to limit the economic development of Brazil to specified lines of economic activity, the
viceroy in Rio de Janeiro opposed textile weaving in Minas
Gerais, since he believed that this would decrease trade
between Minas, Rio de Janeiro, and Portugal. Activities
other than gold mining were opposed as trade with other areas,
and therefore toll revenues, would decrease. Similarly, direct foreign trade by São Paulo through the port of Santos
rather than through Rio was opposed because Rio would lose
tax revenue. In general, regional officials "viewed the economic gains of a neighboring administrative unit as likely to
affect adversely the income of their own branch of the Royal
Treasury."[150]

These policies were adopted despite earlier concern with
promoting economic activity because the Marquis of Pombal
fell from power in 1777. The privileged groups who replaced
him used their influence to obtain the adoption of more rigid
mercantilist policies. In 1785 textile factories were prohibited in Brazil, and those already in existence were ordered
to be closed, except for those producing rough cloth for
slaves and packaging. Iron manufacture appeared to be protected
by the heavy import duties on iron implements, and the rich
iron beds available in Minas Gerais. However, "anyone who knew
how to cast iron was automatically suspected of harboring extreme and subversive opinions and became the victim of every
kind of persecution."

The prohibition against goldsmiths has already been noted; in addition, government tax policy handicapped the leather curing and meat preserving industry, since salt was subject to a royal monopoly, and consequently expensive.[151]

At the same time that restrictive policies were adopted, the decline of gold mining led to a shortage of gold coin, and the necessity of producing at home goods which could no longer be imported. The economic activity of Minas Gerais diversified. Portugal, however, believed that the "gold decline" was merely one more device used to defraud the government. Strong efforts to collect taxes and enforce restrictive laws were made. In 1789 a dentist, "Tiradentes," in Minas Gerais was the nominal leader of a conspiracy to overthrow the Portuguese regime. An independence conspiracy was discovered in Rio de Janeiro in 1794, and an independence uprising occurred in Bahia in 1798. Independence, however, was not the only solution proposed. Others presented were separation, federation, the liquidation of Portuguese merchants and masons, the abolition of slavery, suppression of the color bar, and the breaking down of class barriers. In Brazil as in Mexico, society was fragmented along racial, economic, and class lines, as well as by conflicting ideologies and country of birth. These divisions prevented the immediate unification of all Brazilian-born for independence.

By the mid-1890s, both strict mercantilism and the independence movements had failed. Some of the harsher features of monopolies and tax farming were abolished, while by 1895, the government explicitly permitted the establishment of iron foundries.[152]

The Brazilian solution to the problems of its colonial status did not result so much from Brazilian action as it did from the removal of the Portuguese royal family from Portugal to Brazil in 1808. Because the presence of the crown in Brazil radically changed Brazil, the colonial period of Brazil, in which Brazil was physically separate from the nation's administrative center, can be said to have ended in 1808, even though independent national status was not achieved until 1822. It is therefore reasonable to ask the questions: "Was owning Brazil profitable for Portugal?", and "How did colonial status effect Brazil?" as of the year 1808.

The effect of the receipt of taxes and private gold shipments on the Portuguese economy was similar to its effect on Spain. An immediate effect was an increased price level, and, therefore, a relative cheapening of imports, which contributed to the destruction of such Portuguese manufactures as can be said to have existed at the time. This could have been countered if Portugal were able to increase its supplies rapidly, or maintain Brazil as a captive market. This did not happen, first of all, because Portugal was too small a nation

to supply goods as fast as the gold came in: Brazil provided
half of the world's gold supply; Portugal could not supply
half of the world's goods. Brazil had to trade through Portugal, but not with Portugal alone, because of the triple treaties of 1642, 1654, 1661, which gave England a preferred position in the Portuguese market, enabling British goods to be
sold to Brazil. The increase in demand that resulted from the
gold and diamond discoveries did not result in an increase
in demand for Portuguese goods, with resulting increases in
output and economies of scale; the favorable effects of the
Brazilian gold and diamond strike were captured by England.
After the Golden Age of Brazil, Pombal's sober policies began
to integrate the Brazilian and Portuguese economies. To the
extent that Pombal's policies were successful in increasing
the supply of goods that Portugal needed in Brazil, and enabling Portugal to produce those goods that Brazil would buy,
colonization "paid off" for Portugal.

An evaluation of Portuguese policy on the future economic
development of Brazil is necessarily mixed. The new industries
developed as a result of the mercantilistic policies held
benefited Brazil; at the same time, the limited development of
industries that were prohibited so that Portugal could
monopolize them inhibited future Brazilian development.

The shipment of taxes and private funds to Portugal decreased the funds available for investment in Brazil. Further,

> the fiscal practices of the Crown itself inhibited the
> formation of capital in the colony. Although a leading
> purchaser of goods and services, the government was a
> notoriously poor payer, a reputation that it admittedly
> shared with most other European governments of the time.
> Nevertheless, colonial merchants and planters whose
> capital was tied up in unpaid government contracts were
> obviously deprived of funds needed for normal operations,
> and lacked surpluses to invest in new activities. There
> can be little doubt that the shortage of both royal and
> private financing handicapped efforts toward economic
> diversification.153

On the eve of economic independence, Brazil contained
some of the diverse skills and industries needed for economic
development. It lacked a strong export, and appeared to be
in a less favorable foreign trade position than Mexico in 1810.
Brazil, at the time, was probably a poorer nation than Mexico.
Agricultural production for the domestic market was hindered
by unequal land distribution and slavery. Both prevented the
formation of a Brazilian market large enough to encourage the
rapid development of manufacturing activities, while Brazilian
produce was less well suited to export than that of temperate

zones. Mexico, because of its mines and trade, and Argentina, because of its climate and free labor, seemed more likely to develop at the beginning of the nineteenth century.

FOOTNOTES

Chapter 8. Brazilian Colonial Economic History

1. Roberto C. Simonsen, História Econômica do Brasil, 1500-1820, p. 53.

2. Ibid., p. 63.

3. Ibid., cited on p. 64.

4. Ibid., pp. 45, 55, 61. The value of the currency declined during this period; therefore, no conversion is given.

5. Hubert Herring, A History of Latin America from the Beginnings to the Present, pp. 218-220.

6. Simonsen, História Econômica do Brasil, pp. 83, 84.

7. Ibid., p. 6.

8. Richard Morse, ed., The Bandeirantes, p. 8.

9. Simonsen, História Econômica do Brasil, pp. 97, 98.

10. Ibid., cited on p. 98.

11. Noel Deerr, The History of Sugar, vol. 1, pp. 108, 109. This is a direct quotation from Deerr, except for substitution of English for Portuguese terms.

12. Ibid., vol. 1, p. 110; vol. 2, pp. 528-530.

13. Simonsen, História Econômica do Brasil, p. 110.

14. Based on Deerr, op. cit., p. 105.

15. C. R. Boxer, The Dutch in Brazil, pp. 277-278.

16. Celso Furtado, The Economic Growth of Brazil, p. 49.

17. Deerr, op. cit., p. 106; Boxer, The Dutch in Brazil, pp. 32, 148.

18. Deerr, op. cit., p. 110.

19. Simonsen, História Econômica do Brasil, p. 113; Furtado, op. cit., pp. 45-52.

20. Mircea Buesco and Vicente Tapajós, História do desenvolvimento económico do brasil, p. 81.

21. Boxer, The Dutch in Brazil, pp. 3, 13, 15.

22. Ibid., p. 66.

23. Ibid., p. 76.

24. Ibid., pp. 76, 77, 78.

25. Ibid., p. 79.

26. Ibid., pp. 81, 82.

27. Ibid., p. 149.

28. C. R. Boxer, A Great Luso-Brazilian Figure: Padre António Vieira, S.J., 1608-1697, p. 17.

29. Deerr, op. cit., I, p. 107.

30. Ibid., p. 110.

31. Ibid.; and João Lucio Azevedo, Epocas de Portugal Económica, pp. 271, 278.

32. Deerr, op. cit., I, p. 111.

33. Buesco and Tapajós, op. cit., pp. 162-163.

34. José Honório Rodrigues, Brazil and Africa, p. 6.

35. Ibid., p. 25.

36. Azevedo, op. cit., p. 285.

37. Ibid., pp. 287-290.

38. Ibid., p. 292.

39. Ibid.

40. Ibid., pp. 296-298.

41. Simonsen, História Econômica do Brasil, p. 151.

42. Ibid., p. 169.

43. Ibid., p. 171.

44. Ibid., pp. 174-176.

45. C. R. Boxer, The Golden Age of Brazil, 1695-1750, pp. 26-29.

46. Cited in E. Bradford Burns, A Documentary History of Brazil, pp. 90-91. Translated from André João Antonil, Cultura e Opulência do Brasil, part III, chap. II, pp. 179, 180.

47. Boxer, The Golden Age of Brazil, 1695-1750, p. 39.

48. Cited in Boxer, Four Centuries of Portuguese Expansion, 1415-1825, pp. 74, 75.

49. Part Three, chap. V, cited in Boxer, Four Centuries of Portuguese Expansion, 1415-1825, pp. 74, 75.

50. Boxer, The Golden Age of Brazil, 1695-1750, pp. 42, 43.

51. Ibid., pp. 44-45, 317-318.

52. Ibid., p. 52.

53. Ibid., p. 47.

54. Ibid., pp. 27, 53, 54.

55. Ibid., pp. 191, 334.

56. Ibid., p. 59.

57. Ibid., p. 206.

58. Ibid., p. 210.

59. Ibid., p. 212.

60. Ibid., p. 220.

61. John Mawe, Travels in the Interior of Brazil, pp. 265-267.

62. Boxer, The Golden Age of Brazil, 1695-1750, p. 177.

63. Ibid., p. 216.

64. Mawe, op. cit., pp. 317-318. Mawe's footnotes are incorporated in the text.

65. Ibid., pp. 319-320.

66. Cited in Boxer, The Golden Age of Brazil, 1695-1750, pp. 216-217.

67. Ibid., pp. 217-218.

68. Simonsen, História Econômica do Brasil, p. 130.

69. Ibid., p. 124.

70. José Honório Rodrigues, Brasil, Periodo Colonial, p. 92.

71. Rodrigues, Brazil and Africa, p. 18.

72. Rodrigues, Brasil, Periodo Colonial, pp. 55, 56; Buesco and Tapajós, op. cit., p. 81.

73. Simonsen, História Econômica do Brasil, p. 134.

74. Rodrigues, Brazil and Africa, p. 49.

75. Azevedo, op. cit., pp. 263 ff.

76. Ibid., pp. 277, 278.

77. Koster, cited in Gilberto Freyre, The Masters and the Slaves, pp. 324, 325.

78. An Irish observer, cited in Boxer, The Golden Age of Brazil, 1695-1750, p. 7.

79. Boxer, The Golden Age of Brazil, 1695-1750, pp. 7, 8.

80. Antonil, op. cit., p. 51.

81. Frank Tannenbaum, Slave and Citizen: The Negro in the Americas.

82. Translation of a Brazilian document, presented in Morse, op. cit., p. 119.

83. Boxer, The Golden Age of Brazil, 1695-1750, p. 171; Sergio Buarque de Holanda, História general da civilização brasileira, p. 25; Herring, A History of Latin America from the Beginnings to the Present, p. 113.

84. Boxer, The Golden Age of Brazil, 1695-1750, p. 170.

85. Ibid., pp. 171-172.

86. Ibid., p. 173.

87. Rollie E. Poppino, Brazil, The Land and the People, p. 59. Alexander Marchant, From Barter to Slavery, pp. 11-20.

88. Marchant, op. cit., pp. 39. 70, 76, 79.

89. Ibid., p. 82.

90. Poppino, op. cit., pp. 59-61.

91. Serafim Leite, S.J., Suma Histórica da Companhia de Jesus no Brasil (Assistência de Portugal), 1549-1760, p. 22.

92. Marchant, op. cit., pp. 96, 97.

93. Leite, op. cit., pp. 24, 28.

94. Marchant, op. cit., pp. 97, 98.

95. Paula Cohen, "What, If Not the Jesuits?", unpublished manuscript, 1965, pp. 6-8.

96. Marchant, op. cit., p. 106.

97. Ibid., p. 98.

98. Leite, op. cit., pp. 72-76.

99. Marchant, op. cit., pp. 114-118.

100. Ibid., pp. 130-132.

101. Ibid., pp. 135-137.

102. Morse, op. cit., pp. 4, 14.

103. Ibid., p. 24.

104. Myriam Ellis, "The Bandeiras in the Geographical Expansion of Brazil," in Morse, op. cit., p. 50.

105. Ibid., pp. 55-59.

106. José de Alcântara Machado, "Life and Death of the Bandeirante," in Morse, op. cit., pp. 68, 73-74.

107. Caio Prado Junior, The Colonial Background of Modern Brazil, pp. 101-102.

108. Morse, op. cit., p. 15. See also A. P. Canabrava, O Comercio Português no Rio da Prata, 1580-1640.

109. Cited in Morse, op. cit., pp. 104-108.

110. Rodrigues, Brasil Periodo Colonial, p. 64.

111. Rodrigues, Brazil and Africa, p. 27.

112. Ibid., pp. 28-29.

113. Rodrigues, Brazil and Africa, pp. 29, 33; Caio Prado Junior, op. cit., p. 270.

114. Prado Junior, op. cit., p. 274.

115. Alan K. Manchester, British Preeminence in Brazil, Its Rise and Decline, pp. 3, 4.

116. Ibid., p. 9.

117. Ibid., p. 12.

118. Ibid., pp. 16-18.

119. Ibid., pp. 22-23; Shep Clough and Charles W. Cole, An Economic History of Europe, pp. 345-346; G. C. Fite and J. Reese, An Economic History of the United States, p. 66.

120. H. V. Livermore, A New History of Portugal, p. 200.

121. Manchester, op. cit., p. 23.

122. Unsigned document cited in Manchester, op. cit., p. 24.

123. Manchester, op. cit., p. 25; Livermore, op. cit., pp. 202-204.

124. Manchester, op. cit., pp. 27, 28.

125. Ibid., p. 35.

126. Pombal's memoirs, cited in Manchester, op. cit., pp. 39, 40.

127. Livermore, op. cit., p. 217.

128. C. R. Boxer, Race Relations in the Portuguese Colonial Empire, 1415-1825, p. 98.

129. Ibid., p. 100.

130. Archivo Trece.

131. Manchester, op. cit., pp. 41-43.

132. For the depressing details of an attempt to establish a rice mill, see Dauril Alden, "Manoel Luis Vieira: An Entrepreneur in Rio de Janeiro During Brazil's Eighteenth Century Agricultural Renaissance," Hispanic Historical Review, XXXIX, #4 (November 1959), pp. 521-537.

133. Cited in Livermore, op. cit., pp. 237, 238.

134. Prado Junior, op. cit., p. 349.

135. Ibid., p. 351.

136. Ibid., pp. 374, 375.

137. Ibid., pp. 375-378.

138. Dauril Alden, Royal Government in Colonial Brazil, p. 280.

139. Ibid., p. 312.

140. Ibid., p. 317.

141. Ibid., pp. 350-352.

142. Ibid., p. 353.

143. Ibid., pp. 353-354.

144. Ibid., p. 381.

145. Ibid., p. 403.

146. Ibid., p. 404.

147. Ibid., pp. 405-408.

148. Ibid., p. 388.

149. Ibid., p. 389.

150. Ibid., p. 387.

151. Hector Ferreira Lima, Formação Industrial do Brasil,
     Periodo Colonial, pp. 135, 167; Prado Junior, op. cit.,
     pp. 261-263.

152. For details of economic development of Minas Gerais in
     the late eighteenth century, see Kenneth Maxwell, forth-
     coming ms.

153. Alden, op. cit., p. 382.

RAILROAD MAP OF BRAZIL

1887

VENEZUELA
COLOMBIA
GUYANA
SURINAM
FR GUIANA
BOA VISTA
MACAPÁ
BELÉM
MANAUS
SÃO LUÍS
FORTALEZA
TERESINA
NATAL
JOÃO PESSOA
RECIFE
PERU
MACEIÓ
ARACAJÚ
RIO BRANCO
PÔRTO VELHO
SALVADOR
CUIABÁ
☆ Brasília
GOIÂNIA
BOLIVIA
BELO HORIZONTE
VITÓRIA
ATLANTIC OCEAN
NITERÓI
RIO DE JANEIRO
PARAGUAY
CURITIBA
SÃO PAULO
- - - - Narrow Gauge
——— Broad Gauge
☆ National Capital
● Capital Cities
FLORIANÓPOLIS
ARGENTINA
PÔRTO ALEGRE
URUGUAY

scale of miles
0   400   800

"Narrow gauge" is a term referring to all gauges other than
broad gauge (1.6 meters). The "narrow gauge" railroads shown
on this map, therefore, are varied and do not form a unified system.

CHAPTER 9

THE TRANSITION FROM COLONY

TO NATION, 1808-1822

The arrival of the royal family and their court in Brazil favored Brazil in four basic ways that underlay many of the changes in policy and administration that were carried out between 1808 and 1822. The first, and most obvious, was that the court spent its money in Brazil, so that even if no other changes took place, the currency shortage would have been alleviated, and business would have revived. Court expenditures also called into existence new industries to meet court needs. That, plus the activity necessary to provide housing and other supplies required by the 15,000 new arrivals, guaranteed an increase in economic activity. The second, and strategically most important way, was that Portuguese mercantilist restrictions had been designed to favor Portugal, keeping Brazil as a supplier of raw materials. When the crown arrived in Brazil, Portugal had been captured by the French; protection of the Portuguese economy was no longer relevant. The goals of national self-sufficiency and industrialization were transferred with the crown from Portugal to Brazil. Thus, restrictions were lifted and manufactures encouraged. Third, at least part of Portugal's tax policy had been influenced by the fact that Portugal imported more from Brazil than she exported to it at the end of the eighteenth century. When England found itself faced with an unfavorable trade balance with its American colonies, it increased taxes to make up the difference, instead of earning the balance by trading elsewhere. When Portugal was faced with an unfavorable trade balance, it reacted as had England, by prohibiting competing economic activities and by levying taxes. Once Portugal was occupied, and Brazilian trade with Portugal reduced, financing of the import surplus was the preoccupation of the French rather than the Portuguese, so that the need to tax Brazil in order to pay for Brazilian imports disappeared. The chaotic conditions governing world trade during the Napoleonic Wars radically changed the needs and policies of the crown. Fourth, the removal of the court to Brazil favored Brazil for the above reasons; yet that same fact had one striking effect that was at best mixed in its influence on future Brazilian economic development. The crown was incapable of guaranteeing its continued independence without English help. Mainland Portugal was occupied by the French, and the Portuguese did not possess either a fleet that could control the shipping lanes and access to European ports or an army capable of effectively resisting a European-aided invasion. Thus Portuguese policy was necessarily circumscribed by the need to maintain English aid and protection by granting many of the concessions the English demanded. In combination, these four factors provide the background necessary to understand Portuguese economic policy in Brazil from 1808 to 1822.

Some notion of the financial impact of the court is given by the fact that the "uxaria," or domestic establishment of the royal family alone consumed 6 million cruzados, equal to some ₤540,000 a year. Its bills were paid punctually.[1] The problems of means of payment were alleviated almost immediately by the creation of new monetary mechanisms. Through most of its history, Portugal had relied on the use of European banks, as it lacked its own national bank. In 1803 the Banco de Troço had been founded in Brazil. When the court arrived, its access to European banks was limited, and to meet its needs, it took over the Banco de Troço, creating the Banco do Brasil in 1808.[2] The Banco do Brasil had an authorized capital of 1,638 contos of reis ($2,309,580 U.S. equivalent in 1808 prices); this sum was completed ten years after the bank was created. Its capital was less than that of the First Bank of the United States, which had an authorized capital of $10 million, of which $2 million was provided by the government. Public acceptance of the Bank was slow: it took a year to sell the first hundred of twelve hundred shares of stock offered:

> At first the subscribers could with difficulty be persuaded to enter into it, even by a liberal distribution of knighthood, although in the sequel they made very large profits: and the directors soon found it particularly convenient to be able to oblige one another, by gratuitous discounts, to the amount of a few hundred thousand milreis for each, without interest, for an indefinite time.[3]

The Bank was authorized to issue notes to bearer, and general letters of credit ("letras"). These notes were limited to 30$000 or less. The bank notes functioned as money. The bank's note-issue power did not aid business directly, but rather favored the government, since virtually all the notes issued before 1822 were for the government.[4] Shortfalls in government income were covered by borrowing from the Banco do Brasil; 160 contos of notes were in circulation in 1810, 1,042 contos in 1814, and 8,071 contos in 1821[5] (see Table 9-1). While notes in circulation increased fifty-fold, the bank's capital increased twenty-fold (see Table

9-2). Since bank notes had increased two and a half times
more rapidly than had the capital which backed them, prices
predictably increased to 263 per cent of their 1808 level by
1821 (see Table 9-3), which indicates that the internal price
level depended almost entirely on the capital/note issue ratio, rather than on external forces. This analysis is rein-
forced by the fact that the value of the currency fell by only
37.8 per cent from 1808 to 1821, from 70.00 pence per milreis
to 51.50 (see Table 9-4). The apparent disparity between the
local rate of inflation and external rate of depreciation of
currency is due to the very weak trade links during this period;
the difficulty of trading during the Napoleonic Wars and their
troubled aftermath meant that imports and exports formed a
very small share of total products in the economy, and that
therefore the prices which they commanded had a limited effect in determining the overall price level. The monetary
experience of Brazil during the Transition Period therefore
gives evidence that although the trade policies and treaties
enforced by the crown were of precedent-setting importance,
their immediate impact on the economy was smaller than their
startling break with tradition would indicate.

On the surface, the prince regent's order opening the
ports of Brazil appears to be an ultraliberal act, rather
than an act of national defense. The text of the order
reads:

Count da Ponte, Member of My Council, Governor, and
Captain-General of Bahia. Friend. I, the Prince Regent, send you greetings as one whom I esteem.

Attending to the remonstrance which you sent to My
Royal Person concerning the interruption and suspension of the commerce of this captaincy with the consequent grave prejudice it does to My Vassals and to My
Royal Treasury because of the critical situation in
Europe and wishing to give to that important matter
prompt attention capable of remedying the ills it does,
I am pleased to order provisionally and temporarily, until I formulate a general law which will effectively
regulate the matter, the following:

First: In The Custom Houses of Brazil shall be admit-
ted all and whatever produce, fabrics, and merchandise
transported either in foreign ships of powers which are
at peace and harmony with My Royal Crown or in the ships
of My Vassals, by paying upon entrance a tariff of
twenty-four percent [on dry goods; includes groceries],
namely, twenty in direct duties and four in special
gift duties as already established. The charges shall
be regulated by a customs list or laws because up to now
each one of the said Custom Houses has made its own

regulations. Wet goods, for example, wines, liquors,
and olive oil henceforth will be charged double duties.
Second: Not only My Vassals but also the above mentioned
foreigners can export to any ports which seem to benefit
commerce and agriculture because I sincerely desire
to encourage trade in all and whatever colonial produce
and products with the exception of brazilwood [diamonds
or other monopoly by law or contract] or other products
notably scarce. Produce leaving the country shall pay
the same duties already established in the respective
captaincies. Royal Letters and other Orders which until
now prohibited trade between My Vassals and foreigners
are suspended and without vigor. Execute all this with
the zeal and activity I expect of you. Bahia, January
28, 1808. The Prince.[6]

The opening of trade with Brazil to all nations was in
fact a declaration of independence from England. In the
course of encouraging the evacuation of the Portuguese royal
house from Portugal for Brazil, the English had aided the
Portuguese to such a degree that the English minister to
Portugal felt that "I have entitled England to establish with
the Brazils the Relation of Sovereign and Subject and to require Obedience to be paid as the Price of Protection."[7] The
"Price of Protection" that England had attempted to charge
was "an open port for British goods on the coast of Brazil."
The opening of Brazilian ports to all comers undercut the
impending English monopoly of the Brazil trade. When the
ports were opened, the English chargé d'affaires in Rio said
that the opening "could not fail to produce a good effect in
England, but that had it authorized the admittance of British
vessels, and of British manufactures upon terms more advantageous than those granted to the Ships and Merchandize of
Foreign Nations, it would necessarily have afforded greater
satisfaction."[8]
    The total duties in the decree were lower than the pre-
ceding rate of 36 per cent. Although during the Napoleonic
Wars, only England in fact was more capable of trading with
Brazil than were other European nations, the prospect of
peacetime competition was not welcome. The degree thus laid
the basis for a decreased dependence on England. Complementary measures to increase Brazil's economic independence
soon followed. On April 1, 1808, the mercantilist provisions
limiting Brazil to the production, for the most part, of raw
materials, were reversed by a decree reading:

I, the Prince Regent, make known to one and all: That
desiring to promote and further the national wealth, and
one of the sources of it being manufacturing and industry

which multiply, improve, and give greater value to the
provisions and products of Agriculture and the Arts and
increase the population by giving work to many laborers and by furnishing means of subsistence to many of My
Vassals, who, for lack of such means, would be left to
the vices of idleness, and that wishing to remove all
obstacles which might diminish or frustrate such advantageous benefits, I am pleased to abolish and revoke
all and every prohibition which exists to this respect
in the State of Brazil and in My Overseas Domains.
Henceforth, it shall be legal for any of My Vassals in
any area in which they live to establish any kind of
manufacture, without any exception, to make goods in
large or small quantities as best suits them. I do
therefore annul the Royal Order of January 5, 1785 and
any other laws or orders which contradict this decision
without making individual and express mention of them.
Therefore, I command the President of the Royal Council,
Governors, Captains-General, and other Governors of the
State of Brazil and of the Overseas Domains and all the
Ministers of Justice and other persons to whom knowledge of this is important to carry out and to fulfill
this My Royal Order and to disregard those laws which I
have hereby revoked and annulled. Given in the Palace of
Rio de Janeiro on April 1, 1803. The Prince.[9]

Raw materials were exempted from import duties and draw-
backs on reexported articles were conceded. National interests
were favored by closing coast-wide trade to foreign vessels
and restricting foreign commerce to the ports of Rio, Bahia,
Pernambuco, Maranhão, and Pará. Tariff advantages for Portuguese, as contrasted to foreigners, were granted on June 11,
1808, in a decree which lowered import duties on dry goods
from 24 per cent to 16 per cent, and reduced the duties on
provisions including wet goods by one third, in cases where
the goods belonged to the Portuguese and were imported in
Portuguese vessels.[10] In 1809, raw materials destined for use
in factories were exempted from taxes, while an annual subven-
tion of 60,000 cruzados, from the yield of the national lot-
tery, was established to aid manufacturers of wool, cotton,
silk, iron, and steel. In addition, exclusive privileges were
given to inventors or introducers of new machines for fourteen years.[11] These decrees not only stimulated Brazilian
economic growth, but also impelled the English to attempt to
regain an economic position in which they were on equal terms
with Portuguese nationals. The Portuguese, who necessarily
relied on England to regain control of Portugal and rethrone
the House of Bragança, were forced into signing a treaty with
England in May, 1810, which

revived all the old treaties, and, specifically, the
English obtained the right to appoint, subject to royal
consent, judges-conservator in Brazil, and the Brazilians received in England (in common with all other
foreigners) "the most strict and scrupulous observances
of the laws . . . through the acknowledged equity of
British jurisdiction and the singular excellence of the
British Constitution"--the phrase "acknowledged equity"
has become a byword in Brazil. Duties on British goods
were limited to 15 percent. . . . According to the
treaty, the special rate was not to be extended to
foreigners, while the appropriate regulations by which
the duty would be assessed would be drawn up by Portuguese and British in equal numbers. Portuguese goods
entering England received most-favoured-nation treatment. . . . It is likely that Strangford did not fully
appreciate that he was wresting concessions in Brazil
in exchange for advantages in Portugal, a fact which
explains the unpopularity of the treaty in Brazil.[12]

The tariff reduction granted the English was more favorable
than the tariff rates which the Portuguese themselves paid,
so that in the interests of equity, the tariff on merchandise
brought in by Portuguese ships was lowered from 16 to 15 per
cent by a decree of October 18, 1810.[13] The treaty further
provided that

Brazilian sugar, coffee, and other articles similar to
the produce of the English colonies were denied entrance
to British markets, although the right was granted to
Portugal to send such produce to England for reexporta-
tion, exempt from the higher duties imposed on such
articles destined for consumption within the British
Dominions, a stipulation which insured British vessels
of cargoes and English merchants of business. Likewise,
the prince regent could set up prohibitory duties on
English articles known by the name of British East Indies goods and on West Indies produce, such as sugar and
coffee.

In addition, a packet line was to be established between England and Rio de Janeiro. The treaty was designated "perpetual and immutable," although it could be modified in fifteen
years if both parties agreed to such modification. The possible objections to the treaty are placed on two different
grounds. The first is that 24 per cent tariffs are high
enough to protect "infant industries" but that 15 per cent
tariffs are not, so that the reduction of the tariff killed
existing Brazilian industries and prevented the establishment

of new ones. The second is that tariffs were levied for revenue purposes, rather than for protection, and that imports
would be demanded as long as foreign exchange was available.
In that case, reduced tariffs simply reduced government income
and increased the income going to the British producer. In
this argument, the reduction of tariffs does not change the
quantity of goods imported. However, it ignores the possibility that tariff reduction makes smuggling less profitable,
so that the increase in revenue would reflect not the change
in total quantity of imports, but the change in quantity of
legal imports. Thus, protection of Brazilian industry was
reduced; the Portuguese claimed that revenue also declined;
in the absence of budget records for the period we are faced
with the choice of accepting their word or believing that they
used the treaty to place the blame on Britain for difficulties whose origin was in Brazil: the latter is possible, because at the time of tariff reductions in the 1820s, import
tax receipts went up and smuggling declined. Despite the
qualifications which foreigners sometimes place on such an
evaluation, Brazilian historians often suggest that by the
treaty of 1810, once again, Portugal traded economic sovereignty for political independence.
     The Portuguese crown, therefore, had in the space of two
years passed acts and signed treaties with contradictory results. The decrees of 1808 served to stimulate local agriculture and manufacture: cotton was planted in larger quantities; the number of sugar and salt factories increased, and
the cultivation of wheat and hemp was encouraged. The treaty
of 1810 exposed such manufacture to the competition of foreign
imports and to that of manufactures produced locally with
newly invested British capital. The protective section of
the decrees of 1808 that were not countered by the treaty of
1810 concerned the promotion of new export crops, and the
founding of the Banco do Brasil. The encouragement of manufactures, however, could be expected to be less effective.
The combined effect of the decrees and treaty can be traced
in Table 9-5, which shows a general increase in the value of
Brazilian exports between 1796 and 1806; the value of total
trade fell sharply by 1819. Leather products and cotton
production grew considerably during this period. Further,
by 1821 coffee had become an important export, accounting
for 16.3 per cent of Brazil's total exports. Throughout the
period, Brazilian exports to Portugal were reexported to
other European ports, a fact which is reflected in the striking parallel between the figures of Portugal's imports from
Brazil and total Portuguese exports. The effect of the treaty
of 1810 on the ability of Brazil to choose its trading part-
ners is clear: Britain accounted for one third of the total

trade with the Portuguese Empire in 1796, three eighths in
1806, and four ninths in 1819.[15] Moreover, England consistently sold more to Brazil than it bought from it.[16] Yet the initial effect of the treaty was to reveal the ignorance and
gullibility of the English, who sent ice skates to Rio: they
rusted. The English sent more goods to be sold in Rio than
could be stored in warehouses. The goods were left in the
open, where the Brazilians liberated them. Incautious English
merchants bought counterfeit gold and diamonds, as well as
poorest quality exports. Eventually, the trade became better
suited to Brazilian conditions. The treaty did, however, have
one striking, immediate effect: the reduction of tariffs was
so great that smuggling and contraband were greatly reduced.[17]
     The effect of the treaty on the structure of the Brazil-
ian economy is less certain, since it cannot be proved that
if manufacturing activities had been protected, they would
have developed either at all, if the requisite skills and
resources were missing, or at a rapid rate, if the Brazilians knew how to manufacture the various tools and consumer
products that they imported. Specifically, Brazil imported
from England fine cloth, dress hats, boots, shoes, earthenware and glass, porter, cheese, butter, mirrors, silk and
cotton hosiery, fashionable dresses for women, pork products,
oil, wine and brandy, cotton, linen and woolen goods, iron
and steel products, salt, hardware, glass, matches, nonfer-
rous metals, gun supplies, and, from the United States, flour,
naval supplies, turpentine, and household furniture. Of
these goods it seems likely that some textiles and iron products could have been produced in Brazil on a craft basis for
the local market, but that even the production of butter required skills the Brazilians lacked, while the low cost
of many of the remaining British products was based on advances of technology and economies of scale so great that
Brazil would have been unable to meet the competition of these
imported goods.
     To the extent that the treaty of 1810 shifted Brazil
away from competing suppliers whose goods would have been
available more cheaply, in the absence of differential tariffs, the treaty encouraged misallocation of world resources, and, possibly, a higher total price, in the long run,
for imports than would have obtained if the most efficient
product had been bought. In the short run, the reduction in
tariffs seriously reduced the income of the government, thereby contributing to its financial difficulties. This is almost certainly the case; only if imports were "price elastic,"
so that a one per cent reduction in price resulted in a more
than one per cent increase in quantity, would the price reduction following tariff cuts result in greater government
revenue. Given the absence of local production of many of the

imported goods, it seems safe to say that they would have been
imported in as large a quantity as possible, as long as
Brazilians had the foreign exchange with which to pay their
suppliers. A tariff reduction therefore could increase the
quantity demanded of British goods, to the extent that funds
released from tariff payments were spent on additional imports, but that it could not directly increase government revenue. An increase in government revenue could occur from a
decrease in smuggling and an increase in taxable trade or could
come from a more roundabout process, by which an increase in
overall production led to an increase in exports, available
foreign exchange, imports, and, therefore, tariff payments.
Yet it was precisely at this time that the Napoleonic Wars
disrupted trade, and domestic inflation reduced the purchasing power value of tariff collections.

As the crown was unable to cover its expenditures by tax
revenue, it had recourse to a number of unfortunate expedients.
The most obvious, borrowing from the Banco do Brasil, has already been mentioned. The next step was the debasement of
silver and copper coin. Spanish dollars, which were worth
800 reis in "strong gold coin" were stamped 960 reis, an operation which yielded a 20 per cent profit. The overvaluation
of the Spanish dollar in terms of reis made it profitable for
Peruvian and Chilean merchants to sell Spanish dollars
against drafts on London or gold in Rio de Janeiro, by which
arbitrage they earned 5 to 6 per cent net profit. Payment
for international trade purposes was demanded in gold, which
was hoarded or sent abroad. Arbitrage was carried out as follows: 28 shillings worth of silver by weight at the overvalued Brazilian price, could be used to buy 36 shillings worth
of gold. The gold was exchanged for inconvertible Brazilian
currency, which could then be used to purchase silver. As the
specie/currency ratio declined, the value of the currency in
terms of foreign exchange also declined (see Table 9-4). This
procedure was extended to copper currency when the court required funds from Pernambuco, which did not have any. Pernam-
bucan officials met this crisis by stamping existing copper
coin at double its face value, and shipping the required (nominal) sum to Rio. Most Brazilian and some north American copper was then shipped to Pernambuco for the obvious profit to
be made; copper for small payments was lacking throughout Brazil, which enabled some financiers to profit through complex
exchanges between silver and copper. Since copper was at a
discount in relation to silver, silver drafts in the provinces
sold at a 15 to 20 per cent premium. Although a new stamp was
placed on the overvalued copper coin, it was readily counter-
feited in Brazil, the United States, and the United Kingdom;
it has been suggested that some Yankee ingenuity was handsomely
rewarded in smuggling copper coin to Brazil.[18]

Tampering with the value of money and granting preferential treatment to the English were unpopular with the Brazilians. Even worse, from the point of view of the planters, was the agreement by the Portuguese crown to limit the slave trade. The English had ended slavery in the United Kingdom, and prohibited its citizens from engaging in this trade, in 1808. The English attempted to persuade, by whatever means necessary, the other European powers to outlaw "the abominable traffic" in slaves. From the English point of view, a powerful economic argument was added to the humanitarian one: it was believed that the British West Indian sugar plantations were threatened by overproduction; this peril could be avoided by the end of the traffic in slaves, since Brazil would thereby be prevented from extending its sugar cultivation through lack of labor. With an arrogance for which they were world-famous, the English wrote of Brazil: "In that vast and fertile territory, an influx of British Capital and British enterprise alone" was "wanting to compleat the ruin of all our Islands in the Antilles. . . ." According to Manchester, "Land was ninety per cent cheaper in Brazil than in Jamaica while most of the supplies for a sugar plantation were raised within the country. Hence the Brazilian planter could sell with profit in Europe at a price which would mean ruin to the West Indian plantation owner, and the European market was essential to the British sugar trade, since England no longer absorbed anything like the total output of the sugar colonies."[19]

Planters from the British West Indies and English exporters to them combined to influence the British government to insist on the abolition of the slave trade as a basic part of any agreement by which Portugal gained access to the British market or obtained British guarantees of independence. They were only partly successful, since the slave trade clause in the Treaty of 1810 did not outlaw the slave traffic, but instead prohibited the trade from any part of Africa not belonging to Portugal. The British enforced the treaty by seizing slave ships off the coast of Africa. More than half of the slave ships sent from Bahia in 1811 were seized by British cruisers; five Bahian commercial houses failed in 1812. The British insisted that only British admiralty courts had jurisdiction, and the Bahians had no court of their own nationality to appeal to for indemnification.

Bahian resentment against the British, and against the Portuguese court, which did nothing to help them, rose, and contributed to the desire for separation from Portugal. It is worth noting that many of the Bahian complaints were justified, since the British were seizing vessels illegally for their military needs from 1810 to 1815 in the South Atlantic, as they did in the North Atlantic. The United States went to war with Great Britain; Portugal was clearly unable to fight

or negotiate for its rights. In 1815, treaties with Portugal
were concluded at the Congress of Vienna whereby the Portuguese
crown was awarded ₤300,000 in payment for seizures by the
British before June 1, 1814. The Bahians protested, since Dom
João was short of funds, and it was feared that the reparation
payments given the crown would never be paid to the shippers
whose claims had given rise to the award. In addition, Portugal prohibited all trade in slaves north of the equator, which
meant that the Bahian trade with the Gold Coast—its most
important source of slaves—was illegal. Transshipping of
slaves south to the legal zone was the easiest way around the
treaty, when it was not ignored altogether.

In 1817 the British, who desired to enforce the existing
treaties, obtained a convention whereby they were enabled to
visit any merchant vessel that

> might be suspected upon reasonable grounds of having
> slaves on board. Guilty slavers should be detained and
> brought for adjudication before special tribunals which
> were to be established. . . . The next article was a
> costly mistake on the part of Castlereagh, for it stipu-
> lated that no seizure was lawful unless slaves were
> actually found on board. Evidence of the recent pres-
> ence of illicit slaves was not sufficient to condemn
> the vessel—a stipulation which resulted in the whole-
> sale dumping overboard of Negroes by slave-traders when
> they were in danger of capture by British cruisers.

Thus, before England's attempt to suppress the slave trade
15 per cent of the slaves died during the voyage, while after
the attempt began, the loss rose to 25 per cent.[20] Since the
Portuguese king was not secure on his throne, he did not actively enforce the limitation of the slave trade: any attempt
to do so would have united the opposition of the majority of
the Brazilian population. Although the Portuguese slave trade
was restricted on paper, more slaves entered Brazil in 1821
than in 1808.[21]

The treaties by which the Portuguese king and emperor of
Brazil Dom João VI had been granted English aid were at the
expense of Brazil. The result was Brazilian resentment of the
king and the British. When it was necessary for a representa-
tive of the House of Bragança to return to Portugal so that
some member of the family could continue on the throne, Brazilian pressure ensured that it was the king, rather than his son,
who left Brazil. The king returned the compliment. In the
words of an unsympathetic observer,

> As a _finale_ to his maladministration of the finances of
> Brazil, Don John, on quitting it in 1822, in order to

resume the government of Portugal, left his loyal and
loving subjects in Brazil an everlasting proof of his
royal and paternal solicitude for their welfare, by empty-
ing the treasury, the bank, and even the museum, of every
article worth taking away, even to the specimens of gold
and diamonds which had for years belonged to the latter
national establishment.[22]

As onerous as the treaties and the financial situation
were, the Brazilian economy contained some elements of
strength at the close of the Transition Period. Some of this
strength became apparent, oddly enough, during the financial
crisis (in 1818-1819). The government was a debtor to the
bank, "and this sum the bank owed to the public, because it
could no longer pay its notes. The bank was therefore the
nominal creditor of Government, but the public the real one."[23]
Despite the lack of specie backing the notes, no one tried to
cash in the notes because of the great increase of agricultural
produce in Brazil, which required an annual increase in the
circulating medium. By 1819, bank notes became "forced legal
currency," which circulated at a discount against silver,
which, in turn, was treated as merchandise. In addition to
the expansion of traditional agricultural exports and the
introduction and production for export of new crops, government aid resulted in the founding of iron factories.[24]
Skilled technicians were recruited from Europe, while businessmen and professionals from England emigrated to Brazil
voluntarily, where their funds, knowledge, and professional
contacts contributed to the growth of the economy. This
growth was reflected in the increase of ships entering Rio
de Janeiro from 810 in 1805 to 1,311 in 1820.[25] Trade with
Portugal grew about 25 per cent from 1806 to 1821. Deflating
for the change in purchasing power of money, this becomes a
decline of 10 per cent. The per capita decline was slightly
greater. As agricultural production increased, while the real
value of foreign trade declined, it is difficult to be certain
of the trend of per capita income.
When Dom Pedro declared the Independence of Brazil in
1822, he inherited, therefore, a growing economy, a bankrupt
treasury, an insolvent bank, foreign treaties designed to in-
hibit Brazil's development of manufactures and make her agriculture more expensive, and an army and navy that were too
small to challenge a major power, but which nevertheless absorbed half of the government expenditures. Political independence from Portugal was easily obtained. Economic independence from England was not. The following chapter, therefore, focuses on the attempt to create a national economy in
Brazil.

FOOTNOTES

Chapter 9.   The Transition from Colony to Nation, 1808-1822

1. John Armitage, The History of Brazil, I, cited in R. A.
    Humphreys and John Lynch, The Origins of the Latin
    American Revolutions, 1808-1826, p. 197.

2. Manoel Pinto de Aguiar, Ensaios de História e económia,
    1° volume, pp. 84 ff.

3. J. J. Sturz, A Review, Financial, Statistical, and Com-
    mercial of the Empire of Brazil and Its Resources:
    Together with a Suggestion of the Expediency and Mode
    of Admitting Brazilian and Other Foreign Sugars into
    Great Britain for Refining and Exportation, pp. 4-5.

4. J. Pires do Rio, A Moeda Brasileira e seu perene caráter
    fiduciário.

5. Victor Viana, O Banco de Brasil, p. 313.

6. Modified from citation in E. Bradford Burns, A Documentary
    History of Brazil, pp. 186-187.   Cf. Manchester, British
    Preeminence in Brazil and Its Rise and Decline, pp. 70-71.

7. Strangford to Canning, F.O., 63/56, No. 103, cited in
    Manchester, op. cit., p. 67.

8. Hill to Canning, F.O., 63/63, No. 3, cited in Manchester,
    op. cit., p. 71.

9. Cited in Burns, op. cit., pp. 186-187; Manchester, op.
    cit., p. 74, says that "permission was given to colonials
    and foreigners of any nation to establish manufacturing
    plants of all kinds."

10. Manchester, op. cit., p. 74.

11. Humberto Bastos, O Pensamiento Industrial no Brasil, p.
    28; Nicia Vilela Luz, A Luta Pela Industrializacão do
    Brasil, p. 15.

12. H. V. Livermore, A New History of Portugal, pp. 256-257.

13. Manchester, op. cit., p. 9.

14. Ibid., p. 89.

15. Calculations based on Simonsen, _História Econômica do Brasil, 1500-1820_, p. 457.

16. Manchester, _op. cit._, p. 98.

17. John Mawe, _Travels in the Interior of Brazil_, pp. 450-471.

18. Sturz, _op. cit._, pp. 2-7.

19. Manchester, _op. cit._, p. 166.

20. Oleveira Martins, _O Brazil e as Colonias Portuguesas_, p. 58, footnote 1, cited in Manchester, _op. cit._, pp. 159-160, 170-174.

21. Manchester, _op. cit._, p. 185.

22. Sturz, _op. cit._, p. 7.

23. _Ibid._, p. 5.

24. Simonsen, _História Econômica do Brasil_, pp. 448-449.

25. _Ibid._, p. 440.

CHAPTER 10

THE ECONOMIC HISTORY OF THE

BRAZILIAN EMPIRE, 1822-1889

The economic history of the Brazilian Empire (1822-1889) is dominated by two interrelated themes: the struggle for independence from England, and the conflict over the abolition of slavery. The handling of these issues depended on who was in power. It is therefore convenient to divide the study of the empire into four periods: the rule of Dom Pedro I (1822-1831), the regency (1831-1840), the consolidation of national power under Dom Pedro II (1840-1870), and the end of slavery, starting with a law declaring that all children of women slaves were born free (1871) and culminating in the abolition of slavery (1888), which was a major factor in the overthrow of the empire in 1889.

The rule of Dom Pedro was devoted to the establishment of Brazilian independence. Recognition of Brazilian independence was aided by England, in exchange for commercial advantages and a promise to end the slave trade.

The Regency was marked by continuing regional revolts, which obtained increased power for the provincial legislatures and reduced export taxes, whose assessment was concentrated by region. Brazilians were convinced that slave labor was necessary for economic expansion, so that British measures to end the slave trade were constantly evaded.

The years 1840 to 1870 established the control of the national government. Domestic control was achieved by reducing the power of the provincial legislatures. The last provincial revolt during the empire occurred in 1849. Increased control over international trade was obtained when the commercial treaty with England lapsed and was replaced by strongly protective tariff legislation, which aided domestic manufacture. At the same time, government promotion of railroads aided exports. The slave trade was ended in 1850, and the release of capital from investment in this trade to investment in other economic activity sparked an economic boom, which benefited from relative world peace and prosperity until 1873.

The final period of the empire was characterized by the gradual abolition of slavery. European immigrants began to arrive, and industry to develop. The government encouraged bank expansion, resulting in a rapid increase in money supply. The increase was used to finance the expansion of economic activity, although prices increased rapidly.

The major bottlenecks to economic development during the empire had been the treaties with England, the presence of slavery, and a credit shortage. The treaties with England were replaced by protective tariffs. Slavery had led to labor short- ages. Its abolition led to heavy immigration and rapid growth. The end of the credit shortage by domestic banking expansion created an adequate financial base for economic expansion.

Yet the length of time needed to achieve these aims was disappointing compared to Argentina or Mexico, while Brazil's export performance was inferior to that of these two nations. The frequency of separatist movements and the final overthrow of the empire suggests that retention of monarchy led to only slightly greater political stability than obtained in Argentina, while regional, economic, and military factors determined Bra- zilian policy. It simply was not true that the combination of a spirit abhorring bloodshed, and institutional continuity created a Brazil that was strikingly different from its His- panic Latin American neighbors.

Dom Pedro I, 1822-1831

The Legal and Historical Background

When the Portuguese court sailed for Lisbon in 1821, they left behind Dom João's eldest son, Dom Pedro, as regent. Bra- zil had been elevated to a kingdom in 1815. The cortes (par- liament) in Lisbon, however, took a number of steps to return Brazil to a colonial status. The reestablishment of economic colonialism was foreshadowed when the opening of the ports was condemned, as Portugal wished to regain the entrepôt trade with Brazil.   Political colonialism appeared to be reestablished when the organs of central government at Rio de Janeiro were abolished and the provinces were made individually responsible to Lisbon. Municipal and provincial juntas were formed which refused to pay revenue to Rio. This step reduced Dom Pedro from regent of Brazil to governor of Rio de Janeiro and the southern provinces. The Banco do Brasil failed in July, and popular hostility to Portugal increased. In January 1822 Dom Pedro declared that he would remain in Brazil. The Portuguese troops attempted to force Dom Pedro to comply with the cortes's or- ders by threatening to bombard Rio de Janeiro. Armed Brazil- ian citizens and militia forced the Portuguese troops to with- draw. A month later, for a price, they were sent back to the mother country. The cortes responded by sending more, which Dom Pedro refused to allow to land. In February, Dom Pedro created a consultative council of all the provinces, and in June he called for a constituent assembly "to establish the bases on

which should be erected its independence." In response, the
cortes abolished the chancery court, the treasury, the junta
of commerce, and other courts and administrative bodies set
up in Brazil under Dom João. At the same time, Dom Pedro was
ordered to return to Portugal to complete his education, and
Brazilians were by edict excluded from political and military
offices, while Dom Pedro's ministers were declared guilty of
treason. Two days later governors-at-arms were appointed
for each of the provinces. The news of these acts reached
Dom Pedro on September 7, 1822. His response, the famous
Cry of Ipiranga, was: "The hour has come! Independence or
death! We have separated from Portugal!"[1]

Although they were united against the Portuguese government, the Brazilians were not united among themselves. One
group, composed mainly of Portuguese in Brazil and some
wealthy Brazilians, favored an absolute monarchy under Dom
Pedro, with a government that was legally independent of
Portugal, but nonetheless united by family ties. The "Brazilian party" wanted a constitutional monarchy independent of
Lisbon; a sizable group within this party favored the establishment of a republic.[2] Above all, the provinces had no tradition of cooperation and few land transport links; the revolt
of Dom Pedro had been confined to the four southern provinces
of Rio de Janeiro, São Paulo, Minas Gerais, and Rio Grande do
Sul. Its success did not bring with it the acquiescence of
the northern provinces. The emperor's minister, José Bonifácio
de Andrada, hired the British admiral, Lord Cochrane, to aid
the army by improvising a navy and driving out the Portuguese
forces. Cochrane was victorious at Bahia, Maranhão, and Belem.
Montevideo and the eastern bank of the Plata, which had been
formally annexed in 1821, were lost due to internal squabbling
between Portuguese and Brazilian troops, and a seige that had
lasted seventeen months before the Portuguese troops left on
orders from the cortes. By January 1824, "by the grace of God
and the British Navy," the territorial unity of Brazil was assured.[3] A constitution was proclaimed in March 1824; it
formed the legal basis of the monarchy until its fall in 1889.

The recognition of the new nation was aided by British
fear that Austria or France would either act to reunite Brazil
and Portugal, or would defend the slave trade in exchange for
commercial advantages. The British, however, were under treaty
obligations to Portugal, which would have required them to
aid Portugal if it entered a war against Brazil. To fore-
stall this possibility, England forced Portugal to recognize
Brazilian independence, so that England could then recognize
Brazil and at least formally abide by its treaty commitments.[4]
The economic aspects of the treaty by which Brazilian independence was recognized were the establishment of a mixed commission with England to determine the indemnity for prizes,

and for confiscated or sequestered property; the compensation
of Portugal for the loss of public property in Brazil; and the
granting of mutual most-favored-nation clauses and a 15 per
cent import tax. A secret additional article stipulated that
Brazil would pay Portugal Ł2 million sterling in compensation
for all losses caused by the independence of Brazil. This sum
included Ł1,400,000 of a Ł1,500,000 loan Lisbon had raised in
London to fight the Brazilians and Ł600,000 for palaces and
other royal properties left in Brazil. The ratification of
the treaties helped to assure Brazilian independence as a
unit, rather than a series of smaller nations. The United
States, which in 1824 had been the first nation to recognize
Brazil, was unable to persuade European powers or provide de-
finitive military and naval force to assure Brazilian independence. The United Kingdom, by its naval and diplomatic
supremacy, forced Portuguese recognition, which was obtained in November 1825. Austria, France, and England followed within the next two months, and many of the remaining
European states, with the expected exception of Spain, by the
end of the year.[5]

Despite the advantages of a relatively peacefully and
inexpensively secured independence, the treaty was anything
but popular in Brazil, as Brazilians believed that their independence was the result of their own efforts, and that they
therefore owed nothing to the king of Portugal, least of all
a Ł2 million indemnity. The payment of funds by Dom Pedro to
his father Dom João increased the Brazilian belief that Dom
Pedro was too concerned with Portugal. This was made worse
when Dom Pedro spent taxes raised in Brazil on attempts in
1828 to place his daughter Maria da Gloria on the throne of
Portugal. Of more lasting consequence were the treaties
with Great Britain signed in 1826 and 1827. Dom Pedro, indebted to Britain for the independence of Brazil, agreed in
1826 to the abolition of the slave trade three years after
the treaty was ratified; thereafter, it would be treated as
piracy. That any treaty on slavery was obtained at all is
an indication of England's determination and strength, since
Dom Pedro had refused a direct offer of recognition from
England in November 1822 on condition that he abolish the
slave traffic. The initial offer had to be refused because
Dom Pedro's government might well fall if he accepted the
terms. Negroes were viewed as neceysary for agricultural
production. The slave trade could be gradually reduced, but
not abolished overnight. Moreover, the crown was influenced
by the prospect of the loss of some Ł200,000 annual income
from the tax on Negroes imported into Brazil. The British
minister, Gordon, insisted that existing treaties between
England and Portugal enabled England to require Portugal to
close its slave ports to Brazilians, who were now a foreign

nation. Thus, Brazilian ships engaged in the slave trade
would be treated as pirates. The English pointed out to the
reluctant Dom Pedro that it was better to grant terms by treaty that which would in any event be taken by force. The British minister, predicting the unpopularity of the measures,
wrote to his government, that the treaty would result in a
tenfold increase of slave traffic during the next three years,
and that it would continue afterwards by a system of contraband with the connivance of the Rio government. The task of
enforcement, therefore, would be left entirely to Great Britain. The treasy was immensely unpopular, and Brazilian
legislation to enforce it was not enacted until 1831, after
Dom Pedro's abdication. Since the terms of the treaty were
not to go into effect until three years after ratification,
the legal date on which its provisions were to be enforced
is 1834.[6]

The treaty of 1827 renewed for fifteen years the special
commercial privileges that Britain had obtained under the
treaty of 1810. Some of the provisions of the new treaty were
unobjectionable to Brazil.

> Peace and friendship were to exist between the two coun-
> tries; consuls were to be appointed with their powers
> clearly specified by the treaty; perfect liberty of
> conscience in matters of religion was guaranteed; the
> inviolability of domicile was assured; deserters were
> to be delivered up on demand; mutual liberty of commerce
> in all ports of both parties was granted, although coast-
> wise trade was restricted to national ships; port duties
> were specified; the packet service was to continue;
> piracy was outlawed; shipwrecked or distressed vessels
> were to be protected; mutual right of warehousing and
> reexportation without payment of consumption tax were
> conceded; drawbacks or bounties on reexported articles
> were declared to be independent of the nationality of
> the vessels receiving such reexported articles; Brazil
> abolished all monopolies or exclusive commercial com-
> panies, except existing crown monopolies; and the Eng-
> lish merchants obtained the privilege of making pay-
> ments to the customs house on the same footing as the
> subjects of Brazil.[7]

In addition, a number of articles especially obnoxious
to the Brazilians were included. The office of "Judge Conservator for the British Nation" was to be continued until a substitute arrangement was established. It never was, so that
British extraterritoriality was maintained as long as the
treaty was in force. Ownership of vessels was defined in a manner that excluded much of Brazil's merchant fleet from the

benefits of the treaty. The British also succeeded in declaring a large number of articles to be war contraband, while the low import duty forced Brazil, by virtue of most-favored-nation clauses, to grant the same low rate to so many nations that on September 24, 1828, Brazil decreed that all nations were granted the 15 per cent rate. This was of extreme importance, since import duties were normally the most important source of revenue for new nations; their reduction was a major cause of the new government's lack of funds. No compensation was forthcoming, for the treaty also recognized England's preferential rate in favor of produce from the British West Indies: Brazil, therefore, could not expand her export of sugar and tropical products to Great Britain.

The two treaties of 1826 and 1827 mark the height of British influence and unpopularity in Brazil. Dom Pedro's misfortunes continued beyond the signing of the treaties. The war with Argentina from 1825 to 1828, which was fought for control of the eastern bank of the La Plata, was ended by the force of Great Britain, which created the modern state of Uruguay out of the disputed territory. The result of three years of war was that Dom Pedro lost money, men, prestige, and--from the Brazilian point of view--the Brazilian territory of Uruguay. Popular dissatisfaction with the emperor increased when his well-liked queen, Leopoldina, died after a violent quarrel about Dom Pedro's mistress Domitila de Castro. After Leopoldina's death, Dom Pedro married a European princess, accepting the condition that he discard Domitila, who had been with him for eight years. In that time, however, the Brazilian Domitila had used her influence with the king to help her friends, so that those she did not aid were added to the opposition. The problem of favoritism in appointments also included reliance on Portuguese rather than Brazilian advisers, and inability to get along with the elected lower house of the legislature. The revived Banco do Brasil was so bitterly resented for its close links to the court that its charter was not renewed in 1829. In France, King Charles X had been expelled from the country following the July Revolution in 1820. When news of his overthrow reached Rio on September 14, the Brazilians demonstrated against their own monarchy in favor of a federal republic. In March 1831, Dom Pedro appointed a ministry composed entirely of Brazilians, only to dismiss it three weeks later, appointing in its place another consisting of unpopular aristocrats--"the ministry of the marquises." When the restoration of the Brazilian ministry was demanded on April 6, Dom Pedro refused on the grounds that that would be a denial of the imperial prerogative. He would "do everything for the people, but nothing by the people." At this, the army joined the revolt, and at midnight Dom Pedro abdicated in favor of his five-year-old son.

Dom Pedro, following his father's tradition, took the remaining gold and silver from the liquidated Banco do Brasil, boarded a British warship, and sailed for Portugal, where he gained the Portuguese throne for his daughter. He died in 1834.[8]

Economic Actions and Development

The course of economic action taken during Dom Pedro's reign reflected the political conditions of the time. The new nation was short of funds, and combined revenge with necessity on December 11, 1822, by authorizing the sequestration of all merchandise in the warehouses belonging to Portuguese subjects; merchandise or cash belonging to Portuguese merchants and all rural and urban buildings they possessed; and, finally, the ships or parts of them belonging to the Portuguese. Exempt from sequestration, however, were the stocks of the Banco Nacional, insurance firms, and the iron factory at Villa de Sorocaba.[9] The sequestration of Portuguese goods was as disappointing in its yield of revenue as had been that of the Jesuits in 1759. Revenue from sequestration provided 2.3 per cent of total government revenue in 1823 and 1.6 per cent in 1824 (see Table 10-1), a total of 876:976$000 reis, which would be equal to $859,417. No funds from sequestration were reported after these years. Thus, a more permanent source of revenue was needed. The government, in hopes of increasing its revenue, raised its import duties on December 30, 1822, from their level of 15 per cent to 24 per cent on foreign stuff, and on Portuguese merchandise. The remaining goods paid flat rates, which are shown in Table 10-2. In 1823 an administrative body was created to collect export and internal taxes. Some of the evils of the colonial administration were avoided, as the government administered most of its taxes, farming only three relatively unimportant contracts.

Following the increase in tax rates, tariff collections rose from 1,851 million reis in 1823 to 2,380 million in 1824, to 2,450 million in 1827. This supports the suggestion made above that Brazilians tended to import to the extent that they earned foreign exchange, and that price changes resulting from a tax increase did not influence the quantity bought sufficiently for a tax rate increase to lead to a decline in tax yield. Nonetheless, when tariffs were reduced to 15 per cent ad valorem in 1827-1828, the real value of import tax receipts did not fall in the following years, 1827 to 1831. This reflects the fact that the reduction in the import duties made smuggling less profitable, so that it is unlikely that a larger share of imports were legally imported and paid taxes. Brazil's earnings of exports were declining in real terms during the reign of Dom Pedro I; the real value of imports also fell, while while Brazil consistently imported more than it exported

(see Table 10-3).   The difference was paid for out of the
proceeds of loans floated in Great Britain in 1824, 1825, and
1829 (see Table 10-4).   If Great Britain had not granted preferential treatment to the British West Indies, then it is
possible that Brazil could have increased its exports to Great
Britain by a large enough sum to pay for its imports.   Brazil
was faced with interest and commission charges on the loans
that would not have had to be paid if the necessary funds
could have been earned directly.   In the short run, therefore, exclusion of Brazilian imports and the granting of loans
was profitable to Great Britain.

The financing of Brazil's trade from 1822 to 1831 can be
summarized as follows: total exports equaled 181,939 contos
of reis (in 1823 prices = U.S. $187,397,000).   Imports were
197,582 contos, which left an import balance of 15,643 contos.
In 1831 the balance of the foreign debt was 26,279 contos.
If imports were directly financed from the British loans, this
would leave 10,636 contos to pay for services and for capital
remitted abroad, and to hold against a further fall in the
value of Brazilian currency.   It seems likely that most of the
sum was used to pay for foreign ships carrying Brazilian imports and expenditures of Brazilian ships in foreign ports,
since the United States, which had a larger fleet, spent 3 per
cent of its import value on such payments.   It is plausible
that Brazilian payments for this item would be somewhat larger.[10]
The British loans helped the Brazilian government's finances,
but they were not the only source of funds.   During this period,
the increase in bank notes was 9,161 contos, 1,475 contos less
than the increase in the Brazilian currency equivalent of the
loans (in 1823 reis).   The total increase available to finance
the domestic economy and to pay for international transactions
other than imports of goods was 19,797 contos.   Because foreign
loans increased at a faster rate than did the domestic money
supply, the fall in the value of the reis was not proportional
to the increase in money supply.   At least part of this increase was anti-inflationary in the long run, since it was
used to finance the 33 per cent increase in the volume of
exports during the decade (see Table 1-2).   The increase in
production did not have the anticipated effect on Brazilian
national income or government receipts, since the prices of
commodities which Brazil produced fell by 33 per cent, while
the prices of imports from Great Britain fell by 28 per cent.
The net result was a decline in the terms of trade of 20 per
cent, which, in the case of Argentina from 1833 to 1850, explains a large share of the government's inability to pursue
a development program more rapidly.

The government was further handicapped in spending funds
on development by the need to provide at least the minimum of
armed force to maintain its control over its territory, and
by the unfortunate war with Argentina, which absorbed 27.4 per

cent of the national budget above the normal military expenditures of some 40 to 50 per cent of the budet (see Table 10-5).
Roughly 7 per cent of the budget was used to support the imperial household and ministry of the empire. Justice and
Foreign Affairs absorbed 5 per cent, leaving 40 to 50 per cent
for the Treasury for the largely administrative expenses of
the government.

Total government expenditures per capita were about $3.00
U.S. during the decade and could not result in a great increase
in per capita income. Although it was difficult to aid development by government investment, an important legal change was
secured. In 1830 the government abolished the 15 per cent tax
that had been collected in some provinces on goods that were
imported from other Brazilian provinces, while the tithes collected in Bahia on exports were no longer levied on exports to
other Brazilian provinces.11 Thus, the government attempted
to establish a national market considerably earlier than had
been done in Mexico (1895) or Argentina (1853). Although the
tax structure was favorable to its establishment, its development was severely limited by the lack of overland transportation; coastwise shipping continued to provide a major trade
link between the various areas of Brazil. Inland trade must
have been much less than coastal trade, where shipping was possible, as the cost of land transport was very much greater.
This, in turn, explains the lack of overland transport wherever
water transport facilities were available. Thus, overland
trade was important between Rio and São Paulo; the direction
of trade links was determined by the source of supply of imports. Export supply areas were linked with ports, which
were in turn linked with Europe. Export supply areas were to
a much lesser degree linked with each other. In this sense,
Brazil was on the periphery of the European market, and did
not constitute a national market (see vol. 2, p. 130 for de-
tailed analysis of this point). Until Brazil could produce
the goods supplied by Europe, it was unlikely that there would
be more internal than foreign trade in products other than
food crops and rough textiles.

An evaluation of the economic achievements of Dom Pedro
I is necessarily mixed. He secured national independence and
the integrity of Brazilian territory, although he definitively
lost Brazil's claim to Uruguay. A constitution was provided,
and the fiscal basis for the creation of a national market
established. However, the useless war expenditures (1825-1828)
contributed to a decline in the value of the nation's money,
and to the fall of the Banco do Brasil. The price paid for
British aid in the treaty of 1827 in the form of low import
duties to some extent hindered the development of Brazilian
manufacturing, although except in some textiles, the major
blockage to development was ignorance of how to produce the

goods in question, rather than cheap foreign products. It
is not true that the treaty of 1827 was responsible for a fall
in government revenue below the amounts that would have been
collected if tariffs had been higher, since more goods would
have been smuggled as the rates rose, and the government would
not have been able to collect the taxes. Much more serious,
however, were the loans contracted during the 1820s, since
the interest and amortization charges would, in the future,
absorb a large share of the government budget. In 1828, for
example, amortization and interest on loans absorbed 11 per
cent of the government budget.[12] As had been the case throughout earlier Portuguese and Brazilian history, the political
basis for future economic development was laid at considerable economic cost.

The Regency, 1831-1840

When Dom Pedro I abdicated in favor of his son, Dom Pedro
II was five years old. A regency was set up to rule in his
name until he was capable of governing the nation. The regency
was beset by factions, which mirrored the unrest throughout
the country. There were revolts in Pará in 1831, in Minas
Gerais in 1833, in Mato Grosso and Maranhão in 1834, a slave
revolt in Bahia in 1835, a ten-year war of secession in Rio
Grande do Sul (1835-1845), and a new series of revolts in
Maranhão. In order to hold the nation together, a number of
reforms were instituted. The constitution was modified in
1834: provincial legislatures were created in which minorities could have a voice, the entailing of estates was abolished,
and the educational system was extended and modernized. Shifts
in education had begun with the introduction of the court to
Rio, which established

> Colleges of Surgery and Medicine in Rio and Bahia, and
> a Naval Academy. A Royal Press began to function. In
> 1810 and 1811 a School of Commerce and a Military Academy
> opened their doors. In 1814 a collection of books--
> the nucleus of [the] present National Library--was put
> at the disposal of the public. The National Museum was
> created in 1818, as was the School of Fine Arts. In the
> same year, with a view to improving agricultural methods,
> and the introduction and acclimatizing of new plants, the
> first steps were taken to create the Botanical Gardens.[13]

The spread of interest and instruction in practical skills is
reflected in the Provincial Budgets, which were included in
the Imperial Ministry budget. For example, in the fiscal year
of July 1831 to June 1832, all of the provinces provided for
public instruction. Many had high schools, specialized

academies, public libraries, and botanical gardens. The
provinces also set aside funds for the catechism of Indians,
medical facilities, vaccinations and public works, while
São Paulo allotted 486$000 reis for its iron foundry.[14] Mea-
sures to promote development continued to be adopted throughout the regency, which

> accomplished something in the way of legal codification,
> improvement of administrative practice, creation of a
> Public Archive and a School of Agriculture. The famous
> Colégio Dom Pedro II was founded by government decree
> in 1837 and became the peculiar concern of Vasconcelos.
> The Regency upheld the liberty of the press at a time
> when liberty was interpreted as unbridled license, and
> greatly stimulated the emergence of a genuine public
> opinion. In the economic sphere it took the first steps
> to promote the construction of railways, and steam navi-
> gation between Rio de Janeiro and the Northern ports.
> The fiscal administration was reorganized on a basis
> that prevailed to the end of the Empire. . . .[15]

The imperial government was willing to spend some funds
on needed infrastructure. Yet, not all Brazilian intellec-
tuals at this time were economic nationalists. At least some
powerful leaders believed in the doctrine of free trade. For
example, Bernardo Pereira de Vasconcelos had unified tariffs
in 1828, saying: ". . . nothing of privileges for industry;
foreign products, whatever they be, being bought with the
products of our industry, which these purchases animate. Our
profit lies not in producing goods in which foreigners have an
advantage over us, but on the contrary, we should apply our-
selves to the products in which they are inferior to us. Protection and oppression signify the same in regard to industry."[16]
Taxes for 1832/33 were set at 10 per cent on sugar, cotton,
coffee, tobacco, unscraped hides, 20 per cent on hides from
Rio Grande do Sul, and 40 per cent from Bahia. According to
Manchester, a growing deficit caused the empire to levy an
8 per cent tax on exports in 1836 to cover the deficit. Carreira, however, gives this as 7 per cent.[17] Vasconcelos' position was politically disastrous because the regions producing
these commodities considered that they were being subject to
discriminatory taxation. Since these taxes were one of the
factors contributing to the separatist revolts, they were removed in 1835 and 1836: for fiscal 1836/37, the 50 reis tax
on hides (Pernambuco and Alagoas), the tax on oil (Bahia),
the tax of 60 reis per sack of exported cotton (Pernambuco)
and 120 reis per sack from Bahia; the 10 per cent tax on
dried meat exports (San Pedro), and 80 reis per tonelada
(Pernambuco), 40 per cent on aguardente (Bahia) and the bridge

tax (San Pedro) were abolished. For fiscal 1837/38, the 20 per cent tax on hides from Rio Grande do Sul was reduced to 15 per cent.[18]

If Brazil was to remain united, it had to grant a measure of regional autonomy in politics, and avoid levying taxes with an incidence that was concentrated by region. Since exports grown in one area of Brazil were not grown in another, consumption, tithe, and export taxes levied on them, if relatively easy to collect, were far more politically inflamatory than virtually any other kind of tax. Import taxes, for example, could be passed on to consumers and, at least in theory, consumers were equally spread among the various provinces. Export taxes, therefore, were nominally reduced. Export tax collections increased both absolutely and as a share of national revenue (see Table 10-6) because smuggling was reduced. Although the quantity of some exports (coffee, sugar, cocoa, and yerba maté) grew during the decade, the overall export quantity index increased by only 1 per cent. It seems clear that tax reductions, by leading to an increase in the prices received by producers, were one factor in the increase of the quantity they produced. Thus the way to increase government revenue was to reduce the tax rate, which, by leading to an increase of quantity of taxable goods produced, increased the total revenue. Nonetheless, the increase in export production again led to a less than proportionate increase in income, since the prices of exports, with the exception of cocoa and yerba maté, fell 13 per cent until 1839, recovering in 1840, while the prices of imports rose 16 per cent, so that the terms of trade moved against Brazil from 129.9 in 1830 to 114.1 in 1840.

Both during the rule of Dom Pedro I and the regency, the combination of industrialization in Great Britain and relatively free trade with Brazil worked as follows. The importation of industrial goods from Great Britain benefited consumers, but to some extent limited the further development of the few existing industries in Brazil. The terms of trade moved against Brazil because the goods which it produced, with the exception of cotton, were not essential for industrial development. Moreover, cotton prices fell as world production of cotton expanded rapidly following the invention of the cotton gin and the planting of increased areas in the United States and Egypt. The price of the remaining exports would increase only if large numbers of new consumers suddenly were able to afford to purchase them. Yet it was precisely the ability of Great Britain to sell its industrial products to the rest of the world, instead of to British laborers, that enabled Britain to avoid raising laborer's income. Thus, as laborers' income did not rise, the increased quantities of exports could only be sold if their prices fell. The difficulties Brazil faced in earning foreign exchange could be alleviated only if (1) Brazil produced exports more essential to industrial production, (2) working class income increased in Europe by an amount large enough to lead to a strong increase in demand for Brazilian exports, while pressure on Brazil's balance of payments could also be alleviated if (3) Brazil produced some of the goods which it had previously imported.

At least some attempts were made to increase Brazilian industrial production. Textiles had been exported from Minas Gerais (1,242,343 varas) in 1818; whale oil had been refined in Bahia and Santa Catarina, and exported to England and France for use in textile factories; in Goiás, wool was used to manufacture hats, while iron was produced in Ipanema (Rio). In 1828 the first Chamber of Commerce (Sociedade Auxiladora da Industria Nacional) was founded. Yet industry did not grow; the first textile firm in São Paulo failed because of the lack of skilled labor capable of using the machines.[19] The slow development of industry is reflected in the fact that in 1835 there were mainly models of industrial equipment, but little equipment itself. Brazilians berated themselves for the lack of foresight, planning, and division of labor which were necessary to make business prosper.[20] In 1835, also, British Parliament passed a law which gave permission to construct a railroad in Brazil, as the Brazilians did not have enough capital to construct a railroad.[21] The lack of roads and canals was signaled as the cause of high transport and warehouse charges, which further inhibited business. In 1850 there were only fifty industrial firms in Brazil, one half of which were saltworks.[22]

The regency was characterized by tumultuous change, not only in domestic politics, but also in the more technical aspects of the nation's economic structure. Shifts in monetary and banking arrangements stand out as an example. The difficulties of establishing an adequate banking and currency system were apparent as early as 1825/26. Metal had almost disappeared from circulation by this time, and attempts "to reintroduce a metallic currency was frustrated, in the first place, by the selfishness of the bank, which kept the Ł600,000 in specie and bullion in its coffers [that had been intended for circulation] under pretence that, if put into circulation, it would soon find its way back to England; whereas its real motive was grounded on the fact, that the circulation of its notes was more profitable to it, the notes having recovered a little from their deterioration on its being known that the bank held so much specie or bullion in its vaults."[23] When the bank charter expired in 1829, it was not renewed. The bank's affairs were then handled by a committee for its liquidation; gold and silver were used in part payment of its notes, "and

the debt of the government having been ascertained to be
16,900,000$, notes of the bank were ordered to be withdrawn
to that amount, and those of the government substituted."[24]
The regency therefore was faced with a system of paper money,
no banking facilities, and a coinage system whose deficien-
cies were discussed in Chapter 9.

An attempt in 1833 to reorganize the Banco do Brasil
failed. The government assumed the task of regulating the
money supply by officially recognizing the decline in the
value of Brazilian currency from 1$600 reis per oitava of
gold (3.586 grams), which were worth 67 pence in 1808, to
2$500 reis per oitava of gold of 22 quilates, equal to 47 1/5
pence, in 1833. Copper currency, about half of which was said
to be counterfeit, was gradually withdrawn, and replaced by
government notes. At the same time, the number of notes in
circulation which had been issued by the Banco do Brasil
were gradually reduced from 20,507 contos in 1829 to 19,017
in 1833-34. For the next twenty years, notes were issued by
the treasury; the total of notes outstanding reached 40,400
in 1840, the year in which Dom Pedro II's majority was
proclaimed. It is important to note the lack of commercial
or land banks, which apparently was due to the fact that the
Brazilians were unfamiliar with them. Sturz claims that Brazilians had not heard of the Louisiana banking system (estab-
lised in the 1820s) until 1836. Under this system the state
government provided capital, and the bank issued notes, and
lent them on current transactions. The Banco Commercial of
Rio de Janeiro was founded in 1833. The first Bank of Deposit
and Discount was established in Ceará in 1836, and proved a
success. Since most banks of emission failed, short-term
paper of commercial banks (as distinct from bank notes) served
as money.[25] No other banks appear to have been successfully
founded during the regency.

The withdrawal of notes from circulation had some effect,
since the value of the currency increased from $U.S. .51 to
$U.S. .80 between 1831 and 1836. Wholesale prices in Brazil
followed a similar pattern, falling from 1833 to 1836/7, and
rising thereafter (see Table 9-3). At least part of Brazil's
monetary difficulty stemmed from the increased expenditures
needed to suppress the various separatist movements; as these
expenditures were not accompanied by an increase in receipts,
deficit finance, inflation, and a depreciation of the exchange
rate necessarily followed. The extent of the inflation and
internal deficit financing was limited, however, by the
authorization in 1838 of a loan to be floated in London,
the proceeds of which were to be used to cover the deficits
of the ministries of the Army, Navy, and Treasury.[26] The
loan was raised in 1839, at a ₤411,200 face value bearing 5

5 per cent interest.* The government received Ł312,500. With
this one exception, the government was able to maintain its
policy of relying on its own resources, or, if need bem printing money or raising internal loans, rather than paying
interest abroad. The avoidance of foreign sources of finance
by Brazil at least in part was the result of increasingly
strained relations with Great Britain over the abolition of
the slave trade.

In 1831 the legislature ratified the treaty of 1826, under
which the slave trade was to become illegal three years after
ratification. Following ratification, the Brazilians attempted
to modify various of its provisions, on the grounds that the
legislature had not been consulted; the emperor had been
thrown out; and the nation needed more time to be able to comply with the treaty. The British loftily refused to consider
breaking a pact, while the Brazilians refused to comply with
a treaty obligation, because they felt the terms had been
dictated by the stronger power to the weaker. The specific
issues were the result of the Convention of 1826, which stipulated that the slave trade was to be prohibited as of March
13, 1830. The traffic was forbidden, but the trade in slave
grew, increasing strikingly just before the expiration date
of legality, falling off slightly owing to the preceding over-
supply of the market, and then steadily increasing (see Table
10-7). The British attempted to force the Brazilians to agree
to an "equipment clause," so that the British could treat as
slavers ships that were "fitted up" for the slave trade,
whether slaves were present on board or not. This, they felt,
was essential to the effective enforcement of the treaty.
During the 1830s the lower house of the Brazilian legislature
repeatedly refused to ratify either international treaties or
domestic laws embodying such a provision.

The condition of Negroes found on ships which the British
captured and brought to shore in Brazil was a source of continuing friction between the two nations. According to the
treaty, such Negroes were to be freed, and each nation bound
itself to guarantee the liberty of those slaves consigned to
it. The Brazilian government, realizing the impossibility of
fulfilling its commitment on Brazilian soil, stipulated in the
law of 1831 that captured slaves should be exported to the
coast of Africa as rapidly as possible. The British minister
"refusing to consider reëxportation on the ground that the

_____
*Oliver Onody, A Inflação Brasileira, p. 191. He gives
a higher face value than does Castro Carreira, discrepancy
probably due to inclusion of commission charges. Ł405,000
in loan "certificates" were issued. (Castro Carreira, História
Financeira e Orçamentario do Imperio do Brasil desde a sua
fundacão, p. 227.)

fate of the Negro sent to Africa would be death on the return
voyage or re-enslavement after landing, demanded that the law
and decree be rescinded at once, and blocked the efforts
of Brazil to secure a safe destination for reëxported slaves.
. . . Brazil was forced, therefore, to continue to dispose of
captured Negroes by auction."[27] The government auctioned
these Negroes to private individuals for a term of years; yet
this system turned into a form of slavery, rather than the
indentured labor for which it was designed.

> Old and worn out slaves were substituted for the _emanci-
> pado_ who became a legal slave in place of the old one;
> Negroes obtained by auction were sent to the interior
> far from the supervision of the government and beyond
> the investigation of the British agent; false certifi-
> cates of death were produced, and . . . "every device
> that unprincipled and unscrupulous cupidity" could "put
> in force, assisted by the connivance or support
> of those whose duty it was to prevent such proceedings"
> were "daily and hourly made use of in this country.[28]

In view of this, the refusal of the British to permit reexport
to possible ports of asylum was high-handed culpable negligence. Similarly, if consent of the governed is necessary for
the enforcement of law, British tactics ensured nonconsent.

> Cruisers assigned to the coast of Africa continued to
> bring in vessels suspected of illicit traffic regardless
> of whether Negroes were actually on board and the com-
> mission continued to release the ships but to refuse
> claims of compensation for time and expense incurred by
> the slavers. . . . In 1844 English vessels were detain-
> ing ships flying the Brazilian flag within Brazilian
> ports before they sailed, although the evident destina-
> tion was another national port.[29]

Thus, defying the British became in part a matter of national
independence and assertion of sovereignty, despite the desire
of many people in the government to end the slave trade. More
to the point, the British could try to rule Brazil without the
consent of the governed, but the regency, which had learned
through the expulsion of Dom Pedro I, could not. Moreover,
the regency had come close to losing control of the outlying
areas through unpopular policies, and could not survive if it
seriously tried to stop the slave traffic, or acceded more to
British demands than to Brazilian ones. The economic effects
of slavery under the regency differed slightly from those of
the preceding period, as taxes could not be collected on contraband imports. The government, therefore, derived no direct

tax income benefit from the slave trade, which continued at
an estimated rate of 43,000 slaves per year. It is important
to note that even those who agreed that the slave trade was
vile did not foresee the immediate end to slavery; some wanted
to maintain the traffic until Brazil could "propagate its
own supply" of slaves, which meant that the slave conditions
would be improved enough so that live births would increase,
and perhaps the average life span of a slave as well. The
institution of slavery would be maintained. The movement to
replace slave labor with European labor did not have many
adherents until after the Brazilians themselves passed strong
antislave traffic legislation in the 1850s, since early
experiments with importing European soldiers and laborers had
failed to provide an adequate substitute labor supply.

The increase in the slave trade was the result of the
rapid increase in the quantity of sugar and coffee exports,
which brought with it a parallel increase in the quantity of
labor demanded. As the quantity of recorded exports was virtually stable, and terms of trade declined, the increase of
Brazilian imports from 32,146 contos in 1832 to 41,040 contos
(in 1832 milreis) in 1839 must have been financed by smuggled
exports or unrecorded long-term suppliers' credit. The increased value of coffee and sugar caused the combined share
of import and export taxes to almost double from 39.3 per cent
of government income in 1832 to 76.0 per cent in 1840. Coffee
export quantities alone increased by 188 per cent; in 1837
Sturz wrote that Brazil supplied nearly two thirds of all the
coffee consumed in Europe. Brazil continued to be closely
linked with Great Britain in international trade: in the
early 1830s consumption of English goods by Brazil was more
than that of all the Spanish Republics together and more than
one third that of the United States. Nonetheless, the prohibition on admittance of foreign sugars continued to impede
trade between Britain and Brazil, since ships returning to Britain from Brazil carried only one third of cargo capacity;
granite was used as ballast, and freight rates per unit of
export were clearly higher than would have been the case if Brazil had had free access to the British market, especially in
the case of sugar. England continued to be more important to
Brazil than Brazil to England, as England supplied five sixths
of Brazilian imports, almost entirely in nonluxury items.[30]
The importance of foreign trade is underscored by Simonsen,
who wrote that during periods of the nineteenth century,
foreign trade represented three quarters of "commercial movement" in Brazil.[31]

There is an intimate connection between export growth,
tax structure, and the ability of Brazil to suppress its regional separatist risings. As Brazil's exports grew, the
share of trade taxes in government income increased, enabling

the government to reduce internal taxes, which fell from 47.3 per cent of the total in 1832 to 16.5 per cent in 1840, and absolutely from 5,286 million reis to 2,780 million reis (2,453 million in 1832 reis). Since internal taxation was one of the causes of the separatist risings, a strong parallel between Brazil and the United States emerges. Each nation felt not only that no taxes without representation should be levied, but also that levying any taxes was apt to provoke disorder, once independence had been achieved. The Whiskey Rebellion in the United States and the separatist revolts in Brazil are both cases in point. Further, both the United States and Brazil relied heavily on import duties for revenue. In the United States, political union was assured by a Constitution reserving wide powers to the states. In Brazil, a turbulent period sharing some features with the Confederation in the United States was resolved when the Brazilian constitution was amended to give increased political power to the provinces. Economic redress was obtained by the provinces with the reduction of internal and some export taxes. It can be argued that national unity would not have been maintained if there had been high levels of taxation on any transactions except international trade. It is possible that only with low levels of taxation was the cost of revolt more than the cost of staying in Brazil. If this is correct, then national unity depended on increased exports which, in turn, required a rapid increase in the labor force. From the Brazilian point of view, this increase could come about (only) through an increase in the number of slaves. Only when the nation had either consolidated its political control, so that difficult economic adjustments would not trigger a revolt, or when the nation's economy had advanced enough so that adjustments resulting from the end of the slave trade could be made with relative ease, was it likely that the Brazilian government could or would agree to actively suppress the slave trade.

The absence of the requisite economic conditions is reflected in the allocation of increasing shares of the government budget to the Army and Navy (41.1 per cent in 1832, 33.3 per cent in 1836, and 55.6 per cent in 1840). Although the expulsion of Dom Pedro I permitted a reduction in imperial expenses, the government had little left with which to buy provincial loyalty or to invest in facilities needed for economic development. The regency, carried out under shifting political groups, had neither the economic nor political strength to enforce the suppression of the slave trade which, in part, made national unity possible.

Dom Pedro II, 1840-1870:
The Transformation of Brazil

The first thirty years of the reign of Dom Pedro II were
marked by a government policy which resulted in the abolition
of the slave trade and an increase in railroads and banks.
The end of the slave trade released capital previously used
in it for investment in the Brazilian economy. Favorable coffee prices led to an expansion of coffee exports, while government promotion of railroads was successful in obtaining 745
km. of railroad construction and favorable freight rates for
exports. Banking expansion contributed to the financing of
new manufacturing and commercial activities. The Brazilian
textile manufacture grew rapidly, but was small in size compared to that of the United States or Great Britain. A major
limitation to further growth was the lack of a large domestic
market, and the lack of a literate and skilled labor supply,
neither of which could be obtained as long as slavery existed
in Brazil.

After a decade of political turbulence, the greatest
need of Dom Pedro II on ascending the throne was to consoli-
date his power, increasing it against both internal and external threats without provoking an unsuccessful war. The
power of provincial legislatures was reduced. "Under the
Regency, judicial and police powers had been combined in the
locally elected judges. By the law of December 3, 1841, the
situation was reversed, judicial functions being entrusted
to police authorities acting for the central government, a
harsh and callous device that 'for forty years maintained a
solidity of the Empire'".[32] The immediate result was a
liberal revolt in 1842 in Minas Gerais and São Paulo, and a
revolt in Pernambuco in 1847/8. These, and the revolt in
Rio Grande do Sul were put down by 1849; there were no further
armed revolts before the end of the empire in 1889. In large
measure this was because the emperor alternated the parties
in power by dismissing cabinets when he felt they no longer
reflected the state of public opinion or the best interests
of the nation. In 1847 this process was formalized by creating the office of the President of the Council of Ministers
(Prime Minister). The president in consultation with the
sovereign chose the other ministers, which lent coherence and
a measure of stability to the cabinets and the parties they
represented. Although property qualifications for office
and indirect nature of elections meant that Brazil was less
than a full democracy, the combination of strong administration
and governing to reflect the will of much of the literate
pooulation made Brazil after 1840 stable and peaceful enough
for political and economic development to increase.

Control over the provinces removed internal threats to

the emperor's sovereignty over Brazil. Whatever the other
merits of the case may have been, it was psychologically necessary to reduce dependence on Britain to assure the fact that
Brazil was an independent nation, rather than a semicolony of
Great Britain. The area open for adjustment of relative status
was trade. The treaty of 1827 was due to expire in 1844. Its
renewal unmodified was opposed by the empire since it stipulated maximum import rates of 15 per cent, and by "most-
favored-nation" clauses was unable to tax the imports of any
other nation at more than that rate. In order for Brazil to
be able to increase her import tax rate, the treaty had to
lapse or be modified.[33] Negotiations were made difficult by
Britain's special treatment of imports from its colonies, on
the one side, and Brazil's unwillingness to allow Britain to
tie a treaty of commerce to any modification of slavery in
Brazil, which was the major act for which Britain would have
granted substantial economic benefit. Further, British merchants in Brazil were not interested in a continuance of the
treaty of 1827, save for a guarantee of equality of treatment.
According to Manchester, "Under various forms English goods
were paying twenty-one per cent., some as high as forty per
cent., and Brazil would be stupid, said the merchants, to load
any more duties on suddenly. Nor were they solicitous about
maintaining the conservatorial courts, for, as they reported,
traders of other nations were not suffering injustice in the
administration of the law although only the British had the
privilege of extra-territorial jurisdiction."[34]

No commercial treaty was signed between Brazil and Great
Britain during the rest of the empire. There was, however,
one specific outgrowth of nonrenewal that created immediate
difficulties. The British Cabinet in 1844 levied a tax of 63
shillings on sugar imported from Brazil, and one of forty-
three shillings on sugar imported "from its other colonies.
This measure was combined with a ferocious campaign against
slavery."[35] According to Bastos, Brazil met "reprisal with
reprisal" in the form of the Alves Branco tariff of 1844,
which raised the rates from the preceding official level of 15
per cent to 30 to 80 per cent on imports.

The ground for the "reprisal" had in fact been prepared
in 1843, when a commission was created to prepare a new list
of tariffs to take effect when the treaty with Great Britain
expired. The key concept in the new tariff was the "law of
similars." This provided that foreign products that had
"similars" in Brazil, or where similar products could be produced in Brazil owing to the abundance of raw materials, were
to pay rates from 50 to 60 per cent. Goods indispensible to
the defense of the state that could be produced in Brazil were
to pay 60 per cent. Crude cotton manufactures were to pay
60 per cent; finer quality cotton textiles from 40 to 50 per

cent, while spinning and weaving machines were exempt from duty. Wines and spirits paid 50 per cent. Goods "of first necessity" for the nation paid 20 per cent; expensive goods imported in small volume were to pay from 2 to 10 per cent; goods imported from India were to pay, in general, 60 per cent when carried in foreign ships; when carried in Brazilian ships belonging to foreigners, 40 per cent, and when in Brazilian ships owned by Brazilians, 20 per cent. Goods not mentioned in the list were to pay 30 to 40 per cent.[36] In the next two years, the aid to Brazilian industry granted under this tariff was extended by reducing the tax on the export of salted hides; although domestic tobacco manufactures were to be lightly taxed for the first time, import duties on foreign tobacco were raised to 60 per cent. In addition, foreign goods exported to Africa were to pay a 5 per cent transit tax.[37] In 1847, Peel's cabinet revoked the tariff on Brazilian sugar; although this helped clear the air somewhat, it failed to end the animosity felt toward the British. In 1850 the Brazilian government was authorized to increase shipping and import taxes on British ships and merchandise.[38]

The Brazilian government, both for revenue and protective purposes, had placed high tariffs on goods competing with Brazilian manufactures, or commodities which Brazil expected it would soon manufacture. A complementary charge, which increased the relative attractiveness of industry, was government action to enforce the abolition of the slave trade. Such action, by raising the cost of most segments of agriculture, would decrease the incentive to invest in agriculture, and raise the incentive to invest in industry. The process by which the government took such action was complex. The treaty of 1826 governing the slave trade expired in 1845. The treaty created a mixed commission to judge the claims of vessels seized as slavers, and granted the British the right to visit and search Brazilian ships in time of peace.[39]

The Brazilians thoroughly hated the treaty, and wanted to end it as an assertion of national sovereignty. Two examples of this attitude from contemporary articles and speeches by Brazilians are: "We who acknowledge how advantageous the produce of the Industry of England, and its capital are to Brazil; we who believe that no Foreign Commerce is more useful to the Country, desire that the former good feeling be re-established and therefore we sincerely wish that the Right of Visit, happily terminated, be interred forever." And a Brazilian speaker who pointed out that the "offended nationality of the Brazilians appeared desirous of supporting the traffic, 'if only in despite of England. If there was not a nation pretending to impose the laws on' Brazilians, certainly their 'Christian feelings, their patriotism'" would have

resulted in "'some steps having been taken to put an end to
the traffic in some manner or other,'" but, treated as they
had been, the Brazilians "'tried to uphold the traffic if it
were only to show' their resistance."[40]

The lapse of the treaty merely provoked the British into
passing a law which implemented the clause of the treaty
that declared the slave trade to be piracy. Under the Aber-
deen Law of August 8, 1845, the British continued to detain
and visit slavers as under the conditions specified by the
treaty of 1826; but instead of taking prizes to the mixed commission, they brought them before British Admiralty or Vice
Admiralty Courts. In practice, the British seized ships
loaded with slaves bound for Brazil, refused to discuss the
issue, and rejected all claims for damages which Brazil
claimed were the result of force and violence, since the right
of search and seizure "was exclusively a belligerent right
and unlawful in time of peace."[41]

According to Manchester, "The simplest solution to the
crisis would be for the Brazilians to stop the traffic by
their own efforts, ignore Great Britain's stand, and maintain
their attitude of hostility until London granted recognition
of the fact that the traditional position in England in Portugal could not be continued in Brazilian affairs."[42] This,
in fact, was the policy adopted. The suppression of the re-
gionalist, slaveowner-backed revolt in Pernambuco brought
centralist Conservatives to power. They soon passed the famous Queiróz Law (September 4, 1850) which provided that

> Brazilian vessels wherever found, and foreign vessels
> found in the ports, bays, anchorages, or territorial
> waters of Brazil, having slaves on board, whose importa-
> tion is prohibited by the Law of the 7th of November,
> 1831, or which may have landed them, shall be seized by
> the authorities, or by Brazilian ships of war, and con-
> sidered importers of slaves. Those which have not
> slaves on board, nor shall have recently landed them,
> shall, if appearances are found of having been employed
> in Slave Trade, also be seized, and considered as at-
> tempting to import slaves.
>
> The importation of slaves into the territory of the
> empire is hereby considered piracy, and shall be punished
> by its tribunals with the pains and penalties declared
> in Article II of the Law of 7th November, 1831. The
> attempting and abetting shall be punished according to
> the rules of the Articles XXXIV and XXXV of the Criminal
> Code.[43]

The law also abolished the auction of captured slaves to private persons; it authorized the sale of vessels with all cargo

on board involved in the slave trade, the proceeds to go to
the captors, "deducting one-fourth part for the informer, if
any," and rewards for the crew of the ship capturing the
slaver. While much of the impetus for the passage of this law
came from within Brazil, the timing of its enactment may well
have come from the issues of formal orders by the British
ministry in the middle of 1850 to its cruisers to enter Brazilian territorial waters and harbors and make captures. Some
ninety slave ships had been captured by British cruisers between August 1849 and May 1851. Once both the Brazilians
and the British worked together to end the trade, the importa-
tions of Negroes fell drastically from an estimated 60,000
in 1848 to 23,000 in 1850, 3,287 in 1851, and 700 in 1852
(see Table 10-7). The importation of slaves, but not slavery
itself, had ended in Brazil. From colonization until 1852 a
total of from 3.5 to 3.6 million slaves were imported. There
probably were half a million imported until 1700, 1,700,000
in the eighteenth century, and 1,350,000 imported from 1800
to 1851. The effects of slavery on the economy, in addition
to those mentioned above, were to prevent the entry of voluntary immigrant laborers, although some skilled technicians
and businessmen immigrated, and to tie up capital in the investment in slaves, because slaves appeared to be a more tangible
and risk-free asset than either free labor or business. Slavery thus diverted capital from investment in industry or infrastructure. When the slave trade was ended, an estimated
15-20,000 contos previously employed in it were transferred
to other activities in Brazil.

For industry to develop, however, a more extensive
infrastructure was required, especially in transport, education, and finance. Brazil lacked a central bank; the number
of private banks was small. Until a financial network was
developed, investment in industry had to be financed out of
profits from agriculture and commerce. In the absence of
banks, it was more likely that the investments would be carried out by the men who had initially earned the profits, or
their families, than that the funds would be advanced
through intermediaries to entrepreneurs not personally known
to the initial suppliers of funds. The lack of a developed
credit system also led to a dependence on foreign suppliers
or the foreign loan market to raise the capital needed for
industrial expansion. Financial innovation and monetary
reforms during the 1840s and 1850s supplied the facilities
necessary for more efficient use of savings in Brazil. In
the private sector, the Banco Comercial do Rio de Janeiro,
whose date of establishment is variously attributed to 1833,
1838, and 1842, was established with the right of deposit and
discount, with permission to emit notes or bearer bonds payable in a ten-day period, whose total was not to exceed one

third of the bank's capital, and could at most reach 500,000
reis. In 1845 the Banco do Bahia was founded with powers of
emission. The Commercial Bank was absorbed into the second
Banco do Brasil in 1853. The second bank had a capital fund
of 30,000 million reis; it was to replace the Treasury emission with its notes, retiring 2.000:000$ per year. The law
of 1852, under which it was created, made it a bank of deposit, discount, and emission of notes or short-term "letras,"
whose total was not to exceed one third of its capital. It
was to have branches in São Paulo and Rio Grande do Sul. The
Banco do Brasil had the exclusive privilege of having its
notes accepted in payment by the government. The smallest
value of notes emitted was 20$ in Rio and 10$ in the other
provinces. The bank was not to emit notes in excess of double
its liquid assets without special authorization by decree.
Bank notes were exempt from payment of stamp tax. Whenever
the bank's capital was increased, the government could request
that one third of the increase be applied to the redemption
of paper money. In 1857 the government was authorized to
deposit funds previously held in the Treasury in the Banco.[45]
(See Table 10-8.) The unique position of the Banco do Brasil
was somewhat weakened from 1857 to 1866 when Minister Souza
Franco gave emission power to other banks, despite the fact
that this step was not authorized by the legislature. This
step has been compared to the United States "free banking" system; its critics claim that it provoked a "banking mania."[46]
The basis for the complaint was that the capital of Brazil's
independent banks had been roughly four times the number of
their notes in circulation from the mid-forties to the mid-
fifties. After emission power was granted to large numbers
of independent banks, this ratio fell to 1.2 in 1858, and
reached 1.9 in 1862 (see Table 10-9). The sharp shift in
independent bank notes outstanding reflected the domestic
economic crisis brought on by the economic crisis in Great
Britain. Despite the difficulties of the late 1850s, the
government had been provided with banking facilities, and the
private sector with a badly needed source of credit. A complementary measure was the revaluation of money on September 11,
1846, according to which the par value of the reis decreased
from its preceding level of Rs. 2$500 per oitava of gold to
Rs. 4$000. The official exchange rate decrease was from
47 1/5 pence per milreis to 27 pence. Despite some fluctua-
tion during the year, the new rate held until 1865, providing
a measure of financial security.

The new period of relative peace and stability, partly
due to world prosperity from 1850 to 1873, sparked the growth
of traditional exports and the initiation of new industrial
and transportation activities by the private sector. The
most striking development in agriculture was the rapid

expansion of coffee exports, and their dominance in Brazilian exports, so that the cry "Brazil is coffee!" was not far from the truth.

Coffee was introduced to Brazil in 1727 in Amazonia, where the climatic conditions were unfavorable for its growth. Its cultivation spread in small quantities to Maranhão and Ceará,[47] and thence to south central Brazil. The profitability of coffee transformed the area in which it was grown from a poor subsistence agriculture into a rich cash crop one: tithes paid in the uplands near Rio had risen from Rs. 500$000 in 1788 for a three-year period to Rs. 59:720$000 by 1820 largely as a result of coffee cultivation.[48] Lands were acquired legally and illegally by coffee planters, from Indians and from squatters, and devoted to coffee cultivation. This was carried out as local experience dictated; there was "no soil analysis to determine where coffee, sugar cane or manioc produce best." By friendship with the powerful, legal battles, and economies of scale, the large coffee planters increased their share of coffee land and production, while the small planters turned to food production.[49]

The incentive to increase coffee production consisted not only in the high prices for coffee paid in Rio, but also in its lighter weight in shipping compared to other crops. At a time when mules were the main means of transport, this was of major benefit in reducing transport costs, as there was a limit of 260-293 lb. to the weight a mule could carry. Further, roads were not sufficiently developed to permit transport by wheeled vehicles, so that transportation considerations limited the choice of crops to produce open to planters.

The coffee cycle began with the felling of virgin forest for coffee land; land to be cleared was chosen by the vegetation growing on it, or, "If the ankle and half the calf sink into the humus beneath the trees, the soil is good."[50] The clearing operation was dangerous, and

> planters often substituted the labor of valuable slaves with that of free, landless squatters who lived in tiny clearings in the fores and who were skilled woodmen. During the early period of settlement they were usually halfbreeds (caboclos). As unclaimed land diminished the propertyless forest dweller was joined by the dispossessed settler who had squatted along the roads, and later by escaped slaves. This group furnished occasional day laborers (camaradas) and from it planters chose a few non-rent-paying tenants (agregados).[51]

When the land was cleared, seedlings were planted. During the three years before the coffee bushes reached maturity, crops such as corn, beans, and manioc were planted between the bushes.   These crops both shaded the trees and provided the owners with food, which helped to reduce the cost of cultivating coffee by providing the mainstay of the slaves' diet. Coffee was planted in vertical rows up and down hillsides, which made both harvesting and soil erosion easier.   The coffee was weeded twice yearly; accounts of coffee harvesting vary.   Either coffee was stripped from the bush with leaves and dead twigs into a strainer, in which it was then winnowed, or all the ripe coffee cherries were thrown on the ground, and the clean ones were then picked up.   According to Stein, "this technique may have been the decisive factor in producing coffee of poor quality."[52]   Poor quality was also assured by setting a quota of coffee to be picked daily; the hurried picking resulted in green, dry and mature coffee cherries being piled together for drying.   After drying, the beans were packed in leather bags and shipped on muleback to Rio, although when labor was available, the coffee was milled on the plantation before shipment.[53]

The conditions which had made the coffee boom profitable were virgin land and cheap labor.   By the 1860s virgin forests had been cut down, while the end of the slave trade led to an aging of the slave labor force, and an increased cost to planters.   Moreover, since credit could be obtained only for planting coffee, subsistence crop production in the coffee area fell, so that coffee planters were increasingly dependent on food produced in other areas, whose costs increased more rapidly than food costs in Rio.[54]

The role played by slave prices in the coffee plantation economy shifted with the end of the slave trade.   While the slave trade continued, the planter was interested in low slave prices, as slaves were worn out rapidly.   After the trade ended, the price of slaves rose, and the slaves began to be viewed more as a salable asset than as a permanent part of the labor force, especially on marginal plantations that were forced to liquidate when faced with rising costs.   Further, slaves were the major asset on which money was advanced. As the number of slaves in the total economy were reduced, their prices had to rise to maintain a steady total asset value of plantations and, consequently, the flow of credit to the rural sector.   The relatively greater profitability of coffee than of other crops produced in Brazil led to a sale of slaves from the remainder of the nation to the coffee areas of Brazil, thus reducing the impact of the end of the Atlantic slave trade.   The end of the slave trade contributed in a number of ways to the increase in prices throughout the economy: capital previously tied up in importing slaves and therefore spent abroad, was free to invest in other activities in Brazil, and was therefore spent in the nation.   Slave prices from

1852 to 1854 almost doubled, and the overall rise in prices
is an indication of the large share of funds that must have
been tied up in the slave trade. The rise in slave prices,
however, was not only a reflection of monetary conditions.
The importation of slaves from other provinces provided a
stopgap, but not a long-term solution to the labor supply.
The end of the slave trade gradually yielded an improvement
in the treatment of slaves: in the early days of coffee cultivation it was common that 75 per cent of slaves purchased
died within three years. In the 1820s the slave population
in one coffee country in Brazil was 77 per cent male, 23 per
cent female. As the need to breed slaves in Brazil was felt,
since it was no longer possible to import according to sex
preference from Africa, the slave population ratio shifted to
63 per cent male in the 1840s and 56 per cent male in the
1880s.[55] The problem of financing the upkeep of relatively
unproductive children, which was more expensive than importing had been, was in part solved by manumitting aged or inca-
pacitated slaves, who had to shift for themselves, or make
do with whatever public charity existed. In part, the
shortage of slaves was ameliorated by interplantation slave
renting and payment of the plantation slaves to work on Saints'
Days and Sundays. At least modest sums were earned in this
way, since itinerant peddlers made a living by selling pri-
marily to slaves.[56]

Even if the planter obtained an adequate labor supply,
he faced considerable difficulties in obtaining cheap and
competent transport. The chief means of transport was a
pack mule, which carried from 260 to 293 pounds of coffee.
One fifth of the plantation's work force worked as muleteers.
On the trip from the plantation to the market in Rio, the
roads were badly kept up; several mules died in the seas
of mud, while the crop was damaged from dampness. In the mid-
1850s it was reported that transport costs absorbed more
than one third of the value of coffee shipped from "up-
country" plantations.[57] The transport situation was drastically changed by the construction, after 1855, of the Dom
Segundo railway through the Parahyba Valley. Mule trails
became obsolete and disappeared; their place was taken by
feeder roads to the railroad line; the new roads were broad
enough for oxcarts, which carried 3,250 pounds, thus reducing
the costs of mules and muleteers. "After the mid sixties,
oxen rapidly displaced pack mules; shortly after 1873 the
price per head of oxen surpassed that of pack animals, within
a few years attaining twice, sometimes three times their
value."[58]

Despite the improvement in transport, profitability of
coffee production was not assured. Aside from the damage
wrought by natural plagues, the planter was harmed by periods

of tight credit, by increased competition from new coffee-
producing nations, and by coffee market crises resulting
from the fall in foreign purchasing power. Ignorance and
routine prevented the planter from successfully fighting
natural damages, from reorganizing plantation crop cultivation and labor practices, and from maintaining influence in
national politics to assure adequate credit on a continuing
basis. The latter, given the deliberate alteration of parties
in power by the emperor, could not have been obtained. Nor
could the planter reasonably expect to influence foreign crop
planting choices or the level of European income. Although
the new difficulties and uncertainties surrounding coffee
production led, on occasion, to the adoption of new machinery, basic agricultural reforms were not undertaken. There
is increasing evidence that coffee planters, rather than
modify a difficult situation, often sold out or invested
some of their profits in new industrial and commercial pur-
suits. The failure to improve coffee plantations, then, was
not entirely a matter of ignorance and bad judgment, but,
rather, at least in part, a reflection of a rational distribution of assets between various investments.

The scope for investment included railroads, telegraphs,
import and wholesale businesses, retailing, banking, and
industry. The means of investment varied from direct investment by owner-operators to purchase of government bonds, the
funds raised being used, in part, for development expenditure. The security of such investments was increased by the
passage of a commercial code in 1850, and laws governing the
incorporation of companies in 1849, 1859, and 1860. The laws
of incorporation made it easier to formally include larger
numbers of family and friends among the stockholders than
under the previous proprietorship and partnership arrangements, but did not radically change the pattern of family-held
operations into one of public ownership.[59]

Many of the new investments were initiated under the
leadership of Irineu da Souza, Baron Mauá, who established the
Banco do Brasil in 1851, before it was taken over by the
government in 1853, and aided the establishment of banks in
Ceará, Maranhão, Bahia, and Pará. He inaugurated steam
navigation on the Amazon in 1850, and constructed Brazil's
first railroad, from the western end of the Rio harbor to
the summer capital of Petropolis in 1854.

The first electric telegraph machines were employed in
1852. During the 1850s, 62 "industrial firms" were founded,
14 banks, 3 "caixas economicas," 20 steam navigation companies, 23 insurance companies, 4 colonization firms, 8 railroad
companies, 8 mining firms, 3 urban transport and 2 gas companies. Of these, the textile firms were most important for the
future industrial growth of Brazil because they produced a

commodity that was widely demanded, and relied in large measure on local raw materials. Further, as the industry expanded, a demand for local production and repair of imported machinery could be expected to emerge gradually. According to Stein, the immediate stimulus to the founding of cotton spinning and weaving mills came from the Alves Branco tariff of 1844, and the lifting of duties on machinery and raw materials in 1846 and 1847.[61] When in 1860 the government increased the tariff for revenue purposes, additional protection was afforded to cotton manufacturers. The government did not, however, extend direct aid to the manufacturers.

The directors of the textile firms faced difficulties associated with innovation in an underdeveloped area. Precise estimates of the capital needs of the new activity were difficult to make; the limitation of the firm to friends and family restricted the mount of funds available. At the same time, banks were conservative in loan policy; a borrower without well-placed connections would find it difficult to obtain funds from a bank, especially if he were engaged in a new, and therefore risky, activity. Firms therefore either called on stockholders to advance new funds as their needs increased, or borrowed with difficulty from banks, or floated loans abroad. The latter policy, acceptable when the exchange rate was stable, resulted in heavy financial burdens when the Brazilian currency devalued, and payments were due in gold or hard currency equivalent.

Once funds were secured, the factor which above all others determined the policies adopted was the technical ignorance of the Brazilian work force. In the early factories, slaves were often used, with a scattering of freedmen. At this time, few Brazilians were literate; yet even literacy was of little help, as the technical manuals explaining the machinery and its operation were in languages other than Portuguese. The millowners petitioned the government to subsidize the translation of such manuals, but this was not done. The millowners, therefore, depended on importing skilled craftsmen, often from England, for a number of jobs within the factory. The English, afraid that they would be replaced by lower-paid Brazilians, told them as little as possible. The Brazilians, lacking in information, could not upgrade themselves, especially as on-the-job training was deliberately denied them. Yet not all Brazilian workers desired "to get ahead." According to Stein, continuous labor was associated with slave status; workers who had a choice often preferred to work just enough hours or days to supply their needs, and then leave. Construction workers had to be paid when machines broke down or when supplies were not delivered on time, because if the work force dispersed, it would be difficult to replace it. The

difficulty in obtaining an inexpensive, skilled labor supply
was in part met by importing textile labor from countries with
relatively low standards of living. The imperial government
facilitated the entry of such immigrant labor by providing
free railroad transportation.[62] Labor, once contracted, often
depended on company stores and houses, the conditions of which
caused a number of early strikes in Brazil.

With labor and financing available, the millowners turned
to procuring machinery. Machines were imported both from England and the United States.   One company wrote that "Both are
very fine and well made; the English machines are more solid,
the American more convenient because they are simpler, use
fewer personnel, are cheaper and operate equally well." Another stated that most equipment came from the "United States,
little from England, we prefer the American for the quality
of the iron, lighter weight, better crating, and cheaper
cost."[63] Yet the lack of a developed iron industry and skilled
mechanics plagued the textile millowners, one of whom wrote
that "we are so dependent that either we tie up funds in
standby machinery or we have to see our machines often halted
to await a small item which can not yet be produced in our
country."[64]

Although Brazil produced indigenous tree cotton of a long
staple, and imported seeds for herbaceous cotton from the
United States, a cotton supply was not assured to domestic cotton mills, since cotton growers sold first to overseas customers,
then to local ones. Further, once the cloth was produced the
mills had difficulty selling the product because of the organization of textile distribution. Cloth importers and urban re-
tailers pressured storekeepers of the interior areas to handle
foreign imports, since importers were often either commission
agents or branch houses of foreign mills. At least one textile mill sold only to accredited cloth houses, rather than
direct to the interior, for a number of years both out of fear
of possible reprisals and because of the uncertainty of dealing
with small and distant businessmen. At times, sales were
promoted by selling at lower prices to the interior than to
the capital. The interior, in turn, protected its own industry: Pernambuco and Amazonas placed a 20 per cent tax on all
cottons brought in from other areas of Brazil. As Brazilian
cheap textiles were profitable, the Portuguese importers began
to invest in and organize the Brazilian textile industry in
the 1880s. Toward the end of the century, cloth merchants
were brought into boards of directors to help assure competent
marketing procedures and wider sales.

Despite the many difficulties, the cotton industry developed from 8 mills in 1853 to 48 in 1885; production increased
from 1,210,000 meters to 20,595,000, while employment grew
from 424 to 3,172 workers.[66] Although the Brazilian cotton

manufacturing industry grew as rapidly between 1866 and 1885, as had its United States counterpart between 1841 and 1860, the Brazilian industry in 1885 was small by comparison. Its 66,466 spindles and 3,172 workers contrasted with 5,235,000 spindles and 122,028 workers in the United States in 1860, and 21,000,000 spindles in Great Britain.[67] The difference in development reflects the size of total population: 12,916,000 in Brazil in 1885, 31,443,321 in the United States in 1860. In the United States, 1,971,135 were slaves. As Brazilian slaves were more apt to be able to earn money on their own account, slave status limited the size of the market less in Brazil than it did in the United States. The United States, however, was wealthier in 1860 than Brazil in 1885. The United States was also favored by a larger share of skilled immigrants, so that a trained labor supply was more readily available. It should be remembered that the United States did not develop much industry in the South before the Civil War, in many cases for reasons that inhibited such development in Brazil. The South was poor in power sources; it shared with Brazil slave labor, little social or economic opportunity for advancement for free labor, and because of the lack of free labor, a limited market for domestic manufactures other than those of the poorest limited quality, bought by plantation owners for their slaves. Further, the South's capital, like that of Brazil, was tied up in the slave trade, and slave owning. Slavery both limited the domestic market, and formed a cultural complex which inhibited Brazil from obtaining the widespread education needed for technical competence that would have permitted the industry to grow based on exports. As long as legal slavery existed, industrial growth was, as a direct consequence of slavery, hampered.

In order to increase both the quantity of exports and the physical and economic size of the market for domestic manufactures, more extensive and cheaper transport and communications facilities than had obtained before 1840 in Brazil's mule-based and sailing-vessel economy were needed. Improvements took the form of railroads, steamships, and telegraphs. They were introduced in the 1850s, in large part as a result of government financial aid.

The imperial government's policy of encouraging railroad development began with the railroad law of 1835 which stipulated the provisions under which concessions might be secured. As no aid was given to private capital, no railroads were constructed under its provisions.[68] The first railroad built in Brazil was constructed by Mauá under a special concession without any guarantee of interest. In order to facilitate investment in railroads, the government enacted the law of June 26, 1852, which stipulated that "(1) No import duties were to be charged on materials used in construction. (2) A privileged zone of five leagues on either side of the right of way was

offered. Within that zone no other company could construct
a railroad without previous permission from the original company. (3) The most important provision was the guarantee of
five per cent on capital invested."[69] The concessions (guarantee) ran from 40 to 90 years.[70]

The guarantee was not great enough to attract foreign
capital, because Russian railroad guarantees were more attractive at this time. The provincial government of Pernambuco therefore added a 2 per cent guarantee to the 5 per
cent already offered by the central government for the line
from Recife to Palmares. This example was followed by the
provinces of Bahia, Rio de Janeiro, and São Paulo.[71] By 1869
the total investment in railways on which the government had
guaranteed interest was 83,820,202 milreis ($31,851,676 U.S.
at the 1869 exchange rate). In fact, however, the participation of the government was greater than the interest guarantee, as the Treasury contributed 35,489,297 milreis of the
above sum as advances to the English railroad companies or in
the form of loans negotiated with the guarantee of the imperial
government.[72]

Disputes soon arose between the railroad companies and
the government over accounting practices used to determine
the amount of capital investment. "Furthermore the guarantee of interest was based upon a fixed amount of capital
investment per kilometer of line. It was, therefore, to the
companies' advantage to make the line as long as possible if,
by so doing, grades, even the slightest, could be avoided.
The method of handling the guarantees of interest fostered
badly laid out systems, some of them more winding than a snake.
Not a few of these still survive."[73]

There were two other reasons for the pattern of railroad
lines. A British observer in 1886 acidly wrote of Parahyba
do Sul, the rich coffee-growing area, that "the whole of this
valley belongs to a comparatively few wealthy important Brazilians, Viscondes and Barões, of such influence that the railway
has had to cross the river five times between Pirahy and Porto
Novo da Cunha by long and expensive bridges to serve the
interests of a Barão on this side, or a Visconde on the other."[74]
Physical convenience as well as political necessity often led
to longer routes, since the ascent from the Brazilian coast
to the interior plateau is quite steep; direct routes were
steeper, difficult to construct, and hampered by erosion during
the rainy season. Construction along direct routes required
the use of such devices as cable systems, rack-and-pinion
systems, and friction rails.[75]

Despite the provision of guarantees, the railroad companies
were not always able to complete the construction of the railroad lines. On July 10, 1862, the government took over the
Estrada de Ferro Dom Pedro II, which later became the Estrada

de Ferro Central do Brasil, because the company was at the end of its resources. The interest guarantee had initially been given in the expectation that the company would be able to aid the government in securing investment funds. As these funds were not forthcoming, it was cheaper for the government to substitute its own bonds for its guarantee of interest on the shares of the company, and operate the road directly.*

The rapid building of railroads did not mean that a railroad network was constructed. Although maps at the time indicated that most railroads used narrow gauge tracks, there were, in fact, thirteen different gauges in use in 1880 on Brazil's 3,971 miles of track.[76]**Operation of the railroads was physically difficult because of the relative shortage of coal in Brazil at that time. The problem was not only fuel for the trains, but also that this lack hampered development of a Brazilian steel industry, so that locomotives, rails, and the metal parts for cars had to be imported, therefore leaving the cost of the equipment and the profitability of the railroads at the mercy of the foreign exchange rate. Operation of the railroads was financially difficult because the railroads were often built in advance of traffic, which limited the earnings of the early years. In addition to the problems caused by fluctuations in the exchange rate, some of the provisions of the decree of October 13, 1853, regulating the 1852 guarantees, effectively placed a ceiling on the dividends a railroad could declare, and, thus, on the effort the railroad would make to develop traffic. The 1853 decree provided that when a railroad company's dividends exceeded 7 per cent, the amount in excess of this sum would be divided between the government and the company. The sum received by the government, after subtracting any funds which had to be paid to the company on interest guarantee account, was to be used to purchase government debt or stock in the railroad company. This, plus the accumulated interest, was to form a fund for future interest guarantee payments. When this fund reached a sum equal to one half per cent of the capital multiplied by the number of years the guarantee had to run, the deduction from the dividends would stop. Under specified conditions, when the fund was no longer needed, two thirds of the fund reverted to the company, one third to the government.

According to the law of 1852, railroad rates could not exceed those of the previous means of transport, and would have to be reduced when dividends exceeded 12 per cent. When

---

*The intermediary company in which the government was the heaviest stockholder was dissolved at this time. Julian Smith Duncan, Public and Private Operation of Railways in Brazil, pp. 28-29.

**See Map 2, page 80.

dividends fell below 7 per cent, the companies were allowed to raise their rates.[77] There was considerable diversity in rates charged, not only between lines, but also along different stretches of the same line.[78] However, it was consistently stipulated in railroad concessions that exports pay less than imports.[79] For example, the Estrada de Ferro Dom Pedro II charged, per tonelada-kilometrico, 20.2 centavos for exports, 30.3 centavos for imports, 15.15 centavos for food products; average rates were 21.88 centavos.[80]

The construction of railroads was further linked to the government's development policy by the 12th provision of the 1852 law, which stated that the government could establish telegraph lines and equipment along the railroad line; the railroad companies were responsible for guarding the wires and equipment and were to transport telegraph agents free of charge. If the government decided not to build telegraph lines on its own account, the railroad company had the right to establish one, with the proviso that it provide free telegraph service to the government,[81] which used the service for government dispatches and fire signals. In the case of the Dom Pedro II railway (1855), the company was required to construct a telegraph line along the entire length of track. In addition, mail and mailmen, public funds, and government employees were transported free, up to stipulated amounts, and at one-fifth the public rate for amounts in excess.[82]

Despite the allegations of some historians of Latin America, the Brazilian government during the empire of Dom Pedro II clearly had a development policy. Although the imperial government had insufficient funds to undertake many projects directly, it provided some financial and considerable legislative aid for education (whose financing was to be undertaken by the provinces according to the Additional Act of 1834), and for a communications network (rail, mail, and telegraph). Moreover, the provincial governments provided assistance when the imperial government ran out of funds, while municipal governments also aided the improvement and growth of Brazilian cities. For example, the municipal government of Rio de Janeiro obtained authorization in 1851 to float a loan, the proceeds of which were to be used to complete a new slaughterhouse.[83] The juridical basis of development was provided by the imperial government by the formulation of the commercial code and laws regulating incorporation of business: these made it possible to place business expansion on a sound legal basis.

It is not accurate, therefore, to state that the imperial government's development policy before 1870 exclusively favored coffee barons or other exporting groups. Obviously, the building of the railroads and the enactment of railroad rates more favorable to exports than to imports helped

exporters. During the same period, however, the government
constructed protective tariffs behind which the modern textile
industry was created, and other commercial and industrial
firms were initiated. Finally, on both humane and economic
grounds, the government's ending of the slave trade laid the
ground for the industrial development of Brazil in two ways
already mentioned: capital previously tied up in the slave
trade was freed for investment; further, the slave trade had
to be stopped before European immigrants would come to Brazil.
This was important, not because of any inherent racial characteristic of Euopreans, but because of the widespread illiteracy
and technical ignorance of Brazilian workers. Importing ex-
perienced factory workers and literate immigrants provided
Brazil, in the short run, with a skilled labor force faster,
and probably less expensively, than a rapid expansion of
educational facilities for free and slave labor could have
done.

The government's development policy strongly influenced
the growth of exports, whose value tripled from 43,192 milreis in 1840 to 140,138 milreis (in 1840 reis) in 1870. The
quantity of exports increased by 147 per cent. British industrial prices fluctuated, so that the terms of trade fell during
the late 1840s, then rose appreciably during the 1850s and
1860s. At the same time, the population increased, both in-
ternally and from rapidly increased immigration. Per capita
exports increased from 8,664 in 1840 reis in 1851 to 13,089
in 1871, which is equal to an increase from $14.78 dollars
in U.S. 1950 prices in 1851 to $20.44 in 1871. Given minimum
survival estimates of $30 per capita, exports accounted for
at most half of the value of Brazilian economic activity in
1851, and probably less.

These years also saw Brazil shift from a position of net
importer of goods (1840-1845, 1851-1861) to a net exporter
(1862-1870). The favorable trade balance did not always lead
to an improvement in the value of Brazil's currency in terms
of foreign exchange. Although the favorable balance contributed to an increase in the value of the milreis from 1846 to
1849, it failed to do so from 1862 to 1870 because of the
extraordinary increase in the money supply. The increase was
used to finance a military expedition to Uruguay in 1864 and
the Paraguayan War (1865-1870). Military expenses absorbed
just over half of the government budget (see Table 10-6).
"At a cost of fifty thousand dead and about $300,000,000, Bra-
zil won some territory and prestige, and a new sense of the
unity of the Empire."[84]

The government's receipts from taxes on foreign trade
increased during these years; however, they were not large
enough to finance the war, so that the level of the budgetary
deficit more than quadrupled during the war years. The

government therefore resorted to a foreign loan to finance
the war, borrowing ₤5,000,000 in London in 1865. The loan
paid 5 per cent, but sold at only 74, which gave rise to
complaints against the government, as preceding peacetime
loans had been floated on much more favorable terms. The
shift in pattern of government external loans is indicated
in Table 10-4. Under Dom Pedro I, loans had been contracted
"for the defense and security of the empire" in 1824 and 1825,
and to cover the government's cash deficit in 1829. They
were guaranteed by the receipts from the customs, especially
those at Rio, which were placed in a special amortization
fund. The only loan contracted under the regency (1839)
was used to cover the deficit of the Treasury, and the Army
and Navy ministries, and had a similar guarantee. The first
loan obtained under "the personal reign" of Dom Pedro II
was floated in 1843 to pay Portugal the sums due under the
treaty of 1825. This was the last foreign loan to have a
specific customs receipts guarantee, the remainder being
floated on the general credit of the nation. The loan of
1852 was also used for the same purpose. Once the political
obligations of the nation had been settled, it was free to
turn to developmental concerns. Loans were floated in 1858
and 1860 to pay the interest guarantee on railroads; loans
for paying previous borrowings were floated in 1859 and 1863,
the latter on more favorable terms than the debt it replaced.
The government's concern during the first phase of the reign
of Dom Pedro II was to (1) establish its legitimacy and financial responsibility by paying past debts; (2) increase the
government's productive capacity and ability to make external
payments by using loan proceeds to help finance railroads;
and, (3) improve the government's financial standing by re-
funding operations. The government made relatively modest
use of internal debt operations, which, at first, were used
(1827) to cover the deficit of 1828, to pay the creditors of
the current public debt, and to withdraw bank notes from
circulation. Until the end of the first period (1840) new
debt issues were used to retire outstanding debt, and to recall bank notes. Carreira Castro states that in 1838 the
combined internal and external debt of Brazil was five times
the income of the government. Although revised estimates indicate that the figure was slightly higher, this compared with
40 times current income for Spain, 15 for England, and 17
for the United States. The internal debt was usually only a
small fraction of the total debt of the Brazilian government.

The mechanism by which Brazil financed its economic
development from 1840 to 1870, the timing of this growth,
and the incidence of its costs and benefits can now be
described. The economy of Brazil was not nationally self-
sufficient, but functioned within the Atlantic economy. For

this reason, Brazilian export earnings would increase when British income increased, or supplies of competing products from the United States decreased. In the years 1855-1870, British income increased steadily, except in 1857/8 and 1867/8. United States supplies of cotton to Europe decreased sharply during the U.S. Civil War (1861-1865). Brazil's export receipts fell during 1858/9 and 1867/8, but increased strongly from 1860 to 1865. Exports continued to increase except in 1867/8, despite the Paraguayan War, which was fought away from Brazil's main export-producing areas. The surprising lack of effect of the Paraguayan War on Brazil's productive capacity is reflected both in the growth in value and quantum of Brazil's exports during these years, despite price declines, and in the lack of growth of Brazil's manufacturing industry to supply the Brazilian army.

The government attempted to protect its credit rating for borrowing abroad by (1) promoting exports, (2) using debt operations to recall outstanding Banco do Brasil notes. Both measures attempted to limit the ratio of milreis to foreign exchange. The government then floated foreign loans; nonetheless, in six out of seven years, the exchange rate fell in the year in which the loan was floated. Shortfalls in income, when not covered by foreign loans, were covered by increased issues of paper money. It is not true that the government relied on a policy of depreciating currency to stimulate exports from 1840 to 1870. The depreciation was small enough that the price of the principal export, coffee, in pounds sterling usually moved in the same direction as the price in milreis: it increased in thirteen out of thirty years, and fell in 17; the price of coffee in milreis increased in 16 years and fell in 14. The difference is statistically insignificant, and confirms the impression that the government regulated its monetary conditions with a view to obtaining loans and investment in Brazil, and that railroad building and preferential railroad rates were more efficient means of promoting exports than exchange manipulation.

The government provided infrastructure and some of the funds for development. It floated external and internal loans, collected taxes, and when necessary, printed money. It also protected local manufactures by tariff legislation, and, in some noncompeting areas, exempted books and machinery needed for local manufacture (and construction of railroads) from import duties. The inflationary burden, which is reflected in a rising wholesale price index and falling exchange rate, affected consumers in general; holders of foreign exchange were cushioned against inflation for domestic purchases, but not usually by very great amounts. The regional distribution of of growth indicates slower than average growth in the sugar-producing areas, and faster than average growth in coffee areas

(Rio and São Paulo), which served as "growth poles." At the
same time, economic activity in regions of the economy characterized by subsistence agriculture increased, so that the
center of economic gravity of the nation shifted south and
moved outward. If not yet rich, Brazil in 1870 was a growing nation with a monetized economy.

The Personal Reign of Dom Pedro, Second Phase, 1871-1889

        Psychologically, and in the long run economically, the
most important act in 1871 was the enactment of the Law of
the Free Womb. The timing of its enactment reflected the Negroes' service in the Paraguayan War, increasing abolitionist sentiment in Brazil, the example of the United States Civil
War, and the Emancipation Proclamation in the United States.
The law provided that

> the children of women slaves that may be born in the Em-
> pire from the date of this Law shall be considered to be
> free. The said minors shall remain and be under the do-
> minion of the owners of the mother, who shall be obliged
> to rear and take care of them until such children have
> reached eight years of age. On the child of the slave
> attaining this age, the owner of its mother shall have the
> option either of receiving from the State the indemnifi-
> cation of 600 [milreis ($U.S. 300)][85] or of making use
> of the services of the minor until he shall have completed
> the age of twenty-one years. In the former event the
> Government will receive the minor, and will dispose of
> him in conformity with the provisions of the present Law.
> The pecuniary indemnification above fixed shall be paid
> in Government bonds, bearing interest at six per cent, per
> annum, which will be considered extinct at the end of
> thirty years.
>   As many slaves as correspond in value to the annual
> disposable sum from the emancipation fund shall be freed
> in each province of the Empire. . . . The slave who,
> through his savings, may obtain means to pay his value
> has a right to freedom.
>   The following shall be declared free: the slaves be-
> longing to the State, the Government giving them such
> employment as they may deem fit. The slave given in usu-
> fruct to the Crown. The slaves of unclaimed inheritances.
> The slaves who have been abandoned by their owners.
> Should these have abandoned the slaves from the latter
> being invalids they shall be obliged to maintain them,
> except in case of their own penury, the maintenance being

charged by the Judge of the Orphan's Court. In general
the slaves liberated by virtue of this Law shall be under
the inspection of Government during five years. They will
be obliged to hire themselves under pain of compulsion;
if they lead an idle life they shall be made to work in
the public establishments. The compulsory labor, however,
shall cease so soon as the freed man shall exhibit an
engagement of hire.[86]

The law, affecting 1,700,000 slaves, was not satisfactory
to the abolitionists, who calculated that at worst, an infant
girl slave would live out her life in servitude, and her
children, would work as slaves until twenty-one; if the last
such child was born when the woman was forty, slavery would
exist for an additional sixty years--until 1931. Most coffee
planters, in fact, incorporated the children of their women
slaves into the labor force. From 1872 to 1874 less than 3
per cent of the slave population was freed by means of the
emancipation fund,[87] which reached 27,075 contos from 1871 to
1878.[88] Free children of slave mothers were not educated;
they were raised in the same conditions as their older
siblings had been before 1871. The only modification seems to
have been that planters added the phrase "only their services"
or "probable services" to the names of such children, who were
included in the planters' lists of slave price and property.[89]
    Although the law itself affected relatively few slaves
immediately, it nonetheless appeared to have ended slavery to
a large enough extent to trigger both massive increases in immigration from Europe and increasing private manumissions
and abolition in various cities in provinces, especially during
the 1880s. More striking, the passage of the law created an
impression of greater unity or compromise on the abolition of
slavery than in fact existed, as abolition brought with it the
fall of the imperial government.
    The arguments for immigration on the part of abolition-
ists strongly paralleled the arguments for immigration of Negro
slaves on the part of those who wanted to abolish Indian
slavery in the sixteenth century. Since the major argument in
favor of slavery was the need for a labor force, the abolition
of slavery for any individual group depended on the assurance
of an adequate labor supply. The fear that slaves, once free,
would refuse to work is clearly present in the Law of the Free
Womb, in the requirement that slaves freed by that law were
under government inspection and were to be forced to work for
the five years following their liberation. Immigrants were
attracted at this time not only because of the policies of
the Brazilian government and of some private persons, but also
because of the wars of national unification in Europe in the
1870s. Germans began to enter Brazil from 1850 on. Italian

immigration surged in the 1870s, while large numbers of
Spaniards immigrated in the 1880s and during the Spanish depression of the 1890s. From 1880 to 1909 Portugal supplied
fewer immigrants to Brazil than did Italy. The influx of
European laborers weakened the argument that slave labor was
necessary for the continued existence of the Brazilian economy. It was therefore possible to shift the argument for
abolition from economic to moral grounds.

In 1883 local abolition societies joined in a national
confederation to pressure the political parties; in the same
year the province of Ceará abolished slavery. In 1884 the
Liberal party endorsed abolition. The province of Amazonas
declared abolition in 1885. The Conservatives, who were the
party in power, declared (in a rear-guard action) that all
slaves over sixty would be freed after another three years
of service. Private owners manumitted their slaves. There
soon were almost twice as many free as slave Negroes. Those
not freed by their masters simply ran away in increasing numbers. In 1887 army officers refused to lead troops in pur-
suit of escaped slaves "as it was beneath the dignity of
officers and gentlemen to employ the national armed forces
for such an ignoble purpose." The Golden Law, which freed
the slaves, was passed by the Senate and signed by the Princess Regent on May 13, 1888. In magnificent simplicity,
it declared that "From the date of this Law slavery is declared abolished in Brazil. All contrary provisions are revoked." Thus, the remaining 700,000 slaves and 300,000 "con-
ditionally free" children were freed; the former owners received no compensation for what they viewed as human property
worth over 280 million U.S. dollars (1888 exchange rate),
while no protection was provided for the newly freed.

Before the passage of the Golden Law, more than a million
slaves had been liberated from 1871 to 1888. The geographical distribution of the last 700,000 slaves to be freed high-
lights the economic structure of Brazil. The North had 18 per
cent of the total, the Center 14 per cent, and the South 68
per cent. The slaves from the North had been sold to the coffee zones, where a good slave, on the average, was bought for
at least 900 milreis ($U.S. 450). The capitalization, amor-
tization of capital used by the slave, and other costs of
maintaining him were 150 milreis per slave. A free worker
earned 400 reis a day or some 10,000 reis a month, so that free
labor was less expensive than slave labor in the Northeast,
which contributed to abolitionist sentiment in the area.
Similarly, by 1888 the majority of labor in the São Paulo area
was free.[90]

The abolition of slavery was the capstone to the nineteenth century modernization of Brazil. In its economic aspect, the freeing of the slaves meant that increased wage

payments to labor led to an increased demand for industrial
products, while the increased level of education (obtained
both by increased numbers of schools in Brazil and the importation of educated workers) meant not only a better quality of
life but also an increase in the productivity of the Brazilian
labor force, so that Brazilian manufactured goods were increasingly able to compete against imports.

The growth of the Brazilian industrial economy is seen
in that Brazil had 2 textile mills, 10 food industries, 2 box
factories, 7 chemical products firms, and 24 saltworks in 1850,
which together had a capital of over 7,000 contos of reis
which, at the 1850 exchange rate, were worth Ł780,000. From
1870 to 1880 the incorporation of 202 firms was approved.[91]
The new emphasis on uniformity and industrialization was resented. In 1874 mobs of "weight breakers" smashed the new
weights and measures required by the adoption of the metric
system.[92]

The Brazilian manufacturing industry continued to grow.
By 1881 Brazil had 44 textile firms which employed more than
5,000 workmen. Half of the factories produced more than 20
million meters of cloth annually. A rapid industrial spurt
began in the 1880s: 150 new firms were founded from 1880 to
1884, and 248 from 1885 to 1889. By 1889 there were 636 industrial firms in Brazil, with a capital equivalent to Ł25 million
(in 1920 prices), employing some 54,169 workmen. The distribution of these firms was 60 per cent textiles, 15 per cent
food stuffs, 10 per cent chemicals, 4 per cent leather, 3 1/2
per cent clothing and toilet articles, and 3 per cent metal-
lurgy.[93]

Much of the new industry was developed in São Paulo,
which began as a center for coffee-milling machinery and textile equipment, and then spread into other branches of industrial activity. The increase in coffee prices and receipts
from 1870 to 1889 generated much of the capital for industrial
investment. Nonetheless, less than 10 per cent of capital invested in Brazil prior to 1885 had been applied to industry;
23 per cent was so invested between 1885 and 1895. During
these years, British investment was overwhelmingly concentrated in government loans, railways, and public utilities.
Investment in industry was low, reaching a peak of 7 per cent
of total British investment in 1885 (see Table 10-10). (A
higher estimate cited in Manchester[94] places British investment in São Paulo alone at between Ł6 million and Ł12 million
by 1888.) This came to less than half of total industrial
investment, thus reflecting the concentration of Brazilian efforts in light industry with relatively small capital require-
ments, and the fact that closely held firms turned to foreign
loans only when no further capital was forthcoming from the
family and friends who were the stockholders.

This industrial growth was, in part, the result of tariff protection and changes in the financial system. Although the level of tariff rates was often set with revenue considerations uppermost, as early as 1844 the tariff structure had been constructed to favor the development of Brazilian industry. In the early 1870s, Brazilian industrialists began to lobby for an increase in tariff rates in order to ensure protection from increasingly efficient and effective foreign competition. Thus, Brazilian hat makers argued that only a tariff of 100 per cent on German hats would allow the Brazilian product to compete on equal terms. This argument was countered by free traders who argued that protection would artificially force the hothouse creation "of urban industries that would flatter the nation's vanity, but would never increase the income or welfare of the people. It would lead to the accumulation of labor in the cities at the cost of rural depopulation, increasing a poverty sadly aggravated by the high price of the most basic foodstuffs."[95]

A mild increase in import duties was achieved in 1876 and 1879; at least part of the reason for the lack of strong protectionist legislation was the split in industrial ranks; spinning firms wanted protection for their product; weaving firms, which wanted cheap thread, did not. The effective amount of protection given depended on the official value set on imports, against which the tariff would be levied. Only importers were consulted in setting these values; the weight of the cloth was the main criteria of valuation adopted. Foreign mills thereupon produced lighter weight cloth to avoid Brazilian tariff levies, which occasioned much protest by competing Brazilian manufacturers.[96]

Among the usual protectionist arguments advanced by Brazilian industrialists, two are particularly striking. In 1881 they wrote to the finance minister that "the local production of coarse cottons . . . is being warred upon by foreign competitors and if legislative measures do not come to the industry's aid, all the effort and capital employed to date will be wasted."[97] This is a trend-setting line of reasoning which is a now familiar part of the Economic Commission for Latin America ideology, and has been especially prominent in Central American Common Market provisions for the creation of monopoly industries in their newly created common market, which are to be protected against foreign competition. The second argument was particularly Brazilian: industrial development should be protected in order to provide employment of labor freed by emancipation.[98] Finally, occasional shortfalls in the coffee harvest and breaks in the coffee price underscored Brazil's need to diversify.

From 1870 to 1889 the quantity of coffee produced increased from 229,620 toneladas to 335,160 toneladas. The price of

coffee increased 24 per cent. Coffee exports thus increased
from 50.3 per cent of total exports to 66.5 per cent, so that
a break in coffee receipts had increasingly serious repercus-
sions throughout the economy. In 1872-74, 1875/6, 1870/80,
1883/4, and 1885/6 the volume of coffee harvested fell sharply below the preceding year's harvest. Coffee prices fell in
1870-72, 1873/4, 1876-78, 1879-81, 1885/6, and 1888. Not sur-
prisingly, total government receipts fell in 1873/4, 1876-78,
1882/3, 1884/5, and 1888, reflecting a fall of export tax revenue as a share of total revenue, which was especially notice-
able during these years.

The Brazilian government followed a policy of "functional
finance" from 1870 to 1889, spending sums necessary to achieve
economic objectives, and raising sums not available from taxes
from domestic and foreign loans. Only in 1872 did the government show a surplus. Loans were relatively easy to obtain as
Brazil had a surplus of goods exported over those imported from
1862 to 1889, with the single exception of 1885/6. At the
same time, the government retired money from circulation whenever its finances permitted, leading to complaints of illiquidity by businessmen. Thus, the fall in coffee receipts did not
determine whether the government had a deficit or not; it did
determine, however, the size of the deficit and the timing of
monetary expansion and foreign borrowing.

Although Treasury and bank notes in circulation increased
only 3 per cent between 1870 and 1889, the amount in circulation varied some 15 per cent during these years, decreasing in
1871-77, 1880-85, and 1886/7, increasing in 1878-80, 1886, and
1887-89. The external debt increased in 1871, 1875, 1883, 1886,
1888, and 1889. Thus, falls in coffee receipts preceded increases in domestic money supply and foreign borrowing. The
overall mechanism was that shortfalls in coffee export tax receipts were covered by increases in issues of paper money and
Imperial Bonds [apólices] issued in anticipation of receipts.[99]
The increase in money supply in relation to foreign exchange
was limited by compensatory foreign borrowing, so that the exchange rate was relatively steady. The exchange rate improved
from U.S. .45 in 1870 to .55 in 1875, fell gradually to a low
of .38 in 1885 and 1886, then rose to .54 in 1889.[100] Except
in years of heavy emission of money, wholesale prices tended
to fall from 1870 to 1884,[101] reflecting the difference in
goods domestically consumed and exported, and the relatively
small share of imports in domestic products.

The periodic crises brought on by falls in coffee receipts were in themselves enough to stimulate economic nation-
alism in the form of demands for tariff protection for industry, and easier credit. These demands could be contained
and economic orthodoxy enforced only as long as no other major
economic group was in opposition to the government, and private

industry was confined to the domestic loan market. The private sector had increasing access to the international loan market, the use of which was necessitated by decreasing liquidity: the supply of bank and Treasury notes per capita declined by 36 per cent from 1870 to 1889. As Brazil's economic activity was expanding, the credit shortage may have been greater than the per capita figure indicates. On the other hand, it is possible that bank deposits increased and that the velocity of monetary circulation increased. Statistical information is not available on this point; if either of these changes took place, then the credit squeeze would be less than the per capita figure indicates. Despite these qualifications, the squeeze was substantial, and increased due to the shift from slave to free labor, since money was needed to pay free laborers, while the money costs of maintaining a slave labor force were lower.[102] For example, more than 50,000 contos were needed to finance the salaries at harvest time on the coffee plantations. Thus the planters joined the industrialists in demanding easier credit facilities.

As long as coffee plantations were profitable, the relatively high cost of credit was not a serious handicap; as the land wore out, and the cash input to plantations increased, planters were increasingly burdened by limited credit facilities, which were more and more channeled to industrial and commercial projects which yielded quicker returns. Similarly, available bank funds were often channeled into the purchase of government securities rather than agricultural loans. Agricultural credit facilities were provided by the creation of a mortgage portfolio within the Banco do Brasil in September 1866. A capital fund of 35,000 contos was provided for agricultural loans bearing an interest of 9 per cent and an amortization of 8 per cent, with a maximum term of six years. In 1872 the Banco do Brasil obtained the reduction of interest to 6 per cent and a lengthening of the term of the loan.[103] By 1876 the credit shortage was so great that the Banco do Brasil made arrangements to accept "secondary money" in the form of "mortgage letters" it issued in payment of mortgage amortizations in its commercial portfolio, but soon abandoned this practice.[104] Two years later, the Treasury lowered the interest on its notes to 3 per cent to alleviate the credit shortage,[105] while the Banco do Brasil agreed to increase mortgage funds to 85,000 contos for loans to agriculture at 4 per cent interest and 5 per cent amortization.[106] As foreign exchange receipts were greated than import expenditures, the credit expansion led to only a moderate fall in the exchange rate, from $U.S. .47 in 1878 to .43 in 1879.

The government attempted to channel limited investment funds into productive activity by the law of November 6, 1875, which authorized a guarantee of 6 and 7 per cent interest on

capital, not to exceed ₤3,000,000, employed in sugar mills for
the manufacture of sugar, brandy, and other products throughout the northern and central provinces. By 1880 these mills
had become a source of speculation for the concessionaires,
who lacked the resources and ability to construct the mills,
and sold their privileges to various companies organized in
London. Many of the concessions were therefore never carried
out.[107] Nonetheless, by 1884 fifty factories with a capital
of ₤2,695,000 were set up under this law while eleven more
operated without a guarantee. Most of the capital employed
in these enterprises was British.[108]

Attempts to channel credit to agriculture were not entirely successful. Bank loans were limited, not only by the
lender's knowledge of deteriorating conditions in the older
coffee areas, but also by legal protection to the planters
which made recovery of loans difficult, and seizure of land
in default of loan repayment almost impossible. According
to Stein,

> The mortgage law of 1863 and supplementary Imperial
> decrees of 1865 creating rural credit companies furthered
> this protection by allowing the "unscrupulous debtor to
> turn himself into the creditor of his creditor." Accord-
> ing to these laws, no loan could exceed an amount equal
> to half the security offered by the mortgager. Where the
> mortgager failed to fulfill his obligation, and the mort-
> gagee obtained judicial approval for foreclosure, the
> former handed over his property, demanding the restitution
> in cash of half the property's value. "This is not just
> a simple hypothesis," added a writer of 1884. "Sucy
> abuses have already occurred." Even a customarily re-
> strained foreign visitor of the same year commented that
> "nowhere in all the world--at least not in Netherland
> India--are agriculturalists granted so many legal securi-
> ties to enable them to cultivate their lands in peace,
> as in Brazil." A third observer was more outspoken in
> denouncing the Brazilian mortgage laws as "defective";
> and made in favor of the fazendeiro who wished to keep
> all the rights.[109]

As private bankers were hesitant in providing loans to
coffee planters, the credit gap was filled by the government's
Banco do Brasil, which more than doubled its loans to planters
in the Province of Rio from 1877 to 1883.[110] Those mortgage
loans granted tended to be based on the value of the plantation's slaves, and not the remainder of the plantation owner's
property.[111] The drop in value of slaves, and its extinction
with abolition left the planters without readily negotiable
assets on which they could obtain loans, precisely at the time

when their cash needs increased. As the empire was politically based in large part on planter support, the government--
which had not paid compensation for slaves on emancipation--
was petitioned to "intervene in our behalf at credit establishments to help our agriculture."[112] In 1888 the government provided roughly 4,300 contos to financial houses, which were to
be advanced for agriculture. In 1889 plantation owners
signed contracts with 17 agencies for 172,000 contos.[113] Although the money supply had fallen in 1888, it increased by
101,735 contos between 1889 and 1890; the impetus came from
increases in credit to agriculture, which began the inflationary process known as the "encilhamento," which lasted from
1888 to 1894.

The term "encilhamento" itself indicates distrust of
the government's role in the inflation, since it refers to the
part of a race track where horses are girthed, and shady bets
were placed if the race itself was not fixed. Yet the changes
that brought about the inflation were tied in with both necessary changes for economic development, and the obvious need of
the empire, and its successor Republic, to buy political support.

Some help had been given to planters by the creation of
a special agricultural section in the mortgage department of
the Banco do Brasil, which had a capital of 12,000 contos,
which could be advanced on various forms of security. In 1889
this capital was increased to 16,000 contos.[114] The basic
changes began with the adoption of a mixed monetary system on
November 24, 1888, under which the Treasury was to lend to
banks which in turn were to advance funds to agriculture based
on a variety of guarantees.[115] Yet it seems unlikely that the
funds released were invested in accordance with the official
aims of the law, as witnessed by the extraordinarily rapid
nominal growth of industry and banks, which competed with
agriculture for funds. In 1888 laws were enacted to promote
the organization of limited liability companies.[116] From independence to 1888 the total capital of banks and industry
incorporated in Rio was 410,879 contos; from 1888 to November
15, 1889 (the end of the empire), 402,610 contos, and from
November 1889 to October 1890, 1,169,388 contos.[117] Not all
of the nominal capital was paid up; at the declaration of the
Republic, banks listed on the Rio stock exchange had a nominal
capital of 491,000 contos, of which 143,340 contos had been
realized. These banks did not have any influence on the circulating medium of the country from 1866 until the law of November 24, 1888, which created a system of "plural bank emission."
Banks were empowered to emit notes up to two thirds of the bank's
capital. Security for the notes took the form of special government bonds bearing 4 per cent interest, deposited in the
Caixa de Amortização. The law established these notes as legal

means of payment which had to be accepted in payment of taxes by the government, and were convertible into Treasury notes.[118] The single exception was that such notes were not accepted in payment of duties on imports, where Treasury notes were required.[119] The banks were required to keep a cash reserve of 20 per cent in Treasury notes against the bank notes emitted. Yet at the same time that credit facilities were expanded, the government was preoccupied with abandoning inconvertible paper currency, and establishing a central bank. In 1889 the government contracted with the newly created Banco Nacional do Brasil (created by the decree of 28 September 1889) for the gradual substitution of Treasury notes by notes convertible into gold; this privilege was to be extended to at most two banks, one of them being in São Paulo, whose bank note emissions had been relatively small.[120] At the end of the empire, the Banco Nacional do Brasil had a nominal capital of 90,000 contos and a paid-up capital of 18,000 contos; it did not have a reserve fund.[121] The government's policy of shifting from inconvertible paper to convertible notes had had too short a time to be put into effect, or evaluated, before the empire fell. Under the plural bank emission system, inflation, and nominal and real economic activity increased. Since the process continued through 1894, an evaluation of the encilhamento is postponed until the next chapter, in which the early Republic is discussed.

The most frequent evaluation of the imperial government's monetary policy from 1870 to 1889 is that "the Treasury emitted paper money not in accordance with the commercial needs of the country, but in conformity with the needs of the government," as the government preferred to emit paper money than to pay interest on loans.[122] This statement is accurate to the extent that the government initially obtained new issues of paper money for its own needs, especially in the years when overall money in circulation decreased, so that the decrease in funds originating in Brazil available to the private sector was greater than the decrease in money supply. Neither in Argentina nor in Mexico during the Porfiriato, did attempts at financial conservatism provide the "institutional conditions" necessary to attract foreign capital investment. By extension, foreign investment in Brazil probably increased as the exchange rate fell. Therefore, it is unlikely that the credit squeeze on internal funds generated equal or greater foreign fund availability to the Brazilian economy, including private, government, and foreign ownership. Nor can it be shown that this policy resulted in a greater availability of credit to the Brazilian-owned part of the private sector (only) than would have been the case if monetary conditions were less stringent.

While the most significant government act in this period was the abolition of slavery, and the most startling economic aftermath of abolition was the encilhamento, the government had pursued a number of important development policies during these years that have often been ignored because of the greater drama of the measures discussed above. These policies affected railroads, immigration, education, and domestic and foreign trade. New legislation encouraged a spurt in railroad construction (see Table 10-11). In 1873 the interest guarantee on capital used in railroad construction was increased to 7 per cent from the preceding level of 5 per cent. As the provincial governments had in fact paid an additional 2 per cent guarantee to attract capital for railroad development, the imperial government in effect took over the burden from the provincial governments on new railroad contracts; the total sum of guarantee in fact paid was unchanged. The new guarantees ran for a term of thirty years, a considerable decline from the forty- to ninety-year guarantees that the lower rates had carried.* Increasing imperial participation in railroad construction was envisioned in a provision which stipulated the conditions under which a construction contract would be let by the government, and provided that the government could construct on its own account.[123] The law of February 8, 1874, made it possible "for roads, although situated wholly within the bounds of a province, to be constructed by the imperial government, provided it could be shown that the proposed line affected the welfare of the nation as a whole."[12]

Under these laws, seven railroads were built by the imperial government, one by the Province of Bahia. The reasons for imperial government construction are varied, including drought relief, defense of the Uruguayan border, and interconnection of existing lines, as well as provision of services for which private capital was unavailable. During this period, the provincial and imperial governments took over four existing railroads, so that by 1889, the central and provincial governments owned 3,044 kilometers, 34 per cent of Brazil's 9,583 kilometers of railroads.

The conditions under which foreign capital could be attracted continued as a subject of major concern. In 1878 the Brazilian ambassador in London reported that a major problem was that of foreign exchange. The handling of profits or losses on remittances due to changes in the exchange rate

_____
*Vieira de Mello e Teixeira Brandão, A Nova Política Ferroviária do Brasil. By 1877, in São Paulo, the Santos Jundiahy railroad dispensed with the government guarantee ten years after the line was opened to traffic and also returned a profit to the government in excess of the specified returns to the company. Manchester, op. cit., p. 324.

had caused disagreements between the companies and the government, which had shifted its policy intermittently. In the
railroad law of 1878, the exchange rate was fixed at 27 pence
per milreis; the length of time before which the government
could recapture a railroad was set at thirty years.[126]
Although the exchange rate set accurately reflected market
conditions in the preceding years, as the milreis weakened,
application of the 1878 legal rate made it possible for the
railroad companies to make a profit on currency conversion.

Toward the end of the empire, sentiment for direct government ownership of railroad lines increased. As early as 1871
a government official argued that early government recapture
of railroads in the states of Pernambuco and Bahia was advis-
able, since their value was being increased by the government's building of extensions to them. The railroad law therefore provided for the recapture of these roads if an agreement
could be reached with the companies. In 1884 a government
engineer argued that the cost of operation by the government
would be less than by private companies. In 1887 the Minister
of Agriculture, Commerce, and Public Works argued against the
system of guaranteed interest and for direct government operation because he believed that government operation was cheaper.
"This is because of the heavy expenses of supervision of the
affairs of the companies, of verifying their accounts, and of
maintaining a commission abroad for coordinating purchase of
material." With the exception of roads having unusually heavy
traffic density, for 1886 "his figures than show an operating
cost of 1,931 milreis per kilometer for the government operated
group and 2,476 milreis per kilometer for the privately-owned
lines. The government can borrow money on its own bonds for
5 1/2 per cent. As its guarantees of interest are usually
for 7 per cent, 1 1/2 per cent can be saved on capital
charges."[127]

"His advocacy of renting the recaptured lines to private
companies does not appear consistent with the contention that
government-operation is cheaper. He wanted the government to
buy the roads through flotation of a bond issue, and then rent
them for operation to private companies. This is precisely
what the government of the federal republic of Brazil later
did."[128] The renting might not be inconsistent with his analysis of the current situation, if he anticipated heavier railroad traffic in the future, since on the lines excluded from
his analysis the ratio of receipts to expenses is slightly
more favorable for private than government railroads.[129] The
government may also have felt that there was a shortage of
skilled administrative personnal available to it. Thus it
paid to argue for a government takeover based on current
operating costs, save the difference between interest guarantee payments and bond interest costs, and also obtain income

from rental fees.   Outright government ownership also made
it easier to proceed with consolidating existing railroad
lines into regional systems with the same gauge.   By obtaining control, the government would be able to save money and
increase efficiency.   The groundwork for takeover was laid
in the 1870s and 1880s.   Takeover itself was not carried out
until after the end of the empire.

The status of Brazil's railroads at the end of the empire was that of 56 railroad companies: 18 operated under an
interest guarantee from the imperial government; 16 operated
under interest guarantee from the provincial governments; and
22 operated without guarantee in the hope of future profits
"which, unhappily, were almost always lacking."130   Track
gauges had been adjusted so that 1,345 km. were broad gauge
(1m60), and 7,585 narrow gauge (1m).   Only 653 km. were of different gauges.   All new lines under construction were of 1m.
gauge.   The total capital invested in railroads through 1888
equaled 517,856 contos (exchange rate 24d), of which 195,636
were constructed by the state, 167,021 were build with interest
on capital guaranteed by the imperial government, 78,272 had
interest on capital guaranteed by the provinces, and 76,927
were built without guarantee.   Carreira Castro notes that the
government lines except for the Dom Pedro II and the Baturité
showed a deficit (government-owned lines including these showed
a balance of 4,725 contos).   They were "compensated by the
indirect profits, carrying the various localities which they
traversed to civilization and prosperity, which later produced
real benefits."131

The length of railroad lines increased substantially from
745 km. in 1870 to 9,583 km. in 1889.   During the same years,
the quantum of exports decreased from 107.5 to 100.0.   The
value of exports in 1840 milreis increased from 140,138 contos
in 1870 to 220,749 in 1889.   Certainly, without the railroads
neither the immigration program, "the indirect benefits of
civilization and prosperity," export receipts, and with them,
national income, could have increased.   As 83 per cent of the
capital invested in railroads was either the result of direct
government investment, or interest guarantees provided by the
imperial and provincial governments, it is clear that railroad
development was the direct result of government policy, which
in regard to attracting investment (which was beneficial) and
maintenance of monetary stability (which was not helpful) was
fairly consistently followed until abolition and the end of
the empire.

The increased demand for Brazilian exports brought with
it an increased demand for labor.   The end of the slave trade
in 1850, and increasing emancipation thereafter, led Brazilian
planters to search for alternate sources of labor.   In 1824
the imperial government established a colony of non-Portuguese

Europeans: Germans were imported to a colony in Rio Grande do
Sul. According to Furtado, "transportation and intallation
costs were paid by the government, and public works were promoted for the purpose of providing jobs for the colonists. . . .
But the life of the colonies was extremely precarious because,
with no market available for production surpluses, the monetary sector soon atrophied and the colony reverted to a rudi-
mentary economic system of subsistence."[132] On the other hand,
Diégues Júnior writes that the colony grew from 126 persons
in 1824 to 4,856 in 1830, and that new colonies were founded
by its members, so that the Province of Rio Grande do Sul became a German agricultural colony.[133]

    Immigration declined after 1830 because of the overthrow
of Dom Pedro I, the succeeding civil wars, and the end of financial aid to immigration. The flow began again in the middle 1840s, and was given special impetus by Senator Nicolau
Verguiero, who imported 400 Germans (80 families) to work as
sharecroppers on his coffee plantations. By 1857 the system
of sharecropping had spread to an additional 26 colonies
which employed 8,152 people. In 1848-1849 the federal government granted the provinces land for immigration: immigrants
either bought or were granted perpetual leases of small lots.
According to the law, the lands could not be cleared by slaves,
or transferred by the colonists who received them. They were
to revert to the provinces if the colonists did not fulfill
these conditions within five years. This system was adopted
in Paraná in 1860.   .

    Yet Vergueiro's system was not considered entirely
satisfactory, as the immigrant was not fully free.[134] Vergueiro
had obtained a subsidy from the government to cover the cost
of transportation. According to Furtado, "In reality, the
actual cost of immigration was entirely paid by the immigrant, financially the weaker party. The government financed
the operation, but the colonist mortgaged his own future
and that of his family, whereas the farmer retained for himself
all the advantages. The colonist was obligated to sign a contract whereby he was committed not to leave the farmer until
his entire debt was paid."[135]

    In the 1860s the demand for coffee increased, while the
number of slaves available from the North of Brazil declined,
owing to the temporary cotton boom that lasted during the
United States Civil War. The planters began to pay colonists,
and guarantee a minimum income to sharecroppers, who were paid
annual salaries for care of coffee trees, plus a wage at harvest time which varied according to the size of the crop. If
immigration were left to private initiative, larger farmers
would be financially more able than smallholders to import
immigrants. At the same time, it was not always possible to
force colonists to stay on one farm to fulfill their contracts.

Since the need for immigrants and their benefit to the economy was general, in 1870 the imperial government took over the cost of transportation of immigrants who were to work on coffee farms. The farmers provided the immigrants with a plot of land on which to grow their food, and paid the immigrants' expenses during their first year of work.[136]

Both because of earlier reports of poor conditions in the immigration colonies, and because of opposition to emigration of a country practicing slavery, German states prohibited emigration to Brazil in 1859 and subsequent years. France and England adopted restrictions in the mid-1870s. Nonetheless, European upheavals limited the effectiveness of these prescriptions, and immigration to Brazil continued to increase. In 1872 there were 388,459 aliens in Brazil, of whom 99,899 were in Rio de Janeiro, 46,900 in Minas Gerais, 41,725 in Rio Grande do Sul, 29,622 in São Paulo, 15,974 in Santa Catarina, 4,191 in Espíritu Santo, and 3,627 in Paraná. From 1850 to 1888, 882,176 immigrants entered Brazil. Italians supplied 33 per cent of the immigrants, Portuguese 31 per cent, Germans 7 per cent, and Spanish, Austrians, Russians, and French the remainder.[137] The immigration was increasingly directed to São Paulo and coffee: 13,000 entered the province in the 1870s, and 184,000 in the 1880s. By 1888, in São Paulo, free labor predominated in coffee.[138] Their presence eased the transition from slave to free labor; although the quantity of coffee harvested fell from 6,075,000 sacks (each sack contained 60 kg.) in 1886/7 to 3,444,000 in 1888, the shortfall in coffee receipts complained of reflects, first, the abnormally high coffee price obtained in 1886/7, and the sharply below average price in 1888. Sufficient stability returned to the coffee plantations by 1889 for a normal quantity of coffee to be harvested.

Immigrants also helped to solve the problems resulting from the lack of schools in Brazil. Despite Dom Pedro's concern with education, and aid to individual students, the ability to provide schools was limited: in 1871 there were 4,096 elementary schools with an enrollment of 138,232 in a five- to fourteen-year-old population of 2,441,728. In 1889 there were 8,157 elementary schools with 258,802 pupils in a school age population of 3,778,485. In 1872, 1,564,481 Brazilians said they could read and write; 8,365,997 could not. In 1890, 2,120,559 Brazilians claimed they could read and write, 12,213,356 could not. By 1900, 3,380,000 Brazilians said they were literate. This increase could not have been entirely produced by Brazil's school system. It seems likely that more than half of the increase in persons who could read and write came from immigrants in the 1890s, and that a substantial share of Brazil's increased literacy was also provided by immigrants in the preceding two decades. Moreover, immigrants were a

major source of entrepreneurial talent, while their savings
helped to finance Brazil's industrial expansion.139

The scope of direct action available to the Brazilian
government is seen by examining its budget. The army's share
of expenditures fell steadily after the Paraguayan War; although naval expenditures increased slightly during the mid
1870s, they soon fell off rapidly, so that by 1889 combined
military expenses absorbed only 16.1 per cent of government
expenditures (see Table 10-12). The fall was useful in freeing funds for development expenditure and disastrous, because
the army felt unappreciated, threw in its lot with the Republicans, and overthrew the empire.

The increasing developmental expenditures are those of
the Treasury, whose debt service expenditure was essential
to promote the flow of foreign capital, agriculture, which included expenditures on government railroads under its jurisdiction, and empire, which included public health, education,
and drought relief. The large empire expenses from 1877 to
1880 reflect the drought and the diseases (smallpox) that were
brought with it: one half of the population of Ceará was
killed between 1877 and 1879; naval expenses were cut to make
funds available for drought relief.

The overall structure of government receipts was remarkably stable from 1870 to 1889. Import duties consistently provided just over half of government revenue. The share of export duties fell from 18.7 per cent to 9.8 per cent of the
total, reflecting a policy of stimulating agriculture by reducing the ad valorem taxes levied on exports. Internal
taxes provided the sums previously financed by export duties;
their contribution increased 3 to 4 percentage points in
the total during most of this period. The government's tax
policies stimulated export production by tax reduction. The
increasing export receipts were spent not only on imports
and tax payments, but also on Brazilian manufactured products,
especially textiles, thereby stimulating domestic economic
activity, increasing total income and employment, and providing an additional internal source of revenue.

In practice, the government's tax policy worked in the
same direction as its railroad, immigration and monetary
policies in stimulating development.

The fiscal policies of the provincial governments were
similar (see Table 10-13): from 1870 to 1890, agricultural
expenditures increased from 3 to 27 per cent of total provincial expenditures, while Treasury expenses fell from 43.4 to
30.8 per cent. Military expenditures fell by more than half,
as demands for internal development increased. However, what
seemed good for an individual province was not always good
for the nation, particularly with regard to revenue. In 1883
the imperial government called attention to the fact that the

provinces were permitted to tax exports 5 per cent in addition to the imperial government's tithe. The Additional Act prohibited the provincial governments from levying duties on imports. Notwithstanding the fact that a number of provinces at that time relied on import duties, despite the Additional Act, they continued to collect the now unconstitutional revenues. The imperial government therefore recommended that the provinces revoke these taxes, covering their deficits by other means. Ceará, Rio Grande do Norte, Parahyba, Paraná, Alagoas, Sergipe, Santa Catarina, and Espíritu Santu complied; it was expected that Pernambuco, Bahia and Maranhão would soon fall into line, while São Paulo declared that it collected no such tax. The government then formed a commission to report on needed changes in the structure of municipal, provincial, and imperial government revenues. Thus, in part as the result of pressure of commercial associations, the imperial government enforced the constitution, enabling Brazil's growing industry to benefit from a unified national market.[140]

Although Brazilian industry began to grow appreciably in this period, the stage of its development is indicated in the fact that Brazil's first cement factory was not established until 1888. The most quantitatively important changes occurring in Brazil were the increase in volume of coffee exports and the development of new exportable products, so that the area of Brazil that was part of the money economy increased. The striking increase in coffee production has been discussed. As old coffee lands in the Province of Rio de Janeiro wore out, new ones in São Paulo were opened. Cotton exports, which had increased sharply during the United States Civil War, stood at 43,024 toneladas in 1870 but fell to 13,575 toneladas in 1889, reflecting a price decline from 1:024$ per tonelada to 513$, which followed renewed United States cotton production and increased world supplies. Total Brazilian cotton production, however, "actually increased to meet the demands of the growing domestic textile industry, which largely offset the loss of revenue from exports."[141]

Rubber, described by Caio Prado Júnior as a more fitting subject for historical novels than for economic history, was first exported in large recorded quantities in 1827, when 31 toneladas were shipped. Its use at first was in waterproofing textiles. As new industrial uses were developed, rubber prices soared, from 290$ per tonelada in 1827 to 533$ in 1840, 1,484$ in 1870, and 1,582$ in 1889. Rubber exports grew to 418 toneladas in 1840, 4,780 toneladas in 1870, and 15,990 toneladas in 1889. The value of rubber exports was 7,093 contos of reis in 1870, 25,295 contos in 1889, reflecting the rubber boom that began in the 1880s and lasted through 1910. "Almost all of the rubber shipped from Brazil originated in the provinces of Amazonas and Pará, where the population at least doubled, exports expanded fivefold, and provincial revenues increased by fifteen times in the last two decades of the empire. On a per capita basis the value of exports from these two jungle provinces in 1888 was higher than that of Argentina and more than twice that of the United States."142

The ability of Brazil to produce rubber depended, above all, on obtaining a manpower supply. The increased production in the 1880s resulted, in large part, from the influx of refugees from drought-stricken Ceará: roughly 60,000 Brazilians from other provinces migrated to Pará and Amazonas between 1872 and 1890. The life of the rubber worker was unenviable.

> Large profits were made by the individuals and corporations wealthy enough to acquire promising tracts of forest lands and to advance passage, tools, weapons, food, and liquor to the rubber gatherers. Few of the latter, however, survived the system of debt peonage and the hazards of life in the jungle to win the fortunes they sought. In variably the rubber worker—known as a seringueiro— was in debt before he reached the isolated stretch of river bank where he lived alone for up to six months at a time. Each man tended two strings of erratically spaced Hevea trees, which were tapped on alternate days. The trees were seldom less than ten minutes apart in the dense forest. The seringueiro also prepared his own crude shelter, hunted for much of his food, and gathered oily nuts and wood for the smoky fire over which the day's collection of latex was cured and formed into large balls. These he was obliged to sell to the company agent at the end of the season, a transaction that was nearly always a simple bookkeeping operation, for the harvest was rarely sufficient to cancel his debt. The seringueiro had little hope of escape. He might flee to another part of the valley, there to begin the process anew with a different employer, but if he tried to leave the Amazon he was subject to arrest by authorities downstream. As a general rule the rubber gatherer remained, growing deeper in debt each year until he met death by accident or disease. Under this inequitable and inefficient system, Brazil was never able to realize the full potential of its immense forest resources or to satisfy the world demand for natural rubber. Nonetheless, as long as rubber prices continued to rise, the lure of wealth in the Amazon attracted enough new workers each year to replace the casualties and to permit a steady expansion in output.143

Cacao production increased steadily throughout the nineteenth century, and increased sharply in 1888 and 1889,

reflecting favorable prices from 1877 to 1886, the time lag
in increased output reflecting the time required for a cacao
tree to reach substantial production.

Brazil's traditional exports faced declining milreis
prices from 1870 to 1889; sugar fell from 212$ to 136$, yerba
maté from 295$ to 173$, tobacco from 465$ to 326$, and
leather and hides from 522$ to 484$. Because of an appreciation of the exchange rate, however, the prices in foreign exchange of traditional exports were about the same at the end
as at the beginning of the period. The quantity of tobacco
exports increased by one third, leather and hides exports
were stable until the drought, after which the decimation of
the herds reduced exports, which were about half their previous level from 1883 to 1888.

Despite yearly variations, sugar exports increased from
138,118 toneladas in 1870 to 329,375 toneladas in 1884, as the
result of a law passed in 1875, which authorized the imperial
government to guarantee interest on foreign capital invested
in the sugar industry to a total of 3 million pounds. In the
next ten years 50 sugar mills were installed with modern
equipment, almost all of them financed by English capital invested under this law.[144] Sugar exports during the middle
and late eighties fell because of the dislocations following
the abolilition of slavery; exports were 105,558 toneladas
in 1889.

Yerba maté production doubled from 10,465 toneladas to
23,165 toneladas. During this time, the share of Brazil's
eight leading exports in total export value increased from
92 to 94 per cent. In order, at the end of the empire, they
were: coffee, 66.5 per cent, rubber, 9.8; sugar, 5.5; leather
and hides, 4.1; cotton, 2.7; tobacco, 2.5; yerba maté, 1.6;
and cacao, 1.3. Despite considerable expansion in the production of exportable commodities--some of which was drained
off to the home market--it was increasingly true that in regard to foreign exchange earnings, "Brazil Is Coffee."

The ability of Brazil's exports to pay for its economic
development is indicated by the shift in commodity terms of
trade, which improved 31 per cent from 1870 to 1879, reflecting a 23 per cent fall in the price of British industrial
goods. Despite the coffee boom, sugar and cotton production
declined, so that the overall quantum and real value of Brazilian exports was roughly constant from 1870 to 1890. Export
development was centered on shifts to more profitable crops,
in the face of declining prices. Overall export growth did
not take place under the empire, at least in part due to the
restrictive credit policies followed. The proof of this is
the response of the export sector to cheap credit during the
rapid inflation (encilhamento) when, despite a price decline
of 15 per cent, the quantity of exports increased 24 per cent.

Thus the presence of slavery prevented the growth of a labor supply that would have made rapid economic expansion possible. The appreciation of the exchange rate led to a decline in milreis receipts of exporters, which decreased their ability to pay off local debts and reduced the profitability of export production, the total quantity of which fell. The appreciation of the exchange rate was achieved by a credit squeeze. Although there was expansion of Brazilian commercial and industrial activity, the fact that economic growth would have been greater had adequate credit facilities been available is demonstrated by the rapid real growth during the encilhamento. Despite the government's promotion of railroads, its economic policies impeded economic development and were an important cause of the overthrow of the empire in 1889.

FOOTNOTES

Chapter 10.   The Economic History of the Brazilian Empire,
              1822-1889

1. F. Assis Cintra, D. Pedro I e o Grito da Independéncia,
    cited in E. Bradford Burns, A Documentary History of
    Brazil, pp. 198-200; Clarence H. Haring, "Secession from
    Portugal," in R. A. Humphreys and John Lynch, The Origin
    of the Latin American Revolutions, 1808-1826, pp. 207-
    220; Alan K. Manchester, British Preeminence in Brazil:
    Its Rise and Decline, pp. 187-188; H. V. Livermore, A
    New History of Portugal, pp. 263-264; Hubert Herring, A
    History of Latin America from the Beginnings to the
    Present, p. 290.

2. Manchester, op. cit., p. 190.

3. C. H. Haring, Empire in Brazil, pp. 20-22.

4. Manchester, op. cit., pp. 193-202.

5. Ibid., pp. 202-203; Haring, Empire in Brazil, p. 32.

6. Haring, Empire in Brazil, pp. 33, 89, 90; Manchester,
    op. cit., pp. 212-215.

7. Manchester, op. cit., p. 208.

8. Haring, Empire in Brazil, pp. 36-43; J. J. Sturz, A
    Review, Financial, Statistical, and Commercial of the
    Empire of Brazil and Its Sources . . ., pp. 14-15.

9. Liberato de Castro Carreira, História FInancéira e
    Orçamentária do Imperio do Brasil desde a sua fundação,
    p. 90.

10. United States Historical Statistics, p. 563.

11. Castro Carreira, op. cit., pp. 154, 158.

12. Ibid., p. 135.

13. João Cruz Costa, A History of Ideas in Brazil, trans.
    Suzette Macedo, p. 35.

14. Castro Carreira, op. cit., pp. 159-164.

15. Haring, Empire in Brazil, p. 55.

16. Cited in Humberto Bastos, O Pensamento Industrial no Brasil, p. 40.

17. Castro Carreira, op. cit., pp. 189, 206; Manchester, op. cit., p. 287.

18. Castro Carreira, op. cit., pp. 205, 210.

19. Bastos, op. cit., pp. 27-41.

20. Ibid., pp. 36, 46.

21. J. Pires de Rio, A Moeda Brasileira e seu perene caráter fiduciário, p. 131.

22. Roberto C. Simonsen, Brazil's Industrial Revolution, p. 22.

23. Sturz, op. cit., pp. 8-11.

24. Ibid., p. 16.

25. Pires de Rio, op. cit., p. 125.

26. Castro Carreira, op. cit., p. 225.

27. Manchester, op.cit., p. 232.

28. Ibid., pp. 231-232.

29. Ibid., pp. 236, 240-241.

30. Sturz, op. cit., pp. 82, 95, 121, 145.

31. Simonsen, Ensaios--Sociais, Politicas e Econômicas, 99.

32. Haring, Empire in Brazil, pp. 58-62.

33. Manchester, op. cit., p. 287.

34. Ibid., p. 292.

35. Bastos, op. cit., p. 110. Cf. Manchester, op. cit., p. 258.

36. Bastos, op. cit., p. 111; Castro Carreira, op. cit., p. 245.

37. Castro Carreira, op. cit., pp. 254-256.

38. Ibid., p. 281.

39. Manchester, op. cit., p. 245.

40. Jornal do Commercio, March 19, 1845, and Junqueira's
     speech in the assembly; both cited in Manchester, op.
     cit., p. 248.

41. Limpo de Abreu, cited in Manchester, op. cit., p. 251.

42. Manchester, op. cit., pp. 252-253.

43. Cited in Burns, op. cit., pp. 232-233.

44. Pires do Rio, op. cit., p. 86. On marriage as a source
     of capital formation, see Warren Dean, The Industriali-
     zation of São Paulo, 1880-1945 (Austin: University of
     Texas Press, 1969), pp. 75, 122.

45. Castro Carreira, op. cit., pp. 696-698.

46. Pires de Rio, op. cit., p. 124.

47. Affonso de E. Tauney, Pequena História do Café no
     Brasil, 1727-1937, p. 31.

48. Stanley J. Stein, Vassouras, A Brazilian Coffee County,
     1850-1900, pp. 3, 4.

49. Ibid., chap. 1.

50. Ibid., pp. 31-32.

51. Ibid., p. 32, note 8.

52. Ibid., p. 35.

53. Ibid., p. 36.

54. Ibid., pp. 45-54.

55. Ibid., pp. 70-77.

56. Ibid., pp. 78-90.

57. Ibid., pp. 91-94.

58. Ibid., p. 108.

59. João Pandía Calogeras, A History of Brazil, translated and edited by Percy Alvin Martin, pp. 195-196.

60. Caio Prado Junior, História econômica do Brasil, p. 192.

61. Stanley Stein, The Brazilian Cotton Manufacture, p. 12.

62. Ibid., p. 51.

63. Ibid., p. 37.

64. Ibid., p. 38.

65. Ibid., p. 71.

66. Ibid., p. 191.

67. Edward C. Kirkland, A History of American Economic Life, p. 304; G. C. Fite and J. Reese, An Economic History of the United States, 2nd ed., p. 209.

68. Julian Smith Duncan, Public and Private Operation of Railways in Brazil, p. 20.

69. Ibid., p. 23.

70. Ademar Benévolo, Introducão a História Ferrovaría do Brasil, pp. 501-503; Vieria de Mello e Teixera Brandão, A Nova Politíca Ferrovaría do Brasil, p. 20.

71. Duncan, op. cit., p. 24.

72. Ibid., p. 25.

73. Ibid., pp. 26-27.

74. James W. Wells, Exploring and Travelling Three Thousand Miles Through Brazil, p. 43.

75. Duncan, op. cit., p. 21.

76. Benévolo, op. cit., p. 217.

77. Ibid., pp. 501-502.

78. Ibid., p. 506.

79. Ibid., p. 508.

80. Ibid., p. 515.

81. Ibid., pp. 443, 444.

82. Ibid., p. 456.

83. Castro Carreira, op. cit., p. 285.

84. Hubert Herring, A History of Latin America from the Beginnings to the Present, p. 737.

85. Burns translates the sum as "dollars." This is an error and should read "milreis," which I have substituted in his translation. Cf. Cálogeras, op. cit.

86. Translation as printed in Burns, op. cit., pp. 257-263.

87. Stein, Vassouras, A Brazilian Coffee County, 1850-1900, pp. 67-68.

88. Simonsen, Ensaios, p. 25.

89. Stein, Vassouras, p. 231.

90. Simonsen, Ensaios, pp. 26-27.

91. Castro Carreira, op. cit., p. 496.

92. João Pandía Calogeras, A History of Brazil, translated and edited by Percy Alvin Martin, p. 800.

93. Roberto Simonsen, Brazil's Industrial Evolution, pp. 18-24.

94. Manchester, op. cit., p. 326.

95. Nícia Vilela Luz, A Luta Pela Industrializcão do Brasil, pp. 47, 48.

96. Stein, The Cotton Textile Manufacture, p. 83.

97. Ibid., p. 82. Italics mine.

98. Ibid., p. 83.

99. Castro Carreira, op. cit., pp. 690-691.

100. Duncan, op. cit., p. 183.

101. Dorival Teixeira Vieira, "A Evolucão do Sistema Monetário Brasileiro," Revista de Administração, Año, 1, #2 (Junho de 1947), p. 376.

102. Simonsen, Ensaios, p. 29.

103. Castro Carreira, op. cit., pp. 443, 450.

104. Ibid., p. 471.

105. Ibid., p. 482.

106. Pires de Rio, op. cit., p. 123.

107. Castro Carreira, op. cit., p. 496.

108. Manchester, op. cit., p. 326.

109. Stein, Vassouras, A Brazilian Coffee County, 1850-1900, pp. 241-242.

110. Ibid., p. 244.

111. Ibid., p. 246.

112. Ibid., p. 248.

113. Simonsen, Ensaios, pp. 29-30.

114. Ibid., pp. 123-124.

115. Ibid., p. 29.

116. Haring, Empire in Brazil, p. 165.

117. Simonsen, Ensaios, p. 31.

118. Castro Carreira , op. cit., p. 568.

119. Piros do Rio, op. cit., pp. 145, 146.

120. Fernando Monteiro, O Banco de Brasil, Breve Notícia Histórica (pages not numbered).

121. Castro Carreira, op. cit., p. 716.

122. Pires do Rio, op. cit., p. 127.

123. Duncan, op. cit., p. 34.

124. Ibid., p. 36.

125. Ibid., pp. 39-40.

126. Ibid., pp. 32, 43.

127. Ibid., p. 42.

128. Ibid.

129. Castro Carreira, op. cit., appendix.

130. Pires do Rio, op. cit., pp. 132-139.

131. Ibid., p. 781.

132. Celso Furtado, The Economic Growth of Brazil, p. 136.

133. Manuel Diégues Júnior, Imigração, Urbanização e Industrialização, p. 31.

134. Diegues Junior, op. cit., pp. 32-25, 41.

135. Furtado, op. cit., p. 138.

136. Ibid., pp. 138-140.

137. Diégues Júnior, op. cit., pp. 47-49; Furtado, op. cit., p. 140.

138. Simonsen, Ensaios, p. 27.

139. Warren Dean, The Industrialization of São Paulo, 1880-1945, ch. 4.

140. Castro Carreira, op. cit., p. 253.

141. Rollie E. Poppino, Brazil, The Land and the People, p. 137.

142. Ibid., p. 140.

143. Ibid., pp. 141-142.

144. Furtado, op. cit., p. 152.

CHAPTER 11

BRAZIL: THE REPUBLIC

The cost of establishing a new government is often greater than that of maintaining an existing regime, since until authority is established, divisive groups must be paid to remain within the political fold; under an established regime, the government can threaten to withhold favors unless support continues. It follows that weak governments must spend more than strong ones to stay in power, and, further, that such expenditures may well result in severe inflations that are one of the causes of the fall of the government from power. This pattern has frequently occurred in Brazil, and was a striking characteristic of the first years of the Republic.

The abolition of slavery, in Brazil as in the United States, had provided neither indemnification for the ex-owners nor means of protection for the newly freed. The ex-owners clamored for easy credit, as the negotiable security on the basis of which they could obtain loans had just been drastically reduced. This problem was greater in the sugar-producing North, which had depended heavily on slaves, than in the coffee-producing South, which had largely shifted to free labor before abolition.[1] As elderly and ill ex-slaves starved, provision had to be made to care for them; the government was morally obligated to take over such social welfare functions as the planters had provided. The industrial and commercial sectors had long complained of the credit squeeze which accompanied the government's program of foreign borrowing, and the armed forces had to be paid off to ensure their loyalty. Thus financial policy was central to the success of the new regime.

The political background against which the encilhamento occurred was the overthrow of the empire by the army on November 15, 1889, and the institution of General Manoel Deodora da Fonseca as the de facto ruler, then president, of Brazil. A new constitution was imposed in 1891. Congress was disbanded on November 3, 1891; as a result of popular pressure, Deodoro resigned in favor of his vice president, Marshal Floriano Peixoto, on November 23, 1891. Under Deodoro's government, "the number of Army officers was more than doubled, and their paychecks were larger than they had ever been under the Empire."[2]

In order to maintain himself in power, Floriano Peixoto supported revolts against governors loyal to Deodoro, which led to armed uprisings against the new president in early 1892

and a naval revolt on September 6, 1893. The commanders of
foreign warships prevented the bombardment of Rio, and a new
navy was purchased and installed by March 13, 1894; it took
possession of the rebel's deserted ships. The Federalist
rebels were defeated; Floriano peacefully left the presidency
in 1894, which was turned over to his elected successor,
Prudente de Moraes Barros. Despite the rapid turnover in
executive personnel, there was somewhat more continuity of
ministers. Chief among them was Finance Minister Ruy Barbosa.

There are two strikingly different interpretations of
the economic policies of Ruy Barbosa. Humberto Bastos suggests
that Ruy Barbosa understood the "structuralist" arguments that
led to the adoption of unorthodox financial mechanisms to promote economic development, and therefore his speeches and acts
as finance minister form a coherent structuralist program.*
João Pandía Calogeras states that Ruy resorted to emission
of paper money, as no other solution was possible; and that he
was not entirely a free agent. Both statements are partly
correct. Ruy did understand the subscribe to much of the
structuralist argument, and therefore wanted to develop national
industry. He also was not completely a free agent, especially
with respect to the two national emergencies not foreseen in
the structuralist argument: the costs of revolution, and the
sudden agricultural credit needs following abolition. The debates and legislation under Ruy reflected and determined major
intellectual currents and shaped financial institutions. They
were at least as important for Brazil as were those of President Pellegrini of Argentina during the same period.

Brazilian recognition of the economic structure which
limited the policy choices open to it was clearly evident
long before the nation was capable of affecting that structure. For example, a Brazilian Parliamentary Commission to
study Agricultural, Industrial, and Commercial Conditions wrote
in 1866:

> Our country is a colonial factory. Without manufacturing
> industries, it is an exporter only of agricultural products
> and raw materials, which it receives afterwards in manu-
> factured products, at double their value. It is an export-
> er of money, not only because it has to pay interest on
> a huge external debt and on foreign capital invested here,
> but also because it provides the huge expenses of our citi-
> zens who live in Europe, or travel there, flaunting their
> leisure; we are not compensated for this, because foreigners

---

*The element of the structuralist analysis that is relevant
here is expenditure of funds in areas of short supply, so that
high prices induce expansion of output, economies of scale, and
eventual price reductions.

do not buy goods in Brazil with the income they earn; on the contrary, we know how much the capital they employ here costs us. A country in these circumstances must never import more than it exports.[3]

By 1880 Brazil had shifted from describing how to live within the structure to prescriptions for changing the structure. Finance Minister Ouro Preto, whose ideas and acts were criticized, but later put into practice, by his successor Ruy Barbosa, wrote:

> Magnificent in theory, the free trade school cannot fail to be proclaimed and followed by those countries whose excess of production over consumption lacks access to all markets. But, for those who encounter themselves in the conditions of Brazil, adopted as an invariable rule, would condemn themselves to a dependence and subjection at times dangerous and benumbing to their own progress. Free trade (concorrencia) presupposes equality of conditions: inferiority excludes it and makes it impossible. In this respect, it seems to me that the examples of the old world are not the ones that most suit us . . . the system adopted by the United States is the secret of its immense prosperity, and it is there that we must learn.[4]

Brazilian economic conditions entailed a great sensitivity to fluctuations in the exchange rate; pressure on the exchange rate would be reduced, according to Barbosa, by the expansion of industry, which would "assure the nation of conservation of capital developed by the exploration of its natural resources, and the activity of its inhabitants."[5] Barbosa --either wilfully or in ignorance--did not (here) consider the possibility of Brazilian producers keeping their profits in foreign exchange as protection against fluctuations in the exchange rate.

In a similar vein, he wrote that trade, especially wholesale activities (o grande comércio), was almost entirely in the hands of foreigners.

> These accumulators of wealth reserve it, in large part, for the country in which they concentrate their hopes, and where they send (retirar) their acquired capital, or the income, which, up to now, was not adequately taxed, at least to save us, for the welfare of the nation, a modest quota of these fortunes gathered at the nation's cost. This tendency constitutes a permanent factor of national depauperization, altering the balance of trade against us.[6]

The crucial question was whether Brazilian industry was
capable of taking the place of foreign capital. Since industrialists claimed that they were hampered in their growth by a
credit squeeze, the simplest way of finding out was by making
funds available to them. In 1889 Ouro Preto had given emission power to the Banco de São Paulo and Banco do Commercio
Rio de Janeiro. Ruy Barbosa, in turn, gave emission power to
the Banco de Credito Real do Brasil (Rio) up to 30,000 contos
(1 conto = 1,000,000 reis), the Sociedade de Comércio (Bahia)
up to 9,000 contos, the Banco Mercantil de Bahia, up to 15,000
contos, the Banco da Bahia, up to three times its gold fund,
the Banco de Pernambuco (Recife) up to three times its gold
fund, the Banco da União de Bahia, up to 24,000 contos, and
the Banco Pelotense (Pelotas) up to three times its gold
funds.[7] In December he decreed that these banks were required
to carry out these emissions up to the value of their specie
deposits, within three months. The banks, however, were
afraid of tying up their metallic deposits, and therefore many
of them lost their emission power; only the Banco do Brasil
and the Banco de São Paulo dared to issue bank notes. In order
to expand the money supply, a new basis of emission had to be
provided.

On January 17, 1890, banks were given the power to emit
notes based on their holdings of government securities (apolí-
ces). Barbosa created three regional banks of emission, at
Bahia in the North, Rio in the Center, and Porto Alegre in
the South, which was also meant to serve Mato Grosso and Goiaz.

> Guaranteed by securities deposited in the Treasury, the
> three banks could emit, respectively, 150, 200, and 100,000
> contos, for a total of 450,000 contos. The notes of one
> region could not circulate in another. The technique of
> emission was that the government sold its securities, which
> yielded four percent, and new notes, to the banks, which
> bought them for old notes, which the government spent.
> Thus the bank got a subsidy of four percent on its capital.
> [This 4 per cent cost of money was low for the government.]
> Depending on the exchange rate, the banks were to get
> either a government guarantee or an exchange premium.
> The mechanics of this manoeuver has been compared to the
> National Banking Act passed during the United States
> Civil War, under which national banks were required to in-
> vest at least one-third of their capital in government
> bonds, and each bank then received a new type of currency,
> national bank notes, equal to 90 per cent of the market
> value of the deposited bonds. National bank notes were
> legal tender and receivable for all obligations except
> payment of tariff duties or interest on the public debt.[8]

The parallel to the United States during the Civil War is one of more than technical arrangements. Defending his policies before the Senate on November 3, 1891, Barbosa stated:

> We decided for plurality, because we did not have a standard of selection. The torrent of federalist sentiments forced us to come to terms with needs of the States. A monopoly of bank emission, at the threat of the federalist revolution, would have been a provocation to force, against which there was not (we had no) power to fight.[9]

For this reason, nine banks received concessions under the law. As the government was under pressure from conflicting groups to increase its economic control, maintain the financial soundness of the currency, and promote the economic development of Brazil by Brazilian industrialists, its actions veered toward the achievement of first one goal, and then toward another— which was often in conflict with the first--in a series of confusing pieces of legislation. It is this series of acts, masterminded by Barbosa, that helped to earn him his "brilliant but erratic" reputation. For example, following the establishment of a plural banking system in January, the government in December decreed the creation of "one grand bank" to substitute its notes for those of the Treasury, and to absorb analagous concessions from other banks. Despite this law, the Banco do Credito Real continued to have emission facilities. The new bank, created by fusing the Banco Nacional do Brasil and the Banco do Estados Unidos do Brasil, was called the Banco da Republica dos Estados Unidos do Brasil. It was to have a capital of 200,000 contos and a duration of 60 years; it was to issue notes up to three times the value of its specie deposits, valued at the official exchange rate of 27 pence per milreis. As the milreis was, in fact, worth only 21 pence, the bank made a profit on the difference.

In 1893 further fusion of the Banco da Republica dos Estados Unidos do Brasil and the Banco do Brasil created O Banco da Republica do Brasil, which was given the right to issue currency up to twice the value of its gold reserve. The new bank and the Treasury were given joint responsibility for the money supply. Their decisions were not readily enforced because of the Federalist revolt and the civil war at Canudos.

The encilhamento lasted from 1888 to 1894. During that time, the exchange rate fell from $.51 U.S. to $.20 U.S. It continued to fall, but more slowly, until 1899, when it reached $.15 U.S. It was also true that there was extremely rapid nominal growth of industry during this period. Nominal imports of railroad equipment rose from 2,973 contos in 1888 to 3,087 in 1889, 8,741 in 1890, and 9,047 contos in the first three months of 1891. In United States dollars for the same

years, these were 1,516,232; 1,666,981; 4,020,862, and 2,714,105.
The phenomenal coffee harvest of 1888-1889, and the borrowing of
Ł20,134,300 sterling in foreign loans during 1888 and 1889, combined with the internal credit expansion, financed the boom in
which the nominal capital of new companies registered between
May 13, 1888, and November 15, 1889, equaled 402,610 contos;
the capital of companies organized during the preceding seventy-
four years equaled 410,979 contos. From November 15, 1889, to
October 20, 1890, new companies were registered with a capital
of 1,169,386 contos. The distribution of new firms by kind of
activity is shown in Table 11-1.

There was sharp debate on the soundness of the government's
policies, since there was some question as to how much of the
above represented real growth. The debates are of interest,
as they anticipate the monetarist-structuralist debates that
dominated Latin American economic circles during the 1950s and
1960s.

Ruy's defense of the Republic's financial policies was
twofold: The inflation began under the impact of policies
adopted during the last days of the empire. The Republic inherited the internal loan of 100,000 contos (August 1889), the
redemption (purchase) of paper money, stipulated by the Banco
Nacional (October), the external loan of 109,694 contos (August),
of which Brazil received 88,744 contos, and contracts with Brazilian banks for 84,500 contos which were to be used for loans
for agriculture. This gave money for seven to twenty-two years
to the banks which were required to lend twice this sum to
agriculture for one to fifteen years at 6 per cent. According
to Barbosa, this led to the prompt liquidation of assets of commercial houses linked to agriculture, and the prosperity of
favored houses who got the government credit, often using it
in speculation of stock of favored banks. Ruy had tried to end
this system by the use of new contracts. The government had
been unable to stop the speculation, as it "did not possess
a talisman by which to transform human nature, and reform the
moral habits of peoples." The government could only moderate
events, and had done so insofar as possible. Thus the origins
of the speculation lay with the empire, and not the Republic.[10]

Further, the issue of a stable exchange rate of gold-
based currency should not be approached by seeking to maintain
convertibility at par. Rather, convertibility at par was the
result of the economic prosperity of the nation. Metallists
invert the terms of the problems, and therefore their creations
are mere houses of cards. Under the gold exchange standard,
favorable balances of trade and international loans determined
the specie circulation and exchange rate. This was an extremely puerile pretension. In revolutionary times, money became
worthless, and the government would be imbecile not to intervene in the market to prevent this. "It was not, therefore,

the Republican government that killed the metallic circulation.
It was hardly an embryo, incapable of life, and died because
of the organic impossibility of living." As the banks held
government debt as backing for monetary issue, this was better
than gold for the purpose. Further, the "metal based paper
standard" led to illiquidity for commercial purposes. "To tie
up gold [in reserves] in a country whose [monetary] circulation suffers for lack of it is to introduce one more patho-
genic element to a debilitated and sick organism. On the contrary, to retire securities from the market would [be to] de-
tach private capital from this sterile investment, and divert
it to industry, and convert the government debits to an instrument of progress." Moreover, a better way of estimating
an adequate money supply (than that entailed by the gold
standard) was to divide the money supply by the population,
and to compare this to the money supply per capita in other
countries. Brazil had less money per capita than other
countries, and the fact that it was inconvertible had nothing
to do with the case.[11]

Challenging this view, Cavalcanti suggested that the
level of industrial development had something to do with the
amount of credit that should be allowed. Although he presented his view in terms used by a businessman rather than
those of an economist, it is clear that Cavalcanti believed
that a given increase in money supply would have a less inflationary result in developed countries, where an increase in demand rapidly led to an increase in quantity supplied, than it
did in underdeveloped countries, where suppliers could not
expand output as rapidly in response to price increases.

Barbosa countered this by introducing an additional set
of institutional differences between Brazil and more advanced
nations: the lack of the use of checks brought with it a
greater need for the use of money. Moreover, small firms and
the salaried class didn't use banks, while agricultural deposits were slow. The large size of the country made the
velocity of money slow. Thus, a greater money stock was needed
in Brazil than in a developed country, for the same total monetary turnover in a given year to be reached.

It was one thing to claim that industry had been stifled
by a lack of credit, and that a credit increase was necessary
to stimulate industry, regardless of the exchange rate fluctuations that were entailed in the short run, since the long-
run development of the country was of overriding importance.
It was another to attempt to finance the government wholly on
the basis of new issues of paper currency, of rapidly falling
value. Private industry, one could argue, had costs largely
payable in local currency; the government had the overriding
responsibility of service and amortization of foreign debt.
If the government were to accept payment of all taxes in paper

money, it would be unable to repay the debt. Further,
industry could always increase prices charged in paper money;
tax increases are more cumbersome to obtain. To protect its
revenues, therefore, the government required that a portion of
import duties be paid in gold, or its officially determined
equivalent. The government's position was that since the in
crease in paper money led to an increase in nominal income and
imports, payment of import duties in gold would tend to limit
them, and would serve as a specific counterweight to the in-
conveniences brought on by inconvertible paper currency. Its
advantages lay in the fact that "import duties in gold did
not necessarily tax the subsistence of the poor, as these consumed foreign goods only in relatively small quantities. Its
tendency, on the contrary, was to protect the working classes
whose interests were benefitted, by the development of national work."[12]

There were Brazilian precedents for this suggestion. From
1867 until 1869, 15 per cent of tariffs had to be paid in gold.
In 1869 these duties were revoked, and their place was taken
by a 40 per cent tax on consumption. In the law of May 1890,
20 per cent of import duties were to be paid in gold, while
the exchange rate was between 20 and 24 pence per milreis, and
10 per cent when between 24 and 27 pence. No gold quota was
to be paid when the milreis reached par. In October 1890, the
gold quota was included in total duties set, at a rate of 22
pence, in order to save time on computations of the sums due
as the exchange rate fluctuated. The fall in the exchange
rate to 14 pence in 1891 led to an increased cost in milreis
of the tariff, and "contributed to the increase in the cost of
living in Brazil. As a result, a strong current of opinion
was formed for abolition of the gold quota, which was abolished
in December, 1891. Its place was taken by an increase of fifteen per cent in the 'additional duties' on imports,"[13] which
reduced the burden of the gold quota by half.

The gold quota may have kept imports from rising even
faster; they rose steadily in real terms (1890 milreis) from
225,520 in 1890 to 311,968 in 1896. Government receipts, however, fell from 195,253 to 135,412. Brazil continued to export
more than it imported, to run a government deficit, and to
cover the deficit with foreign borrowing and new money issues.
The establishment of the Republic changed the economic rela-
tionships within Brazil more than the economic relationship
of Brazil with foreign powers, as can be seen by the doubling
of British investment in Brazil from ₤47,641 thousand in 1885
to ₤92,988 thousand in 1895 (see Table 10-10). In the latter
year, government loans absorbed 56 per cent of British investment, railways 36 per cent, public utilities 4 per cent, raw
materials 1 per cent, and industry and miscellaneous, 3 per
cent, down from the 7 per cent of the total registered in 1885,

both relatively and absolutely. This reflects both increasing
need of the government to borrow abroad, to maintain order at
home, and the ability of industry to obtain credit at home,
and therefore, of industry's decreasing need to borrow abroad.
Expansion of credit to industry was an important part of Brazil's increasing economic nationalism--which was also registered
both in the Constitution of 1891 and in the increasingly protective tariffs enacted during the 1890s.

The Constitution of February 24, 1891, replaced that of
the empire. In theory, under the empire the central government
set provincial budgets and collected the taxes,[14] although in
fact, as we have seen earlier, provincial assemblies circum-
vented the constitution and often levied taxes as they wished
to fill local needs. Economic difficulties were attributed
by the Republicans to excessive centralization. In the Constitution of 1891, they therefore provided that States generally
were to have all power not specifically denied them (Art. 65
#2). Nonetheless, since "if the Union depends on the States,
the Union is dead,"[15] some financial powers were reserved to
the central government. The financial powers of the states,
enumerated in Article 9, were taxes on export of merchandise
produced within the state, rural and urban real property,
transfers of property, industries and professions, stamp duties
on state government acts, and "contributions" on state telegraph and postal services. Traffic between the federal states
was free of all taxes, and the export tax was collected by the
states of origin of the exports. According to Conty, the export tax was the most important single tax among those collected
by the states. It was easy to collect, and was a substitute,
in part, as an indirect tax on rent (foncier), agricultural
exports being easier to evaluate than land.

The financial powers of the federal government were taxes
on imports of foreign goods, naval duties, stamp duties
(except those reserved to the states), "contributions" on federal postal and telegraph services. Banks of emission were
to be created by the federal government. Although import duties for revenue purposes were reserved to the federal government, the states were permitted to tax the importation of
foreign goods to protect local industry, but the revenue from
such taxes went to the federal government, while Congress had
the power to revise the rate of import duty set.

The state and federal governments were prohibited from
levying transit taxes. This completed the "free liberty of
commerce among the States of the Republic." A judicial decision extended this prohibition to municipalities. Article 12
of the Constitution permitted the state and federal governments to create those taxes not otherwise mentioned. Ruy Barbosa indicated that consumption taxes, income taxes, and
property taxes were envisaged under this provision.[16]

Under the conditions of strong regionalism which obtained
in the 1890s, it is unlikely that union of all parts of Brazil
to the Republic could have been obtained unless states had
economic independence of the federal government and control
over export collection, which had provided 12 per cent of imperial government revenue, and, after the foundation of the Republic, contributed just under half of the states' revenue.
Thus "the prosperity of the States was now tied directly to
the volume of exports"; state actions and pressure on the central government to favor export promotion could be expected
to increase with the promulgation of the Constitution of 1891.
At the same time, the federal government--according to Poppino
--"could not erect an effective tariff wall against foreign
manufactures without risking a sharp reduction in its reven-
nues."[17] The latter statement seems a bit sweeping. When the
quantity demanded of imports is constant, regardless of price,
a tax increase would yield increased revenue to the government, but no decline in quantity purchased. In the case where
the same amount of funds is spend on imports, whether a few
at a high price or many at a low price, then a tax increase
will yield both a revenue increase to the government and a
decline in quantity of foreign goods purchased, so that protection to domestic industry could be achieved without reducing
federal government revenue. Only in cases where demand for imports was such that the increase in price yielded a decrease
in quantity of imports to an extent that total revenue fell
would the government have to reduce its tariff rates to maintain its revenue collections, at the cost of reduced protection of domestic industry. One might expect that tariffs
set on various imports would depend on the relative strength
of the various industrial groups, and that there would be
considerable variation among them in the tariff treatment they
received from the government.
    In fact, there was a continued protectionist tendency
in Brazilian tariff legislation, but the degree and objects
of protection varied with political influence and the state of
government finances. In 1890 the government imposed a light
tariff increase in order to finance its deficit. There was no
general law covering exemptions from import duties, and the
law of 1890 stipulated only that such exemptions should not
include articles similar to those produced in the country and
whose production could be sufficient to supply the domestic
market. This was promulgated despite the fact that imported
machinery was already exempt from tariff duties and only subject
to an "expedition tax" of 5 per cent. Exemptions from duties
were arranged by special laws, budget laws, and contracts with
individual enterprises. This system, naturally, gave rise
to favoritism, the proliferation of administrative interces-
sion, as well as diminishing the national treasury. It was

alleged that beneficiaries of special privileges imported
goods in excess of their own needs for resale. In 1892 pro-
industrial sentiment reached new heights, and the legislature
enacted a law which reduced, by 30 per cent, duties on
machines, work implements, agricultural machines, raw materials, dyestuffs, chemicals used in industry, and other articles used in industrial operation, despite the fact that this
law in effect voted a reduction on taxes which did not exist!
At the same time, a light increase in taxes levied on luxury
goods was imposed. The haphazard imposition of tariffs gave
way in 1896 to a protectionist tariff reform, a major aim
of which was the development of industries based on Brazilian
raw materials. The new tariff rates were calculated on the
basis of 12 pence per milreis, not the preceding 24 pence; the
increase in effective rate brought about by this change was
estimated at 25 per cent. Special protection was given to
beer, matches, and cotton spinning and weaving. The tariff
remained in effect for only two years.[18]

   After 1896, the absolute level of import duties collected
fell, and total government revenue along with it, because the
price of coffee fell sharply from the high of Ł4.09 per sack
of 60 kilos in 1893 to Ł1.48 per sack in 1899. The increase
in coffee production was not great enough to counteract the
price fall, and total export receipts in constant (1890) milreis fell from 348,007 contos in 1895 to 267,878 contos in
1898, and not recovering the 1895 level until 1901. Although
the state, not the federal government collected export duties,
federal revenues suffered, since the fall in export earnings
led to a fall in imports, which fell, in constant 1890 milreis, from 311,968 contos in 1895 to 180,601 contos in 1901,
not recovering their 1895 level until 1905. As the federal
government depended on import duties, the sharp fall in imports
created a financial crisis. As export earnings fell, the government's difficulties in meeting its external obligations
increased, and the cost of foreign exchange increased with it.
Tbe cost of obtaining imports also increased, giving rise to
the complaint that only if the coffee harvest were highly profitable could the country afford to protect Brazil's industrial
sector. Tariff revision was turned over to a commission headed
by a well-known free-trade advocate, Leopoldo de Bulhões, who
designed the tariff of 1897 which reduced Brazilian tariffs, on
the whole, by 25 per cent, while rates on individual articles
were reduced by as much as 75 to 85 per cent. Industrialists
complained bitterly of the new competition; they modified their
position, however, to favor tariffs less onerous to the consumer, and to be levied on goods produced by already existing
"viable" Brazilian industries, the attempt to create Brazilian production of goods by levying tariff duties on foreign
supplies being dropped for the time being. The government's

interests were almost overwhelmingly financial. Its major
tariff program simplified tariff classification schemes,
unified rates, and increased the efficiency of tariff collection. In some cases, to increase revenue, rates were raised,
so that increased protection was a by-product of the government's search for funds. Thus the tariff of 1900 was characterized by rates of 50 per cent, and a number of levies from
60 to 80 per cent of value. The share of duties collected
in gold was raised by the tariff to 25 per cent of the total.[19]
The changeable history of the Brazilian tariff indicates that
Poppino's statement that the federal government "could not
erect an effective tariff wall against foreign manufactures
without risking a sharp reduction in its revenues" does not
stand, in all cases examined.

The heavy dependence on import duties led the government to search for additional sources of revenue less vulnerable to the fluctuations in foreign trade. A variety of
"extraordinary" taxes provided a large share of government
revenue in 1890 and 1891. They continued to be levied in one
form or another; by the end of the decade, the most important
of them were the income from the sale of national property,
the tax on industries and professions, and the tax on the
transmission of property.

Pressing military expenditures from 1892 to 1896 impelled the government to impose a 10 per cent "additional"
tax on the "expedition" of goods free of existing import,
lighthouse and waterfront duties. The Brazilian government
also adopted the same expedient utilized by the Argentine
government in that epoch, by establishing consumption taxes.
These became increasingly important, so that they contributed
7.1 per cent of government revenue in 1897, and 11.9 per cent
in 1900, when tobacco, drinks, matches, salt, shoes, candles,
perfumes, drugs, vinegar, conserves, playing cards, hats,
muslin, and thin cloth were taxed.[20] (See Table 11-2.)

Interior taxes provided about one fifth of government
revenue during the 1890s. This category included income from
government-owned railroads, mail and telegraph services, the
transport tax and the stamp tax, as well as a host of minor
levies. Since taxes on exports were levied on groups whose
income was above the national average, and sales taxes were
paid by all Brazilians with enough money to buy matches or
shoes, the abolition of the export tax at the federal level
and its substitution by the sales tax decreased the progressive-
ness of the national government's tax structure during the
1890s. Although export taxes were paid to the states, it is
likely that exporters exerted greater influence at the state
than at the national level, so that the level of export duties levied may well have been less than it would have been
had such duties continued to be controlled by the federal

government. The overall tax collection system increased in
regressiveness following the establishment of the Republic.
The "class" attitude of the price-gouging planter who over-
charged his ex-slaves on goods he sold them, declaring "The
government robbed me of my slaves. Now the Negroes are going
to pay me back"[21] influenced national as well as local policy.
The government's expenditure pattern, because of the local
revolts, was of less immediate economic benefit than it had
been under the empire. War expenses rose, as did those of
the Treasury for borrowed funds. Direct expenditure on public
works, commerce, and roads fell from over 30 per cent to one
fifth of the total in 1897 (see Table 11-3).

The government ran a deficit in all years from 1890 to
1898, except for 1891. Measured in 1890 milreis, the real
deficit fell, except in 1894, and its per capita burden shrank
as the population grew from 14,333,915 in 1890 to 17,438,434
in 1900, as immigration continued despite the revolts. Despite
the break in coffee prices, Brazil continued to export more
goods and services than it imported in amounts greater than the
budget deficits. The relative stability of the exchange rate
gave way to a rapid fall in the price of Brazilian currency
from $.46 U.S. in 1890 to $.30 in 1891, $.24 in 1892, and
$.15 in 1898, reflecting the serious financial difficulties
which accompanied the encilhamento. These difficulties were
in part attributable to Ruy Barbosa's successor as minister of
finance, Alencar Araripe, who took office in 1891, and of whom
Bello wrote:

> at no time did he show any interest in the affairs of
> his department. Wishing to recast the policies of his
> predecessor, who had become the target of every kind of
> criticism, made in good faith and bad, he compounded
> Ruy's possible errors to the extreme. . . . The banks
> kept issuing currency without even bothering to print
> paper bills, using instead those of the Treasury, on
> which they simply imposed their own imprint. Bankrupt-
> cies followed one after another, and security values
> dropped. Public confidence was badly shaken.
>
> Lucena, the de facto head of government, took over
> the Ministry of Finance, but did not improve matters.
> He cancelled the payment of customs in gold and sold
> or loaned the Treasury's gold to more or less insolvent
> banks. The merger of the Banco do Brasil with the
> Banco dos Estados Unidos do Brasil (both in bad shape),
> the issuing of 100,000 contos in Treasury bonds for
> "national industries," the reorganization of the Banco
> da Republica with permission to issue up to 600,000
> contos, and the failure of the General Railroad Company
> with liabilities in excess of 300,000 contos were the

chief fiscal events of the Lucena government's time in office.[22]

The government, unable to obtain enactment of its financial reform measures, obtained a loan of one million pounds sterling from the Rothschilds, repayable in eighteen months, and took possession of a 4 million pounds sterling loan granted to the Minas Railroad company in 1893. The Treasury was permitted to issue up to 100,000 contos in bonds to meet the needs of industry and agriculture; the amount of Treasury currency in circulation increased. The government began to rely heavily on foreign loans, and continued to do so until the Great Depression. The government raised £9,293,700 net of commission and interest charges from 1893 to 1895; the repayment obligation increased by £11,520,000. An attempt to increase Brazil's tax collection capacity had been made in December 1892 by then Finance Minister Serzedelo Correia, who reorganized the administrative structure of the Treasury.[23] This was followed by an attempt to reestablish control over the money supply in 1896, which stripped the Banco da Republica do Brasil of its emission powers. Treasury notes were to replace bank notes. The Treasury notes were to be based on one third of the revenue from the sale of government securities, loans from the Banco da Republica, and railroad profits.[24] In addition, the government issued an internal loan of 60,000 contos. From the establishment of the Republic to 1897, the banks and the Treasury had increased currency in circulation by 583 million, so that the money supply quadrupled in nine years. The increase in expenditures from protracted wars and the catastrophic break in coffee prices left the government virtually bankrupt. The financial crisis facing the government was thrown into relief when Congress voted a budget for 1898 that carried with it an estimated deficit of £5,408,000 (48,606 contos in gold).

> The sale of warships to the United States, then at war with Spain over the liberation of Cuba, and the conversion into 5 per cent paper bonds of the 4 per cent internal gold loan, reduced the deficit by about 1 million pounds. The government would have to acquire the remaining 4 million pounds in the open exchange market, which was then being juggled by the foreign banks. Congress had calculated the cost of converting paper into gold at the 1897 average rate of 8 pence to the milreis. The rate had since fallen to 5 pence. The paper needed to meet the gold demands, including a Treasury note of 1 million pounds that would fall due that year, therefore amounted to 240,000 contos out of a total gross revenue estimated at 343,000 contos.[25]

The Treasury could not meet these commitments; rather
than obtain a foreign loan under conditions reflecting Brazil's poor credit rating, the Brazilian government decided to
follow the precedent set by President Sáenz Peña of Argentina,
who had refunded Argentina's external debt. In April 1898 the
president elect of Brazil, Manuel Ferraz de Campos Sales,
sailed for Europe. The London bankers themselves proposed a
settlement, as British capital invested in Brazil amounted to
more than 80 million pounds.

> They proposed a loan of 10 million pounds, to be guaran-
> teed by all of Brazil's customs duties, and by the reve-
> nue of the Central Railroad of Brazil and of the water
> supply services in Rio de Janeiro. For its part, the
> government was to withdraw from circulation paper equal
> to the value of each loan installment, figured at 12
> pence per milreis. This paper was to be turned over to
> the foreign banks, in trust, and burned in public. The
> government would further agree not to contract any new
> debts during the period of the moratorium.
> In London, Campos Sales obtained from the Rothschilds
> some changes in their original proposal. The rate of ex-
> change for the paper currency withdrawn from circulation
> was set at 18 pence instead of 12; the time allowed for
> interest payments was increased to three years, and for
> amortization payments to ten years; and the special guaran-
> tees for the loan were limited to the customs duties col-
> lected in Rio de Janeiro, the other customs houses becom-
> ing subsidiary. Although the government planned to burn
> the paper money, it was to have the option of leaving it
> on deposit to be used to purchase future bills of ex-
> change.26

The Funding Loan of £10,000,000 was sold at par; after
deduction of interest costs and commission charges, Brazil
netted £8,613,717. The bonds bore interest at 5 per cent,
and amortization payments, beginning after ten years, for one-
half per cent. The loan was to run for 63 years.27
The Funding Loan bailed Brazil out of its immediate difficulties. It also permitted foreigners to determine an
important aspect of Brazilian economic policy, and tied future
income to repayment of the loan, thus reducing the flexibil-
ity of the government in fnancial and tax matters, as ear-
marked taxes rose from 5 per cent of government revenue in
1900 to 26 per cent in 1904, gradually falling to 11.5 per
cent in 1914.
The government's financial difficulties determined its
railroad policy as well as its monetary policy. The government had issued interest guarantee contracts to railroad

companies, many of which were denominated in gold. Moreover,
railroads could profit from the decree of October 16, 1890,
declaring that "if the capital is obtained in a foreign country to rate of exchange in all operations shall be 27 pence
to one milreis."[28] The depreciation of the milreis from 1889
to 1898 increased the amount of milreis needed to pay the gold
obligations due. It has been estimated that the additional
amount needed for this purpose in 1898 was equal to 110,000,000
milreis ($16,038,000 U.S., 1898 prices) of a total budget of
343,000,000 milreis. The increasing interest burden impelled
the government to reduce its commitments payable in gold.
The line of action finally adopted had been suggested by the
Minister of Communications in 1891, who argued that the government should rent the lines it already owned, recapture lines
having guarantees of interest, and, once recaptured, rent these
also. The minister believed that government operation was more
costly, "first, by reason of the greater number of employees
under government administration, and second, by reason of the
provision of pensions and other benefits, not furnished by private companies, which must be provided for government employees."
These costs resulted in only one government-owned line yielding a net operating profit.[29]

In 1896, the railroad law enacted stated that "in order
to reduce the amount of paper money in conformity with the law
of the 11th of September 1846 and also to repay the foreign
debt and better the financial situation of the country, the
government is authorized to rent, following the submission of
competitive bids, the railways of the government.[30] The rental
policy set provided for the payment of a fixed sum on rental,
and a payment based on an annual percentage pf the net operating income, to be worked out as the circumstances warranted
in each case, and for tariff schedules movable with the exchange rate.[31]

The recapture aspect of the government's railroad policy
was put into effect beginning in 1900. At that time, the total mileage having guarantees of interest payable in gold
was 3,110 kilometers and the total annual net burden was
Ł964,248 sterling. By 1902, 2,148 kilometers were recaptured;
the price paid was Ł14,605,000 sterling in government bonds
payable in gold and bearing interest at 4 per cent. The last
operation in this plan was carried out in 1905, when the total
amount of mileage having an interest guarantee payable in gold
was reduced to 903 kilometers, and the total annual net burden
to Ł235,195 sterling.[32] The rental of the railroads was carried out to permit one firm to control many lines and construct
others within a region, thus facilitating uniformity of road
gauges and increasing the efficiency of railroad operation within
each region.

Although the interest guarantee burden was heavy, and the

cost of government operation of railroads high during the
first ten years of the Republic, the railroad net increased
from 9,583 kilometers in 1889 to 15,680 in 1902, and contributed to Brazil's increasing export production. This railroad policy was carried out through the end of the period
studied. By 1914 the government's consolidation policy led
to the establishment of four major railroad systems in Brazil:
Great Western of Brazil Railway (1,476 km.), centered in Recife; Companhia Ferroviaria Este Brasileiro (1,708 km.) centered in Bahia; Red Sul Mineiro (1,249 km.); and Viação Fer-
rea do Rio Grande do Sul (2,172 km.). Railroad gauge was made
uniform between São Paulo and Rio; a total of 26,062 kilometers
were constucted by 1914 under gold guarantees, construction
contracts with renting companies, and guarantees payable in
paper currency. The extent of the government policy of increasing its owned mileage through recapture, and increasing
private operation through renting, is seen in Table 11-4.

The government's policy of requiring the railroads to
collect export taxes on goods shipped on them led to complaints
by the railroads, who believed that their customers failed to
distinguish between tax payments and freight charges. Spokes-
men for the Great Western argued in 1909 that freight charges
were lower than tax payments, as shown in Table 11-5. The
relatively low transport charges were probably a major factor
in stimulating production for export, the growth of which
was essential to the government's financial policy. Under
President Campos Sales (1898-1902), this consisted of obtaining foreign funds and reducing the amount of domestic currency
outstanding. This was supplemented by reduction of foreign
claims against Brazil. Campos Sales' policy was successful
in improving the exchange rate for Brazilian currency. Its
effect on the condition of the Brazilian economy, and on the
inflow of foreign funds, must also be considered for a full
understanding of the impact of this policy.

The inflow of foreign funds depended both on conditions
in the supplying and in the borrowing country. Until World
War I, Britain was the most important supplier of funds to
Brazil. The inflow of British funds had virtually doubled
between 1885 and 1895, but increased by only a third in the
following decade. British income increased 30 per cent from
1885 to 1895 (42 per cent in real terms), and 23 per cent
from 1895 to 1905 (11 per cent in real terms), so that supply
conditions indicate that the rate of growth of British investment in foreign countries would have declined unless foreign
investment opportunities became spectacularly more attractive
than those in Britain. The demand for British funds increased
as the increase in the rate of supply fell, especially because
of British expenditure on the Boer War, which limited the availability of funds for investment. The overall share of Latin

America in net new issues fell from 25.45 per cent in 1886-1895 to 12.14 per cent in 1896-1905.[33] Since net new calls in the British market were almost constant (₺768,307 from 1886 to 1895 and ₺789,986 from 1896 to 1905), the British invested more in Brazil than they did in most other Latin American countries during 1896-1905, but less than they did in the rest of the world, in comparison with their investment patterns in the preceding decade.

The Brazilian government's preoccupation with reducing its foreign exchange interest burden had led it to reacquire railroads with interest guarantees denominated in gold. British holdings of Brazilian railways decreased from ₺33,314 in 1895 to ₺24,022 in 1905. It is not clear if the money received for the railroad shares was reinvested in other sectors of the Brazilian economy or used for other purposes. The largest increases in British investment were directed to government loans, raw materials, and public utilities. Interest in investment in industry remained minimal. Since government foreign debt operations were exclusively directed to debt consolidation and lowering foreign currency obligations of the government, the Campos Sales regime clearly was less able to obtain productive foreign investment than had its predecessors, whose foreign-bond-financed railroad extensions had massively increased the productive capacity of Brazil, as reflected in an increase of 35 per cent in quamtum of exports from 1885 to 1895, compared to the 20 per cent increase from 1895 to 1905. A defense of Campos Sales' policies therefore must rest on the dubious assumptions that (1) a rising price for Brazilian currency was necessary to obtain foreign investment; (2) new foreign investment was either greater in quantity or more strategic in category of investment than would be domestic investment that dried up in the liquidity crisis provoked by the terms of the funding loan; and (3) that export activity stimulated by foreign investment was greater in amount and qualitatively more important than any other category of activity that would have attracted domestic capital.

The effect of the Campos Sales economic program on the Brazilian economy was to cause immediately a crisis because of the decrease in available credit. Money in circulation fell from 779,966,000 milreis in 1898 to 675,547,000 in 1902. On a per capita basis, money supply fell from 46 to 36 milreis. Although the value of the milreis increased from .15 to .24 (U.S.), the crucial point for local businessmen was that debts had been contracted in milreis with a lower purchasing power, and that they had to pay them off at a time when prices were falling; a number of firms that would have required constant or rising prices to survive therefore failed.   As the government accepted Social Darwinism, these failures were accepted as a natural consequence of the competitive struggle, and, ultimately beneficial to the nation. The most spectacular and important failure which followed the cancellation of emission powers by the Brazilian Congress on July 20, 1899, was that of the Banco da República in 1900.

The government's revenue policies were clearly at the expense of the lower classes, and perhaps only accidentally beneficial to domestic industry. The percentage of import duties payable in gold was increased from 10 to 15 per cent in 1899, and in the following year, the tax system was thoroughly revised. While duties on imports were raised, the share payable in gold in 1900 rising to 25 per cent,35 ostensibly for revenue purposes, the protection that this gave to domestic manufactures was in part limited by the increase in taxes on domestic goods which were levied at the same time. Thus the government's tax policy limited foreign competition, but, by taxing domestic products, also limited the size of the domestic market for Brazilian manufactures. Local industry was therefore harmed both by a credit shortage and an increase in taxes, which, on balance, were probably more important than the tariff protection, since foreign credit went to the agricultural sector rather than to manufactures. The relative importance of industry within Brazil appears likely to have declined to the extent that government policy affected the balance between industry and agriculture. If the new foreign investment in the years immediately following Campos Sales was more than the domestic investment that would have been possible in the absence of the credit shortage, then the Campos Sales policies would have led to higher levels of income at a lower degree of economic development, and with greater dependence on world markets.

On balance we conclude, however, that the policy of exchange rate stabilization carried out by Brazil was better than that carried out by Mexico because it was accompanied by a greater degree of protection of Brazilian industry than was Mexico's (see vol. 1, p. 158). Thus Campos Sales was merely booed as he left office, while the protracted unemployment in Mexico led to the Mexican Revolution. The Brazilians were also luckier in that they undertook their stabilization policy earlier and therefore had a breathing space of four to five years before they were faced with the additional hardships of the 1907 recession. Finally, the Brazilian policy was closer to that of Argentina than that of Mexico. In the latter country, silver had been used as a means of payment. In Argentina and Brazil, metal did not circulate. In Brazil, the "gold" quota of taxes was calculated in terms of "gold milreis," whose price was set by the government in terms of paper milreis. A greater number of paper milreis was therefore used to pay the "gold" quota of taxes; gold itself was

not paid. The government thus obtained greater taxes, but
not a greater supply of foreign exchange with which to dis-
charge its external debt. The system of foreign borrowing
and higher taxes would work only if (1) the loans were used
to increase the productive capacity of Brazil, and (2) the
price of foreign exchange were roughly constant. The loans
obtained under Campos Sales indirectly contributed to an increased productive capacity of Brazil. Funds borrowed by
the government where overwhelmingly directed to port and railroad construction. Increased confidence in the Brazilian
economy was indicated by the increase in share of total investment funds obtained by private groups, especially for investment in public utilities and finance, both of which served to
provide the infrastructure needed for industrial expansion.

The government's development policy was largely restricted
to external debt and monetary matters, and railroad promotion
and regulation; direct government expenditure for economic
development was limited by heavy Treasury expenses incurred
by its previous borrowing and striking increases in military
expenditures from 1900 to 1909. The government of Rodrigues
Alves (1902-1906), in addition to railroad and port works,
reconstructed Rio de Janeiro, opening new streets, widening
others, constructing parks. Even more important, it largely
eliminated yellow fever and smallpox. Despite protests,
and issuance of writs "to protect the inviolability of private domiciles against the housecleaning efforts of public
workers," the government managed to eliminate yellow fever
within three years. While the government overcame the opposition to the "mosquito swatters," it had considerably more
difficulty over compulsory innoculation against smallpox. A
league founded to oppose compulsory vaccination became the
center of revolutionary activities against the government;
street riots broke out on November 10, 1904, and spread to
the Military Academy, where the rebellion was largely crushed
on November 15. The government remained in office, and health
began to improve, despite the wishes of much of the population!

Rodrigues Alves also managed a political and economic
coup by acquiring the territory of Acre, on the disputed border
with Bolivia. The territory of Acre was the most productive
of Brazil's rubber exporting regions; rubber accounted for
some 20 per cent of the nation's exports. Although nomimally
Bolivian, the area was settled mainly by Brazilians. The
uncertainty of sovereignty and control had been highlighted by a se-
aratist revolt in 1895, and was thrown into full relief by an odd
expedient adopted by Bolivia in 1901. The government, unable
to govern Acre, had signed a contract in 1901 with a group of
North Americans, called the Bolivian Syndicate, which gave them
civil control of Acre and the right to exploit all of the disputed territory. The prospect of "Yankee Imperialism" on the

Brazilian border was unwelcome. A Brazilian rebellion in 1902
succeeded in gaining control of the region. The Bolivians
rescinded the contract with the syndicate, which, it turned
out, had been bought out for £126,000 by the Rodrigues Alves
government. In 1903, the Treaty of Petropolis gave Brazil
69,500 square miles in exchange for an indemnity of £2,000,000
paid to Bolivia and a commitment to build a railroad from
Bolivia to the Madeira River in Brazil, giving Bolivia an out-
let to the Atlantic.

Rodrigues Alves was clearly committed to increase
Brazil's export capacity. He was not committed to the special
interests of Brazil's exporters when they conflicted with his
general development plans. Thus an area of conflict was
monetary policy. Rodrigues Alves was committed to a high and
stable price for foreign exchange. Exporters, however, benefited from a falling or low rate of exchange, which gave them
an increased amount of milreis for each unit of foreign currency earned. In 1906 the coffee crop reached 22 million bags;
4 million remained unsold from previous crops, and the annual
demand was 10 million, which left 16 million bags in excess of
world consumption, which threatened to force future coffee
prices still lower. The coffee growers asked for government
help to control surplus stocks in order to maintain prices,
and also for price supports and a special rate of 12 pence per
milreis for coffee transactions. (The going rate was 16 pence
per milreis, so that coffee exporters would obtain a 25 per
cent advantage in converting their foreign exchange earnings
to milreis if their plan was adopted.)

The governors of the three most important coffee-growing
states, São Paulo, Rio de Janeiro, and Minas Gerais, met in
Taubaté in São Paulo in 1906 and agreed to support coffee
prices, but failed to first clear the agreement that they signed
with the federal government. The three states obligated themselves to maintain a price of 55 to 65 gold francs per bag
delivered to their ports for export, and also to hold back bags
delivered in excess of world consumption. They were to promote
coffee production and establish grading procedures. A tax
of three francs in gold per bag was to be levied on coffee exported, and used to pay interest and amortization on special
loans obtained to finance the coffee price stabilization scheme.

The president, Rodrigues Alves, refused to endorse the
scheme and rejected the proposed special exchange rate for coffee, stating that it threatened to disrupt the government's
ability to maintain the exchange rate. His analysis of the
consequences of the proposed policy was correct; this did not
prevent his successor in office, Afonso Pena (1906-1909),
from adopting it. The desire of the coffee interests for
government protection of their revenue, combined with the usual
protectionist clamors of industry, united the two sectors,

which had previously fought each other's claims, in a dis-
avowal of classic economic theory in favor of government in-
tervention.   The new president declared that "the state's high
mission also embraces caring for the people's welfare and bet-
tering their lives; it must act beneficently in social matters
whenever individual initiative, in its various forms, shows
itself to be incapable or insufficient."[36]   The government therefore was dedicated to stimulating the economy through protective tariffs, increased immigration, and development of internal
communications.   The newest initiative was that of establishing
a special department for "peopling the land" and agencies to
recruit immigrants in Europe.   The agencies were remarkably
successful; immigration, which had reached a low point of
32,941 in 1903, stood at 72,332 in 1906; 86,751 in 1910; and
190,333 in 1913.   Despite the dominance in the popular mind
of Italian and German immigration to Brazil, the largest
groups entering Brazil from 1903 to 1913 were Portuguese and
Spanish.

     It was possible for the government to carry out its com-
mitment to the coffee exporters at least in part because a
series of small harvests and increasing world income led to
higher prices for coffee, which rose from Ł1.82 in 1907 to
Ł3.85 per sack in 1912.   The foreign exchange value of coffee
rose by 3/7, so that it was not difficult for the government
to repay the 3 million pounds sterling borrowed to finance
the Taubaté agreement.   The part of the agreement not approved
by Rodrigues Alves had stated that

> Article 7.   The products of the surtax, referred to in
> the preceding article, will be collected by the union,
> and is destined to the payment of interest and amortiza-
> tion of the capital necessary for the execution of this
> convention, the surpluses being applied to defray the
> expenses demanded by the services of the said convention,
> and the collection of the surtax will begin after the
> realization of the dispositions contained in article 8.
> Article 8.   For the execution of this convention the
> State of S. Paulo is from this date authorized to pro-
> mote in this country or abroad, with the guarantee of
> the surtax of three francs referred to in article 6, and
> with the conjoint responsibility of the three States the
> necessary credit operations up to the amount of 15 mil-
> lions sterling, which will be applied as a gold reserve
> for the department for the emission and conversion of
> gold notes, which may be created by Congress for the
> fixing of the value of the currency.   The product of the
> emission against this reserve will be applied, in the
> terms of this convention, to the regularization of the
> coffee trade and its valorization, without prejudice to
> other endowments created by law.[37]

The details of the monetary reform adopted by Afonso
Pena were slightly different from those proposed in the Taubaté convention. The legal standard from the empire of 27
pence per milreis was maintained (32 milreis per ounce of 22
carat gold). The government set up a conversion fund into
which proceeds from foreign loans, and foreign currencies
entering Brazil, were to be deposited. Against this deposit,
paper could be issued at the rate of one milreis per 15 pence,
up to a limit of 20 million pounds. The Treasury's reserves
were to be added to the fund, and, whenever the exchange rate
rose to legal parity (27 pence), the conversion fund's paper
would be redeemed at the fixed rate.[38] As both the value of
foreign exchange in Brazilian currency and the price of coffee
declined, the stabilization scheme prevented the further rise
in the value of Brazilian currency, and thus benefited coffee exporters. This move, coupled with the increase in tariff
revenues, also aided industrial producers by increasing the
protection they had against foreign competition. With the end
of the Boer War (1902), foreign investment increased. While
coffee exporters benefited from the ability to obtain the currency issued by the Conversion Office, the nation's importers
were able to obtain more foreign exchange per milreis for the
Treasury's inconvertible paper money. Brazil, in fact, was
on a two-currency system, which it had increasing difficulty
in maintaining. In 1909 President Pena died, and was succeeded by his vice president, Nilo Peçanha, who did not share
all of the former president's views. European funds piled up
in the Conversion Office beyond the amounts anticipated, so
that as gold was acquired, new paper money was not issued.
The new president and his finance minister adhered to the
classical theory of economic analysis, and therefore set the new
rate of currency conversion at 16 pence per milreis, which was
the actual free market rate, and increased the amount of gold
legally acceptable by the Conversion Office to 60 million
pounds. At the same time, the Funding Loan repayments were
begun a year earlier than stipulated in the Campos Sales agreement. Thus as much as domestic political pressure permitted,
Nilo Peçanha reduced Brazil's foreign indebtedness and worked
toward the establishment of money markets free of government
interference.

The following regime, of Hermes da Fonseca (1910-1914),
was less successful in its economic performance than that of
Nilo Peçanha because of the coffee stabilization scheme it
inherited, the break in the rubber market, and the economic
disruption caused by World War I. Loans of ₤7.5 and ₤4.2
million were negotiated in 1914 in order to support the price
of coffee under the Taubaté agreement. Annual monetary increases of 800-900,000 contos had been absorbed by the nation's
economic expansion. However, the fall in the quantity of

exports produced after 1910 reduced the nation's foreign
exchange supply, and meant that large new issues of paper
money could not be absorbed, but instead would cause a fall
in the price of Brazilian currency in terms of foreign exchange. The foreign exchange crisis that resulted was
produced because the value of exports fell 1/7 in 1913, and
2/7 in 1914. This led to a deficit in the balance of payments in 1913 and a 50 per cent decline in imports in 1914.
The value of Brazilian currency declined by one third, while
the government deficits increased from 46,386 contos to
222,898 (in 1890 reis) from 1908 to 1914 (see Table 11-6).

The government raised a foreign loan of ₤11 million in
1913 to meet its expenses. When attempts to raise additional
foreign funds were unsuccessful in 1914, the government suspended the redemption of its notes, and relied on printing
money. The government then obtained a second funding loan of
₤14,502,396 in 1914. Interest payments on the loan were
postponed for three years and amortization payments for thirteen years. At this time, inconvertible Treasury money
amounted to almost one million contos, and Conversion Fund
notes to only 150,000 contos.[39]

Although Brazil was seriously harmed by the decline in
its share of world rubber exports, and the onset of World
War I, the effectiveness of economic policy under the Republic was greater than that under the empire. Exports grew
80.5 per cent from 1889 to 1914, compared to a 7.5 per cent
decline from 1870 to 1889.

The government policies could be viewed as successful
if Brazil grew at least as rapidly as other countries in a
similar stage of development. Although gross national
product estimates according to sector or origin are not
yet available before 1920, information is available on which
a tentative opinion can be based. Looking first at industrial growth, it is clear that the most important manufactures until the twentieth century were textiles, whose manufacture grew remarkably during the 1890s. In 1950 there had
been perhaps 50 industrial firms in Brazil. In 1889 there were
636 establishments with a capital of 401,631 contos. By 1895
there were 1,088 firms with a capital of 613,345 contos.
Some notion of the growth of the manufacturing center is given
in the details of São Paulo's expansion. In 1888 São Paulo had
ironworks, oil factories, founderies, sugar mills, lime kilns,
sawmills, furniture works, hat factories, paper factories,
drink processing plants, and milk processing plants. By
1901 São Paulo had 165 industrial firms, of which 60 had been
founded in the preceding twelve years. The new firms were devoted to new lines of goods; they operated using more than
50,000 workmen, of whom the largest number were Italian.[40]   In
1907 the Centro Industrial do Brasil carried out the first

census of Brazilian industry, which indicated that there
were 3,258 manufacturing firms in the country. They employed
151,841 workers. The results are not completely consistent
with the 1901 data for São Paulo: in 1907, São Paulo reported
326 establishments with 15,426 workers. The value of manufactures produced in Brazil was 477,747 contos; the value of manufactured goods imported into Brazil was 133,196 contos. Although São Paulo occupied third place with respect to manufacturing in Brazil (behind the federal district and Minas Gerais),
the increasing profitability of the São Paulo region, financed
under the Taubaté agreement, led to rapid industrial expansion, so that by 1910, São Paulo had become the leading industrial area of Brazil. São Paulo continued to contribute more
to the national treasury than it received from it. Cincinato
Braga claimed that from 1856 to 1914, the net contribution of
São Paulo was Rs. 1,521,020 contos.[41] Although industrial
growth from 1907 to 1910 throughout Brazil had been slow, due
to the recession of 1907 and the defeat of an increase in the
level of tariffs, 166 new firms appeared; with world economic
recovery, Brazil grew too; its number of manufacturing plants
doubled between 1910 and 1915. By 1914 the nominal value of
Brazilian manufacturing production reached 956,667 contos of
reis ($U.S. 277,433,430 in 1914 prices), of which 30.7 per cent
was produced in São Paulo. The doubling of manufacturing
output from 1907 to 1914 implies an average annual growth
rate of 12.4 per cent. At the same time, price supports to coffee could be expected to increase the number of persons attracted to coffee producing, and to increase the quantity of
coffee produced. Further, the cacao boom had begun, with
virgin lands, cheap labor, and few competitors. A weak spot
was the declining importance of the Brazilian rubber industry
on the world market. The British smuggled the seed of a rubber tree out of Brazil to Malaya and Ceylon; this formed the
basis of Oriental rubber production, which passed that of
Brazil in 1913 and was more than twice Brazil's rubber production in 1914.[42] Rubber produced in the Orient was not subject
to the natural enemies it faced in Brazil, so that Asian production was more efficient. The rubber-producing North of
Brazil suffered a severe decline as a consequence of its inability to meet the new competition.

The overall price index for exports from 1870 to 1914
increased by 20 per cent; the quantity index increased by 68
per cent. In regard to obtaining heavy machinery, Brazil
still was in an export or die situation. Manufacturing continued to be concentrated in light industry, especially textiles and food processing.

Although Brazil was not a modern industrial nation in
1914, the groundwork had been laid for considerable economic
growth. The end of slavery made rapid immigration of skilled

workers possible. The government had promoted railroads,
provided credit facilities, and protected some of its manufacturers and its leading exporters. A domestic market for
Brazilian manufactures was created by these measures (although some of the coffee subsidy funds were spent abroad),
and by the increased wages earned by ex-slaves and immigrants.
The government's greatest failure was in its lack of adequate
provision of educational facilities and in its regressive
tax structure.

Brazil's economic policy was superior to that of Mexico
during this period, while its manufacturing growth rate was
greater than that of Argentina from 1907 to 1914. Although
Argentina was probably richer than Brazil in 1914, Brazil had
a stronger tradition of local industry and maintenance of
export income, both of which helped moderate the effect of
world economic fluctuations on the Brazilian economy. Thus,
although Argentina had employed better economic policy than
Brazil during the nineteenth century, Brazil had an ideology
that enabled it to protect its national interest to a far
greater degree than Argentina in the twentieth century.

FOOTNOTES

Chapter 11. Brazil: The Republic

1. Hubert Herring, <u>A History of Latin America from the Beginnings to the Present</u>, p. 141.

2. <u>Ibid.</u>, p. 748.

3. Cited in Humberto Bastos, Ruy Barbosa, <u>Ministro da Independência Econômica do Brasil</u>, pp. 224-225.

4. <u>Ibid.</u>, cited on p. 249.

5. <u>Ibid.</u>, p. 224.

6. <u>Ibid.</u>, p. 63.

7. J. Pires do Rio, <u>A Moeda Brasileira e seu perene caráter fiduciário</u>, p. 151.

8. Pires do Rio, <u>op. cit.</u>, pp. 151-156; and <u>inter alia</u>, G. C. Fite and J, Reese, <u>An Economic History of the United States</u>.

9. Ruy Barbosa, <u>Finanças e Política da República</u>, p. 36.

10. <u>Ibid</u>. "A Papel e a Baizo do Cambio," discourse in the Senate 3 November 1891, pp. 9, 10, 25.

11. Ruy Barbosa, <u>Finanças e Politica da República</u>, pp. 32, 75, 76.

12. Ruy Barbosa, <u>Os bancos emissores--o projecto oficial</u>, pp. 257-261.

13. Ruy Barbosa, <u>Relatório do Ministro da Fazenda, em janeiro de 1891 (Obras completas de rui barbosa</u>, vol. XVIII, tomo III), pp. 152-158; and Nícia Velela Luz, <u>A Luta Pela Industrialização do Brasil</u>, p. 11.

14. François Conty, <u>L'Indépendence Financière des Etats Fédérés du Brésil</u>, p. 13.

15. Senator Ubaldino do Amaral, cited in Conty, <u>op. cit.</u>, p. 17.

16. Conty, op. cit., p. 20.

17. Rollie E. Poppino, Brazil, The Land and the People, p. 218.

18. Vilela Luz, op. cit., pp. 107-114.

19. Ibid., pp. 113-118.

20. Directoria Geral de Estatística, Balance Geral, 1890-1900.

21. Cited in Stanley Stein, Vassouras, A Brazilian Coffee County, 1850-1900, p. 268.

22. José Maria Bello, A Hsstory of Modern Brazil, 1889-1964, p. 83.

23. Augusto de Bulhões, Ministros da Fazenda do Brasil, 1808-1954, pp. 108-114.

24. Fires do Rio, op. cit., p. 164.

25. Bello, op. cit., pp. 159-160.

26. Ibid., pp. 160-161.

27. Percy Alvin Martin, note, in J. P. Calogeras, La Politique Monetaire du Brésil, p. 303.

28. Julian Smith Duncan, Public and Private Operation of Railways in Brazil, p. 46.

29. Ibid., p. 49.

30. Ibid., p. 53.

31. Ibid., pp. 53-54.

32. Ibid., pp. 50-51.

33. Based on preliminary estimates by Prof. Matthew Simon. I am indebted to Prof. Irving Stone for releasing this material to me. It is subject to further revision by Prof. Stone.

34. Calogeras, op. cit., p. 344.

35. Ibid., p. 358.

36. Cited in Bello, op. cit., p. 198.

37. Cited in E. Bradfoed Burns, A Documentary History of Brazil, pp. 327-328.

38. Bello, op. cit., p. 201.

39. Ibid., pp. 227-228.

40. Manuel Diegués Júnior, Immigração, Urbanização e Indus-trialização, pp. 227-228.

41. Cincinato Braga, Questões Económico-Financeiras, pp. 116-121.

42. Ibid., p. 27; Bello, op. cit., p. 227.

APPENDIX A

TABLES

Table 8-1

Prices of White and Muscovado Sugar at Retail
in England, 1521-1702
(in pence per lb.)

Year	White Sugar	Muscovado Sugar
1521–30	6.75	
1531–40	7.82	
1541–50	11.02	
1551–60	13.93	
1561–70	9.40	
1571–82	17.23	
1583–92	17.10	13.84
1593–1602	19.10	15.67
1603–12	20.27	14.20
1613–22	17.94	13.09
1623–32	19.14	13.80
1633–42	21.56	13.33
1643–52	19.33	14.35
1653–62	12.50	7.36
1663–72	10.80	9.00
1673–92	9.50	6.75
1693–1702	12.76	7.16

Source: Noel Deerr, The History of Sugar, Vol. 2, p. 528.

Table 8-2

Anticipated Profit on Brazil Sugar Production, 1620, Pounds Sterling

Profit Rate %	Quantity (tons)	Category	Purchase Price in Brazil (per lb.)	Cost in Brazil (£)	Sale Price in Amsterdam	Receipts in Amsterdam	Freight and Cost	Profits
118	5,000	White*	8 groots	183,333	18 groots	412,500	22,000	207,167
176	5,000	muscovado	4 groots	91,667	12 groots	275,000	22,000	161,333
252	5,000	panela	2 groots	45,833	8 groots	183,333	22,000	115,500
Total	15,000			320,833		870,833	66,000	484,000

Source: Noel Deerr, The History of Sugar, Vol. 1, p. 105, citing Reese, De Suikerhandel van Amsterdam (Haarlem, 1908), I, p. 187.

* = 20,000 chests of 500 lb. per chest.

Table 8-3

Exportation of Sugar from Netherlands Brazil,
1637-1644

	Amount Exported by the WIC	Amount Exported by Private Traders
White sugar	332,425 arrobas	1,083,048 arrobas
Muscovado	117,887	403,287
Panela	51,961	71,527
Total	502,273	1,557,862
Valued at	₤ 692,521	₤ 1,845,586

Source: C. R. Boxer, The Dutch in Brazil, 1624-1654, p. 148.

Table 8-4

Range of Prices of Raw Sugar, 1623-1939

Range of Prices of Raw Sugar in Amsterdam, 1623-1806, in Shillings per Cwt.
Conversion Made on the Basis of 1 Gulden Equal to 1.818s. and
Amsterdam Lb. Equal to 1.089 English Lb.

Year	Price	Year	Price	Year	Price	Year	Price	Year	Price
1623	56	1691	33	1717	25	1738	16	1759	38
1633	45	1692	32	1718	26	1739	21	1760	30
1640	65	1693	32	1719	26-38	1740	26	1761	34
1641	56	1694	40	1720	24	1741	21	1762	34
1642	56	1695	36	1721	21	1742	23	1763	26
1643	56	1696	46	1722	26	1743	26	1764	22
1644	56	1697	28	1723	24	1744	29	1765	27
1677	27	1698	33	1725	26	1745	38	1766	19
1678	26	1699	36	1726	25	1746	29	1767	27
1679	26	1700	38	1727	22	1747	27	1768	26
1680	26	1701	50	1728	27	1749	25	1769	25
1681	20	1702	38	1729	23	1750	14	1770	33
1682	19	1703	41	1730	19	1751	18	1776	14-19
1683	19	1704	45	1731	18	1752	19	1788	19-25
1684	25	1707	37	1732	16	1753	17	1795	35-49
1685	20	1709	35	1733	19	1754	23	1797	93
1686	18	1710	31	1734	17	1755	33	1800	74
1687	17	1712	40	1735	15	1756	28	1801	50
1688	19	1715	30	1736	14	1757	27	1804	79
1689	27	1716	26	1737	15	1758	35	1806	60

Note: Quotations from 1623 to 1644 do not state origin of the sugar.
From 1677 to 1699 the prices refer to Surinam sugar, and from 1700 to 1806 to
Essequebo sugar.

Range of Prices and Average Price of Raw Sugar (Cost, Insurance, Freight)
in London, 1728 to 1939, in Shillings Per Cwt.

Year	Price	Year	Price	Year	Price	Year	Price	Year	Price
1728	24	1745	40	1762	27-47	1779	50-59	1796	61-78
1729	24	1746	39	1763	26-38	1780	45-59	1797	52-75
1730	22	1747	43	1764	28-40	1781	55-72	1798	59-83
1731	20	1748	32	1765	32-48	1782	26-63	1799	26-87
1732	18	1749	29	1766	29-42	1783	22-48	1800	32-70
1733	17	1750	28	1767	33-42	1784	18-46	1801	32-75
1734	26	1751	30	1768	32-41	1785	26-42	1802	26-55
1735	19	1752	39	1769	33-42	1786	29-48	1803	30-58
1736	19	1753	33	1770	31-43	1787	24-47	1804	46-66
1737	25	1754	36	1771	32-44	1788	34-36	1805	48-59
1738	22	1755	36	1772	29-43	1789	31-47	1806	39-49
1739	26	1756	35	1773	28-44	1790	38-46	1807	32-38
1740	32	1757	37	1774	27-43	1791	47-65	1808	32-50
1741	30	1758	42	1775	26-39	1792	48-76	1809	36-51
1742	21	1759	31-47	1776	30-50	1793	41-73	1810	43-54
1743	27	1760	32-48	1777	35-60	1794	32-67	1811	35-45
1744	31	1761	32-50	1778	40-64	1795	42-75	1812	42-49

Table 8-4 (Continued)

Year	Price	Year	Price	Year	Price	Year	Price	Year	Price
1813	51-75	1839	39	1865	22	1891	13/6	1917	31/6
1814	54-97	1840	49	1866	21	1892	13/6	1918	33/0
1815	57-75	1841	40	1867	22	1893	14/3	1919	38/5
1816	49-60	1842	37	1868	22	1894	11/3	1920	58/0
1817	44-54	1843	37	1869	24	1895	10/0	1921	18/3
1818	47-55	1844	33	1870	23	1896	10/9	1922	15/3
1819	36-51	1845	33	1871	25/6	1897	9/3	1923	25/9
1820	34-37	1846	33	1872	25/6	1898	9/6	1924	21/9
1821	29-35	1847	27	1873	22/6	1899	10/6	1925	12/9
1822	28-34	1848	26	1874	21/6	1900	11/3	1926	12/3
1823	27-37	1849	22	1875	20/0	1901	9/3	1927	13/9
1824	30-34	1850	23	1876	21/6	1902	7/3	1928	11/7
1825	32-41	1851	23	1877	24/6	1903	8/6	1929	9/0
1826	30-39	1852	20	1878	20/0	1904	10/3	1930	6/7
1827	32-36	1853	22	1879	19/0	1905	11/0	1931	6/4
1828	32-38	1854	20	1880	20/6	1906	8/6	1932	5/9
1829	26-30	1855	24	1881	21/3	1907	9/3	1933	5/3
1830	23-25	1856	28	1882	20/0	1908	9/9	1934	4/9
1831	23-25	1857	34	1883	19/0	1909	10/3	1935	4/8
1832	23-30	1858	24	1884	13/3	1910	11/0	1936	4/9
1833	26-31	1859	23	1885	13/6	1911	11/6	1937	6/4
1834	31-33	1860	24	1886	11/9	1912	11/0	1938	5/5
1835	30-38	1861	22	1887	11/9	1913	9/6	1939	7/4
1836	38-45	1862	20	1888	13/0	1914	11/7		
1837	33-37	1863	21	1889	16/0	1915	14/4		
1838	33-42	1864	26	1890	13/0	1916	24/3		

Source: Noel Deerr, The History of Sugar, Vol. 2, pp. 530-531.

Note: The maximum price is 97s., in 1814, and the lowest 3s. 10½ d., reached in 1934.

Table 8-5

Brazilian Sugar Production in 1711

State	Factories	Tons	Tons per Factory
Bahia	140	6,850	47
Pernambuco	246	4,970	20
Rio de Janeiro	136	4,850	35
Total	528	16,670	29

Source: Noel Deerr, The History of Sugar, Vol. 1, p. 110.

Table 8-6

Consumption of Sugar in the United Kingdom, Lb. Per Caput Per Year

Period	Consumption	Period	Consumption	Period	Consumption
1700-09	4	1790-99	13.0	1870-74	49.2
1710-19	5	1800-09	18.0	1875-79[b]	53.2
1720-29	8	1810-19	17.0	1880-89	67.9
1730-39	9	1820-29	17.6	1890-99	78.9
1740-49	8.	1830-39	17.8	1900-09[c]	84.7
1750-59	8	1840-44	16.4	1910-14	90.8
1760-69	8	1845-49[a]	22.6	1915-19[d]	70.1
1770-79	11	1850-59	30.1	1920-24[e]	69.2
1780-89	12	1860-69	38.7	1924-29[f]	87.8
				1930-37	98.1

Table 8-6 (Continued)

Source: Noel Deerr, The History of Sugar, Vol. 2, p. 532.

[a] First year of progressive removal of duties, 1845.

[b] First year of no duty, 1875.

[c] First year of imposition of duty, 1901. Consumption in 1901 93 lb. per caput, the then maximum.

[d] The Great War, 1914–1918.

[e] Period of excessive prices, 1920–1924.

[f] To 1932 in terms of raw, afterwards in terms of refined, the factor of conversion being approximately 100 raw to 93 of refined.

Table 8-7

Cattle Prices in Colonial Brazil

North:

1711   cow 4$000-5$000
      ox for wagon 6$000-7$000
      ox already trained 12$000-13$000

1768   ox 3$200-4$000

1800   ox 1$500

South and Center:

  end C 16, São Paulo
  cow 1$000
  ox 2$000

1711   Jacobinas, ox 2$500-5$000

1710   mineracão, ox, 100 oitavas

1800   ox 4$800

1800   ox Rio Grande do Sul 1$000 at estancias

Source: Roberto C. Simonsen, História Econômica do Brasil, 1500-1820, pp. 154-164; Celso Furtado, The Economic Growth of Brazil; Ivan Pedro Martins, Introdução à Economia Brasileira, pp. 38-39.

Table 8-8

Commodity Composition of Exports, Colonial Period

	Value				Percent of Total	
	1560	1710	1560	1710		
Commodity	Ł1,000		Gold (Kg.)		1560	1710
Sugar	133	2,012	977.6	14,788.2	79	64
Brazilwood	24	38	176.4	279.3	14	1
Tobacco		274		2,013.9		9
Gold		487		3,579.5		16
Hides		161		1,183.4		5
Other	11	156	80.9	1,146.6	7	5

Source: Mircea Buesco and Vincent Tapajós, História do Desenvolvimento Económico do Brasil, p. 27.

201

Table 8-9

Capital Remittances from Brazil to Portugal,
1714-1791
(thousands of reis)

Year	Royal Revenues	Private Funds	Unspecified	Total
1714	67,200	1,075,200	10,400,000	11,542,400
1717	-	-	960,000	960,000
1720	600,000	1,800,000	-	2,400,000
1721	118,896	1,144,738	9,530	1,273,164
1724	-	-	4,216,000	4,216,000
1725	-	-	19,520,000	19,520,000
1727	1,286,765	3,600,000	-	4,886,765
1729	-	-	3,200,000	3,200,000
1730	-	-	2,000,000	2,000,000
1731	2,662,938	-	4,880,000	7,542,938
1733	2,960,000	4,400,000	-	7,360,000
1734	1,011,200	-	-	1,011,200
1735	130,238	158,730	-	288,968
1736	-	-	600,000	600,000
1737	4,420,378	3,218,022	-	7,638,400
1738	1,200,000	1,200,000	580,911	2,980,911
1739	-	-	7,500,298	7,500,298
1740	-	-	391,991	391,991
1742	4,784,701	11,343,505	-	16,128,216
1743	-	-	1,222,962	1,222,962
1745	360,000	1,040,000	-	1,400,000
1746	459,162	2,936,800	-	3,395,962
1749	1,405,888	5,027,373	6,433,260	12,866,521
1771[a]	-	-	-	2,000,000
1772	1,000,000	1,800,000	-	2,800,000
1773	1,200,000	1,900,000	-	3,100,000
1774	·427,396	715,209	-	1,142,605
1775 / 1776	664,692	3,624,131	-	4,288,723
1777	297,179	2,065,962	-	2,363,141
1778	127,865	-	-	-
1791	80,741	-	-	-

Source: Dauril Alden, Royal Government in Colonial Brazil, pp. 328, 331.

[a]Includes shipments from Rio only.

Table 9-1

Money in Circulation, 1810-1914
(millions)

Year	Treasury	Conversion Office	Banks	Total	Index
1810	-	-	160	160	0.2
1811	-	-	104	104	0.1
1812	-	-	60	60	0.1
1813	-	-	130	130	0.2
1814	-	-	1,042	1,042	1.5
1815	-	-	1,200	1,200	1.8
1816	-	-	1,862	1,862	2.7
1817	-	-	2,600	2,600	3.8
1818	-	-	3,632	3,632	5.4
1819	-	-	6,518	6,518	9.6
1820	-	-	8,566	8,566	12.6
1821	-	-	8,071	8,071	11.9
1822	-	-	9,171	9,171	13.5
1823	-	-	9,994	9,994	14.7
1824	-	-	11,391	11,391	16.8
1825	-	-	11,941	11,941	17.6
1826	-	-	13,391	13,391	19.8
1827	-	-	21,575	21,575	31.8
1828	-	-	21,356	21,356	31.5
1829	-	-	20,507	20,507	30.3
1830	-	-	20,350	20,350	30.0
1831	-	-	19,017	19,017	28.1
1832	-	-	19,017	19,017	28.1
1833-4	-	-	19,017	19,017	28.1
1834-5	-	-	30,703	30,703	45.3
1835-6	34,299	-	-	34,299	50.6
1836-7	35,000	-	-	35,000	51.6
1837-8	39,475	-	-	39,475	58.3
1838-9	39,475	-	-	39,475	58.3
1839-0	39,475	-	-	39,475	58.3
1840-1	40,200	-	-	40,200	59.3
1841-2	43,689	-	-	43,689	64.5
1842-3	46,521	-	-	46,521	68.7
1843-4	48,267	-	-	48,267	71.2
1844-5	50,380	-	-	50,380	74.4
1845-6	50,668	-	-	50,668	74.8
1846-7	48,784	-	-	48,784	72.0
1847-8	47,802	-	-	47,802	70.5
1848-9	47,532	-	-	47,532	70.1
1849-0	46,884	-	-	46,884	69.2
1850-1	46,684	-	-	46,684	68.9

Table 9-1 (Continued)

Year	Treasury	Conversion Office	Banks	Total	Index
1851-2	46,693	-	-	46,693	68.9
1852-3	46,684	-	-	46,684	68.9
1853-4	40,685	-	15,331	56,016	82.7
1854-5	45,693	-	21,063	67,756	100.0
1855-6	45,693	-	40,128	85,821	126.7
1856-7	43,677	-	51,540	95,217	140.5
1857-8	41,665	-	50,905	92,570	136.6
1858-9	40,701	-	55,172	95,873	141.5
1859-0	37,599	-	50,391	87,990	129.9
1860-1	35,109	-	46,904	82,013	121.0
1861-2	33,324	-	45,740	79,064	116.7
1862-3	30,594	-	51,129	81,723	120.6
1863-4	29,094	-	70,449	99,543	146.9
1864-5	28,091	-	72,558	100,649	148.5
1865-6	28,901	-	83,963	112,864	166.6
1866-7	42,560	-	74,600	117,160	173.0
1867-8	81,749	-	42,937	124,686	184.0
1868-9	127,230	-	35,995	163,225	240.9
1869-0	149,398	-	43,129	192,527	284.1
1870-1	151,078	-	40,728	191,806	283.1
1871-2	150,807	-	38,000	188,807	278.7
1872-3	149,579	-	35,432	185,011	273.0
1873-4	149,547	-	33,548	183,095	270.2
1874-5	149,501	-	32,367	181,868	268.4
1875-6	149,380	-	30,042	179,422	264.8
1876-7	149,348	-	30,000	179,348	264.7
1877-8	181,279	-	27,654	208,933	308.4
1878-9	189,258	-	27,654	216,912	320.1
1879-0	189,200	-	26,478	215,678	318.3
1880-1	188,155	-	24,129	212,284	313.3
1881-2	188,111	-	24,129	212,240	313.2
1882-3	188,041	-	22,956	210,997	311.4
1883-4	187,937	-	21,680	209,626	309.4
1884-5	187,344	-	20,518	207,862	306.8
1885-6	194,283	-	19,300	213,583	315.2
1886-7	184,335	-	17,956	202,291	298.6
1888	188,869	-	16,419	205,288	303.0
1889	185,819	-	11,337	197,156	291.0
1890	171,081	-	127,911	298,992	441.3
1891	167,611	-	346,116	513,727	758.2
1892	215,100	-	346,116	561,216	828.3
1893	285,745	-	346,116	631,861	932.5
1894	367,359	-	345,000	712,359	1,051.4
1895	337,352	-	340,714	678,066	1,000.7

Table 9-1 (Continued)

Year	Treasury	Conversion Office	Banks	Total	Index
1896	371,641	–	340,714	712,355	1,051.4
1897	439,614	–	340,714	780,328	1,151.7
1898	778,365	–	247,103	779,966	1,151.1
1899	733,727	–	–	733,727	1,082.9
1900	669,632	–	–	669,632	988.3
1901	680,451	–	–	680,451	1,004.3
1902	675,537	–	–	675,537	997.0
1903	674,979	–	–	674,979	996.2
1904	673,740	–	–	673,740	994.4
1905	669,492	–	–	669,492	988.1
1906	664,793	37,272	–	702,065	1,036.2
1907	643,532	100,033	–	743,565	1,097.4
1908	634,683	89,387	–	724,070	1,068.6
1909	628,453	225,729	–	854,182	1,260.7
1910	621,005	303,990	–	924,995	1,365.2
1911	612,520	378,483	–	991,003	1,462.6
1912	607,026	406,036	–	1,013,062	1,495.2
1913	601,488	295,347	–	896,835	1,323.6
1914	822,496	157,787	–	980,283	1,446.8

Source: Dorival Texeira Vieira, "A Evolucão do Sistema Monetário Brasileiro, Revista de Administracão, Año 1, #2 (Junho de 1947), pp. 314-315.

Note: Figures presented in contos of reis.

Table 9-2

First Banco do Brasil, 1809-1829

Year	Capital (millions of reis)	Capital From Bank Tax (millions of reis)	Reserve Fund (millions of reis)	Government Shares	Privately Held Shares	Total Shares	Dividends Distributed (thousands of reis)	Dividend Per Share[a] (reis)
1809	116	–	–	–	116	116	–	–
1810	120	–	0.251	–	4	120	1,255	104,583
1811	122	–	1	–	2	122	3,756	307,869
1812	172	–	2	–	50	172	5,064	294,419
1813	397	63	6	62	225	397	18,049	454,635
1814	502	122	14	122	105	502	43,268	861,912
1815	581	183	29	183	75	581	74,114	127,563
1816	690	272	53	272	109	690	120,298	174,345
1817	1,189	336	83	336	499	1,189	153,409	129,025
1818	1,719	411	122	411	530	1,719	202,027	127,526
1819	2,037	484	163	484	318	2,037	208,073	102,147
1820	2,215	500	207	500	178	2,215	227,139	102,546
1821	2,235	500	275	500	20	2,235	353,224	158,042

Table 9-2 (Continued)

Year	Capital (millions of reis)	Capital From Bank Tax (millions of reis)	Reserve Fund (millions of reis)	Government Shares	Privately Held Shares	Total Shares	Dividends Distributed (thousands of reis)	Dividend Per Share[a] (reis)
1822	2,248	500	329	500	13	2,248	281,892	125,397
1823	2,357	500	404	500	109	2,357	391,778	166,219
1824	2,662	500	485	500	305	2,662	424,004	159,280
1825	3,600	500	570	500	938	3,600	451,204	125,334
1826	3,600	500	692	500	-	3,600	640,029	177,786
1827	3,600	500	819	500	-	3,600	669,402	185,945
1828	3,600	500	954	500	-	3,600	716,216	198,949
1829	3,600	500	1,083	500	-	3,600	686,493	190,693

Source: Dorival Texeira Vieira, op. cit., p. 292.

[a]The total distributed dividend includes cash dividend plus 5 percent interest calculated on the reserve fund.

Table 9-3

Price Index, 1808-1884

Year	Average — Three Commodities	Average — Six Commodities	Index (1821=100)	Moving Averages		
1808	1$300		38		100	
1809	1.702		50		131	
1810	1.806		53		106	
1811	1.838		53		102	
1812	1.281		37		70	
1813	1.662		48		130	
1814	2.283		66		137	
1815	2.542		74		111	
1816	2.554		74		100	
1817	2.513		73		98	
1818	3.156		92		126	
1819	2.984		87		95	
1820	2.967		86		99	
1821	3.438	4$880	100	100	116	100
1822		4.278		88		92
1823		3.863		79		82
1824		3.614		74		100
1825		3.925		80		128
1826		4.017		82		87
1827		4.965		102		115
1828		5.429		111		100
1829		5.076		104		112
1830		4.971		102		96
1831		5.001		102		89
1832		4.644		95		83
1833[a]		4.685		96		100
1834		4.906		101		110
1835		4.698		96		82

Weighted Average

Year	Value	Year	Value
1821	237	1852-3	187
1822	216	1853-4	230
1823	177	1854-5	226
1824	177	1855-6	277
1825	228	1856-7	276
1826	199	1857-8	297
1827	228	1858-9	282
1828	247	1859-60	316
1829	281	1860-1	348
1830	268	1861-2	304
1831	235	1862-3	362
1832	199	1863-4	366
1833[a]	200	1864-5	404
1833-4	216	1865-6	393
1834-5	179	1866-7	374
1835-6	188	1867-8	381
1836-7	160	1868-9	430
1837-8	172	1869-70	433
1838-9	215	1870-1	351
1839-40	205	1871-2	324
1840-1	189	1872-3	398
1841-2	187	1873-4	418
1842-3	183	1874-5	372
1843-4	177	1875-6	421
1844-5	173	1876-7	380
1845-6	193	1877-8	355
1846-7	165	1878-9	372
1847-8	165	1879-80	440
1848-9	160	1880-1	413
1849-50	199	1881-2	322
1850-1	182	1882-3	286
1851-2	197	1883-4	283

Source: Dorival Teixeira Vieira, op. cit., pp. 375-376.

Note: The index refers to wholesale prices. The indices before 1821 are not comparable with those after that date.

[a] First six months.

Table 9-4

Brazilian Exchange Rate, 1808-1914

Year	Pence per Milreis	Index	Dollars per Milreis
1808	70.00	254.0	1.41
1809	72.00	261.2	1.45
1810	73.25	265.8	1.48
1811	71.5	259.4	1.44
1812	74.00	268.5	1.49
1813	77.75	282.1	1.57
1814	85.5	310.2	1.73
1815	73.75	267.6	1.49
1816	58.25	211.3	1.18
1817	64.5	234.0	1.30
1818	71.5625	259.6	1.45
1819	66.00	239.5	1.33
1820	57.00	206.8	1.15
1821	51.5	186.8	1.04
1822	49.0	177.8	.99
1823	50.75	184.1	1.03
1824	48.25	175.1	.98
1825	51.875	188.2	1.05
1826	48.125	174.6	.98
1827	35.25	127.9	.71
1828[a]	31.0625	112.7	.63
1828-9	24.625	89.3	.50
1829-30	22.8125	82.8	.46
1830-1	25.00	90.7	.51
1831-2	35.125	127.4	.71
1832-3	37.375	135.6	.76
1833-4	38.75	140.6	.79
1834-5	39.25	142.4	.80
1835-6	38.4375	139.5	.78
1836-7	29.5625	107.3	.60
1837-8	28.0625	101.8	.57
1838-9	31.625	114.7	.64
1839-40	31.00	112.5	.63
1840-1	30.3125	110.0	.61
1841-2	26.8125	97.3	.54
1842-3	25.8125	93.7	.52
1843-4	25.4375	92.3	.51
1844-5	25.4375	92.3	.52
1845-6	26.9375	97.7	.55
1846-7	28.00	101.6	.57
1847-8	25.00	90.7	.51
1848-9	25.875	93.9	.52
1849-50	28.75	104.3	.58

Table 9-4 (Continued)

Year	Pence per Milreis	Index	Dollars per Milreis
1850-1	29.125	105.7	.59
1851-2	27.4375	99.5	.56
1852-3	28.5	103.4	.58
1853-4	27.625	100.2	.56
1854-5	27.5625	100.0	.56
1855-6	27.5625	100.0	.56
1856-7	26.625	96.6	.54
1857-8	25.5625	92.7	.52
1858-9	25.0625	90.9	.51
1859-60	25.8125	93.6	.52
1860-1	25.5625	92.7	.52
1861-2	26.3125	95.5	.53
1862-3	27.25	98.9	.55
1863-4	26.75	97.1	.54
1864-5	25.00	90.7	.51
1865-6	24.25	88.0	.49
1866-7	22.4375	81.4	.46
1867-8	17.00	61.7	.34
1868-9	18.8125	68.3	.38
1869-70	22.0625	80.0	.45
1870-1	24.03125	87.2	.49
1871-2	25.00	90.7	.51
1872-3	26.09375	94.6	.53
1873-4	25.78125	93.5	.52
1874-5	26.21875	95.1	.55
1875-6	25.34375	92.0	.51
1876-7	24.5625	85.4	.50
1877-8	22.9375	83.2	.47
1878-9	21.75	78.9	.43
1879-80	22.09375	80.2	.45
1880-1	21.90625	79.5	.44
1881-2	21.15625	76.8	.43
1882-3	21.5625	78.2	.44
1883-4	20.6875	75.1	.42
1884-5	18.59375	67.5	.38
1885-6	18.6875	67.8	.38
1886-7	22.4375	81.4	.46
1887-8	22.4375	81.4	.46
1888	25.25	91.6	.51
1889	26.4375	95.9	.54
1890	22.5625	81.9	.46
1891	14.90625	54.1	.30
1892	12.03125	43.7	.24
1893	11.59375	42.1	.24
1894	10.09375	36.6	.20

210

Table 9-4 (Continued)

Year	Pence per Milreis	Index	Dollars per Milreis
1895	9.9375	36.1	.20
1896	9.0625	32.9	.18
1897	7.71875	28.0	.16
1898	7.1875	26.1	.15
1899	7.4375	27.0	.15
1900	9.453125	34.3	.19
1901	11.265625	40.9	.23
1902	11.906250	43.2	.24
1903	11.953125	43.4	.24
1904	12.125	44.0	.25
1905	15.781250	57.3	.32
1906	16.03125	58.2	.33
1907	15.078125	54.7	.31
1908	15.015625	54.5	.31
1909	15.015625	54.5	.31
1910	16.078125	58.3	.33
1911	15.968750	57.9	.32
1912	16.000	58.0	.32
1913	15.933125	57.9	.32
1914	14.656250	53.2	.29

Sources: Dorival Teixeira Vieira, "A Evolucão do Sistema Monetário Brasileiro," Revista de Administracão, Año 1, #2 (Junho de 1947), p. 367; Julian Smith Duncan, Public and Private Operation of Railways in Brazil, p. 183.

[a]1.º semestre.

Table 9-5

Brazilian Exports to Portugal, 1796-1821
(millions of reis)

Category	1796	1806	1819	1821[a]
Provisions	5,761	6,532	4,590	
Gold	1,856	940	26	
Cotton	2,201	3,544	1,784	4,284
Leather	739	2,249	625	2,774
Drug products	162	285	52	
Wood	31	36	13	
Tobacco	640	566	367	892
Total	13,193	15,948	7,517	
Portugese Exports	16,013	23,256	11,291	

Source: Roberto G. Simonsen, História Econômica do Brasil, 1500-1820, pp. 385-387, 457.

[a]Total exports.

Table 10-1

Percentage Distribution of Government Revenue, 1823-1831

Source	1823	1824	1825	1826[a]	1827	1828[b]	1829[c]	1830	1831
Imports	42.0	23.1	49.7	44.5	20.3	28.1	45.4	25.3	22.1
Exports	11.0	5.2	12.1	11.1	7.4	4.6	4.0	5.3	7.1
Maritime	.3	.2	.4	.4	.4	.2[f]	.4	.2	.2
Interior	33.0	27.6	31.9	21.9	21.9	67.1[f]	13.3	32.2	28.0
Loans	10.0	4.3							
Sequestrations	2.3	1.6							
War and navy subscriptions	.8	.7							
Voluntary contributions	.8	.1							
Extraordinary	-	37.2[e]	5.9	3.5	45.2	[f]	36.9	37.0	42.6
Total A millions	3,802	9,618	4,749	5,394[a]	12,068	7,258	14,406	18,213	22,141
B millions	4,400	10,311	4,749	5,394	12,068	7,258	14,464	24,760	22,141

Source: Based on data from Liberato de Castro Carreira, História Financeira e Orçamentaria do Imperio do Brasil desde a sua fundação.

Interpretive Note: This table is not consistent with Table 11-6. The major reason for the discrepancy is that Table 11-6 does not include extraordinary receipts. After adjustment for this item, however, a small discrepancy in total between Table 10-1 and Table 11-6 remains for some years.

Note: Total A equals sum shown in source. Total B shows total of individual components shown in source; Total B = 100.0.

213

Table 10-1 (Continued)

[a]The total may be a misprint. The components add to 4,392. If the 5,394 figure is accepted, 18.6 percent of the total is unaccounted for. The Anuário Estatístico do Brasil, 1956, from which Table 11-6 was constructed, shows 4,372.

[b]First semester only.

[c]Fiscal 1828/29. Fiscal years obtain hereafter.

[d]Includes provincial contributions.

[e]Includes London loan.

[f]Both Interior and Extraordinary are included in Interior in 1828.

Table 10-2

Tax Rates in 1822 and 1823

Item	Unit	United States Equivalent	Rate
1822:			
Portuguese merchandise, foreign snuff			(Ad. Val.) 24 percent (Per unit)
Wine	pipa	2 hogsheads	12$000
White wine			24$000
Oil			7$000
Vinegar			2$000
Red wine	12 bottles		400
White wine			800
Liquor and aguardiente			1$200

Table 10-2 (Continued)

Item	Unit	United States Equivalent	Rate
1823:			
Export of Brazilian products			2 percent
Coffee and miuncas (lambs, pigs, chickens, etc.)			10 percent
Aguardiente manufactured in Brazil	pipa		4$000
Goods manufactured in the province	(subsidio litterario)		20
For pipa that entered the city	(2 hogsheads)		1$600
Tobacco	arroba	32.5 lb.	400
Local produce			siza
Slaves		media	siza
Coffee houses, taverns			tax

Source: Liberato de Castro Carreiro, História Financeira e Orçamentaria do Imperio do Brasil desde a sua fundacão, pp. 90 ff.

Note: In addition to the above, salt, reexport, wheat, the equivalent of the tobacco contract, warehouse charges, stamps, and sugar were taxed in 1827.

Table 10-3

Real Exports and Imports, 1821-1914
(Millions)

Year	Exports	Imports	Balance
In 1821 currency:			
1821	20,119	21,260	- 1,141
1822	20,761	23,645	- 2,884
1823	21,397	20,119	1,277
1824	21,308	22,753	- 5,448
1825	22,081	23,592	- 1,491
1826	12,549	14,116	- 1,567
1827	16,596	17,911	- 1,315
1828	16,955	16,864	90
1829	16,373	17,410	- 1,037
1830	18,832	22,537	- 3,705
1831	26,423	27,363	- 866
1832	25,516	25,781	- 265
In 1832 currency:			
1832	31,815	32,146	- 331
1833[a]	20,522	17,820	2,702
1834	36,284	36,394	- 110
1835	33,949	37,638	- 3,689
1836	41,856	41,608	249
1837	26,526	35,168	- 8,642
1838	24,698	30,038	- 5,340
1839	34,526	41,040	- 6,514
1840	35,158	42,620	- 7,462
1841	33,129	45,893	- 12,764
1842	27,515	39,453	- 11,938
In 1840 currency:			
1840	43,192	52,359	- 9,167
1841	40,714	56,399	- 15,686
1842	33,808	48,475	- 14,668
1843	34,145	42,132	- 7,987
1844	35,566	44,895	- 9,329
1845	38,584	45,287	- 6,703
1846	46,604	45,357	1,248
1847	47,361	50,333	- 2,972
1848	46,688	38,164	8,524
1849	46,946	43,009	3,936
1850	51,015	54,846	- 3,831
1851	63,653	72,226	- 8,573
1852	58,976	82,181	- 23,205

Table 10-3 (Continued)

Year	Exports	Imports	Balance
In 1840 currency:			
1853	67,680	80,258	- 12,578
1854	68,467	76,483	- 8,015
1855	80,631	75,717	4,914
1856	83,850	82,481	1,470
1857	98,396	107,570	- 9,174
1858	79,269	107,338	- 28,069
1859	86,280	102,833	- 16,653
1860	93,981	94,039	- 58
1861	101,493	101,945	- 452
1862	102,491	93,841	8,650
1863	107,660	87,164	20,496
1864	113,229	108,479	4,750
1865	113,727	106,231	7,496
1866	122,852	107,760	15,093
1867	113,005	103,534	9,471
1868	101,544	77,049	24,496
1869	123,039	101,187	21,852
1870	140,138	119,661	20,477
1871	130,200	125,860	4,340
1872	153,704	121,142	32,562
1873	180,731	133,299	47,432
1874	157,641	126,977	30,664
1875	183,058	147,108	35,950
1876	150,003	140,646	9,357
1877	154,886	124,254	30,632
1878	137,898	121,003	16,896
1879	140,596	112,655	27,941
1880	158,537	123,809	34,728
1881	163,060	126,846	36,214
1882	143,328	124,478	18,850
1883	136,938	132,233	4,704
1884	144,788	135,088	9,700
1885	135,762	107,059	28,703
1886	117,562	119,094	- 1,532
1887	190,524	149,808	40,716
1887[b]	90,498	74,930	15,568
1888	168,014	152,615	15,398
1889	220,749	185,566	35,183
1890	204,324	204,324	18,306
1891	211,203	211,203	12,223
1892	239,908	239,908	35,391
1893	249,384	249,384	45,126

Table 10-3 (Continued)

Year	Exports	Imports	Balance
In 1890 currency:			
1890	280,665	255,520	25,145
1891	289,800	273,029	16,771
1892	329,564	280,946	48,618
1893	342,735	280,718	62,018
1894	326,066	290,285	35,784
1895	348,007	311,968	36,040
1896	302,977	298,130	4,847
1897	281,980	250,403	31,509
1898	267,878	252,001	15,877
1899	273,755	241,795	31,959
1900	279,762	180,601	99,161
1901	428,692	223,280	205,412
1902	387,840	248,277	139,563
1903	392,852	257,353	135,500
1904	416,909	275,260	141,649
1905	479,134	318,042	161,093
1906	567,765	354,493	213,272
1907	581,962	435,978	145,984
1908	469,351	377,236	92,115
1909	676,032	394,263	218,769
1910	668,862	508,270	160,592
1911	709,775	561,157	141,548
1912	793,894	674,521	119,372
1913	694,109	712,299	- 18,189
1914	490,480	364,642	125,837

Source: Computed from Anuário Estatístico do Brasil, 1936-1966.

Note: The years 1821-1832 and 1888-1914 are calendar years. All other years are fiscal years (July 1-June 30). The number 1887 refers to the fiscal year 1886-1887, and similarly for all fiscal years. Totals are presented in contos of reis.

[a]First six months.

[b]Second six months.

Table 10-4

Brazilian Foreign Debt, 1822–1914

Year	Nominal Debt	Funds Received[a]	Purpose of Loan	Source of Funds
1824	£ 3,686,200	£ 3,000,000	Establish independence	U.K.
1825	2,000,000	–	Owed to Portugal for independence	U.K.
1829	769,200	400,000	Pay interest due on 1824 loan	U.K.
1839	411,200	312,500	Government expenditure	U.K.
1843	732,600	622,702	Payment of 1825 obligation to Portugal	U.K.
1852	1,040,600	954,250	Payment of obligation to Portugal	U.K.
1858	1,526,500	1,425,000	Prolongation of Dom Pedro II railway	U.K.
1859	508,000	508,000	Payment of 1829 loan	U.K.
1860	1,373,000	1,210,000	Aid to three railroad companies	U.K.
1863	3,855,300	3,300,000	Payment of past loans and floating debt	U.K.
1865	6,693,000	5,000,000	Paraguayan War expenses	U.K.
1871	3,459,100	3,000,000	Payment of debt and railroad expenses	U.K.
1875	5,301,200	5,000,000	Payment of debt and railroad expenses	U.K.
1883	4,599,000	4,000,000	Government expenses	U.K.
1886	6,431,000	6,000,000	Government expenses and consolidate debt	U.K.
1888	6,297,300	6,000,000	Consolidate floating debt and make funds available to pay newly freed work force	U.K.
1889	19,837,000	17,213,000	Consolidate debt	U.K.
1893	3,710,000	2,968,000	Railroad extension	U.K.
1895	7,442,000	6,325,700	Refund floating debt	U.K.
1898	10,000,000	8,613,717	Moratorium on foreign debt	U.K.
1901	16,619,320		Purchase of gold interest-guarantee railroads	U.K.
1903–5	8,500,000	7,860,000	Rio de Janeiro Port Works	U.K.
1906	1,100,000	1,100,000	Payment of Debts of Loide Brasileiro	U.K.

Table 10-4 (Continued)

Year	Nominal Debt	Funds Received[a]	Purpose of Loan	Source of Funds
1907	£ 3,000,000	£ 2,850,000	Taubaté (coffee price stabilization)	U.K.
1908	4,000,000	3,840,000	Government expenditure	U.K.
1908-9	fr. 100,000	100,000	Railroad	France
1909	gold francs, 40,000,000	38,000,000	Port of Recife	France
1910	£10,000,000	8,750,000	Conversion of 1893 and 1907 loans and railroad construction	U.K.
1910	1,000,000	900,000	Annual subsidy to Loíde Brasileiro	U.K.
1910	gold francs, 100,000,000	78,981,284	Railroads	France
1911	£ 4,500,000	4,140,000	Rio de Janeiro Port Works	U.K.
1911	2,400,000	1,992,000	Railroads	U.K.
1911	gold francs, 60,000,000	49,800,000	Railroads	France
1913	fr. 25,000,000	10,670,000	Port works, railroads and payment on treasury bonds	U.K.
1914	£14,502,396	14,502,396	Second funding loan	U.K.

Source: Jose do Nascimento Brito, Economia e Financas do Brasil; Liberate de Carriera Castro, História Financeira e Orçamentaria do Imperio do Brasil desde a sua funacão.

[a] Before commission and other funds are deducted.

Table 10-5

Percentage Distribution of Government Expenditure, 1810-1831

Destination	1810-11	1822	1823	1824	1825	1826	1827	1828	1829	1830	1831
Royal Household	32.0	17.4	6.9	3.0	3.0	3.5	[a]				
Ministries:											
Empire						3.8	14.3	3.2	6.5	7.2	6.6
Justice	1.7	1.7				1.3	1.0	1.3	1.0	2.5	2.3
Foreign Affairs						3.5	5.2	1.3	2.2	2.3	4.1
Navy	28.1	10.6	36.4	16.1	17.9	26.6	20.8	24.0	20.9	17.5	11.8
Army	22.4	10.2	28.7	19.6	21.7	24.7	17.8	30.0	26.2	26.6	22.8
Treasury	12.4	4.6	27.6	61.3	30.0	36.7	40.9	40.2	43.2	43.8	50.0
Extraordinary	3.4				27.4						
Unspecified		55.5	0.4								2.4
Total A millions	3,014	9,771	4,702	9,618	4,749	9,408	11,842	10,679	13,911	18,213	19,778
Total B millions	3,014	9,771	4,702	9,618	8,356	6,909	11,842	10,684	13,911	18,213	19,303

Source: Based on data from Liberate de Castro Carreira, História Financeira e Orçamentária do Império do Brasil desde a sua fundação (Rio, 1889).

Interpretive Note: This series is not consistent with that presented in Anuário Estatístico.

Note: Total A equals sum shown in source. Total B shows total of individual components shown in source. Total B = 100.0.

[a] Royal Household included in Empire.

Table 10-6

Percentage Distribution of Government Income, 1832–1889

Source:	1832	1833	1834	1835	1836	1837	1838	1839
Imports	32.7	28.4	52.5	42.9	50.9	51.2	57.9	57.7
Exports	6.6	3.7	6.3	4.8	6.2	14.7	19.0	19.1
Maritime	0.4	0.6	2.1	1.6	1.8	2.1	3.5	3.9
Interior	47.3	27.2	37.3	35.3	37.4	15.3	16.8	14.6
Extraordinary	12.9	40.0	1.7	15.4	3.8	16.7	2.8	4.6
Special								
Total A millions	15,440	20,200	12,472	14,820	14,135	14,477	12,673	14,970
Total B millions	11,172	20,200	11,711	14,820	14,135	15,477	12,276	15,059

Source:	1840	1841	1842	1843	1844	1845	1846	1847
Imports	52.3	62.4	63.9	56.0	48.2	50.6	48.9	48.2
Exports	23.7	18.1	17.6	18.4	14.2	14.0	15.8	14.1
Maritime	3.3	3.6	3.6	3.7	3.2	2.2	1.9	1.7
Interior	16.5	11.4	10.9	16.0	14.2	16.7	15.3	16.0
Extraordinary	4.2	4.4	3.9	5.8	20.2	3.2	2.6	4.3
Special						13.3	15.5	15.6
Total A millions	15,948	16,311	16,318	15,493	21,351	24,805	26,199	27,628
Total B millions	16,848	16,311	15,376	15,493	22,013	24,805	26,199	27,638

Table 10-6 (Continued)

Source:	1848	1849	1850	1851	1852	1853	1854	1855
Imports	46.6	59.1	61.8	62.7	67.6	65.0	65.4	66.3
Exports	16.7	14.7	13.5	14.4	12.3	13.1	10.7	12.5
Maritime	2.1	2.2	2.0	1.6	1.5	0.5	0.6	0.7
Interior	16.2	19.8	17.3	16.7	12.2	15.4	17.3	17.4
Extraordinary	3.1	4.3	5.3	4.6	6.3	6.0	6.0	3.1
Special	15.4							
Total A millions	24,732	26,163	28,200	32,697	35,787	36,391	34,516	36,985
Total B millions	24,732	26,163	28,200	32,697	36,727	38,103	35,952	35,744

Source:	1856	1857	1858	1859	1860	1861	1862	1863
Imports	65.9	65.4	64.3	60.5	61.1	59.9	59.3	56.4
Exports	12.1	13.8	13.3	15.4	12.5	14.5	15.6	17.2
Maritime	0.6	0.4	0.5	0.6	0.6	0.5	0.5	0.5
Interior	19.8	17.1	19.4	20.0	22.6	23.2	21.8	22.6
Extraordinary	1.2	3.2	2.5	3.6	3.2	1.9	2.8	3.2
Special								
Total A millions	38,634	49,156	49,747	46,920	43,807	50,052	52,489	48,620
Total B millions	38,660	50,243	50,065	48,002	44,618	50,138	52,873	48,620

Table 10-6 (Continued)

Source:	1864	1865	1866	1867	1868	1869	1870	1871
Imports	55.5	59.4	55.7	56.6	49.7	51.0	55.0	54.2
Exports	16.4	16.6	18.3	16.2	21.3	20.9	18.7	15.3
Maritime	0.4	0.4	0.4	0.4	0.4	0.4	0.5	0.5
Interior	20.9	19.5	19.0	20.7	23.8	21.8	23.4	23.9
Extraordinary	6.7	4.0	6.5	6.1	4.8	5.8	2.4	6.1
Special								
Total A millions	54,801	56,996	63,333	64,777	71,201	87,543	94,847	97,737
Total B millions	55,458	58,078	60,001	66,487	72,116	88,923	95,206	97,737

Source:	1872	1873	1874	1875	1876	1877	1878	1879
Imports	55.7	54.2	53.9	52.1	52.9	53.4	51.3	50.9
Exports	16.4	17.4	16.6	17.6	15.7	16.1	14.8	15.6
Maritime	0.5	0.5	0.6	0.3	0.2	0.1	0.1	0.1
Interior	21.5	22.9	24.3	25.8	25.6	26.2	25.6	27.3
Extraordinary	4.9	3.6	4.0	3.0	4.2	2.9	7.3	0.9
Special	1.0	1.4	1.2	1.1	1.3	1.2	0.9	5.1
Total A millions	105,136	112,131	105,009	106,490	103,500	101,064	110,746	116,461
Total B millions	105,136	111,131	104,457	106,490	103,500	101,064	110,746	116,461

Table 10-6 (Continued)

Source:	1880	1881	1882	1883	1884	1885	1886	1887	1888	1889
Imports	53.6	51.7	54.7	56.4	57.2	52.9	54.8	55.1	59.2	56.1
Exports	15.4	15.6	14.7	12.7	12.5	13.5	11.6	12.4	9.8	10.8
Maritime	0.2	0.3	0.3	0.3	0.4	0.3	0.3	0.3	0.3	0.3
Interior	28.1	27.7	26.5	27.6	24.8	28.5	27.8	25.0	24.5	24.9
Extraordinary	1.7	3.7	2.7	1.1	3.6	3.2	4.2	3.0	2.5	7.9
Special	1.0	1.0	1.2	1.8	1.6	1.5	1.2	4.2	3.8	
Total A millions	120,762	131,275	131,987	129,698	134,569	124,156	130,309	221,659	145,896	160,840
Total B millions	120,762	131,175	131,987	129,718	134,569	124,156	130,309	221,659	145,869	160,840

Source: Based on data from Liberate de Castro Carreira, op. cit., for 1832-1888. Diretoria do Serviço Estatístico, Finanças do Brasil, for 1889.

Interpretive Note: This series is not consistent with that presented in Anuário Estatístico do Brasil.

Note: Total A equals sum shown in source. Total B shows total of individual components shown in source. Total B = 100.0

Table 10-7

Negroes and Freedmen Imported Into and Living
in Brazil, 1570-1852

Year	Total In Brazil	In Minas Gerais	Imported to Pernambuco from Africa
1570	2- 3,000		
1590	9-10,000		
1600	12-15,000		
1601-1630			75,000
1631-1636			6,000
1637-1645			23,163
1646-1647			2,000
1648-1652			2,000
1717		27,240-33,000	
1723		41,512-50,000	
1735		135,339	
1736		136,865	
1737		135,699	
1738		136,802	
1739		132,075	
1740		130,102	
1741		130,316	
1742		128,972	
1743		129,134	
1744		124,491	
1745		126,690	
1746		124,435	
1747		119,450	
1748		119,279	
1749		117,064	
1776		167,000	
1786		196,498	
1805		211,293	
1808		180,972	
1821		202,135	

Table 10-7 (Continued)

Year	Total Imported	Living in Brazil
1801	9,067	1,600,000 (1798)
1802	7,325	
1803	17,746	
1804	23,338	
1805	20,634	
1806	20,680	
1807	7,879	
1808	-	
1809	15,036	
1810	2,011	
1811	4,414	
1812	15,092	
1813	14,124	
1814	-	
1815	15,543	
1816	13,061	
1817	11,719	
1818	11,050	
1819	19,976	
1820	15,020	
1821	24,134	
1822	27,363	
1823	29,180	1,148,000
1824	32,724	
1825	28,638	
1826	33,999	
1827	29,787	
1828	43,555	
1829	52,600	
1830–1839	429,307	
1840	30,000	
1841	16,000	
1842	17,435	
1843	19,095	
1844	22,849	

228

Table 10-7 (Continued)

Year	Total Imported	Living in Brazil
1845	19,453	
1846	50,324	
1847	56,172	
1848	60,000	
1849	54,000	
1850	23,000	2,500,000
1851	3,287	
1852	700	

Sources: Mauricio Goulart, Escrivadão Africana No Brasil, pp. 99, 100, 106, 112, 113, 122, 139, 140-44, 169, 265-272; Clarence Haring, Empire in Brazil, p. 92.

Table 10-8

The Second Banco do Brasil
(millions of reis)

Year	Paid Up Capital	Reserve Fund	Liquid Assets	Redemption of Treasury Notes By The Banco do Brasil
1854	11,000	49	8,179	-
1855	15,900	149	9,879	-
1856	19,752	257	10,762	-
1857	22,560	474	10,850	1,000
1858	22,560	740	11,380	2,016
1859	22,560	825	7,170	2,012
1860	22,560	911	9,485	964
1861	22,560	1,025	8,535	3,102
1862	26,400	1,232	7,308	2,490
1863	29,752	1,552	12,328	1,785
1864	33,000	1,888	10,299	2,730
1865	33,000	3,211	14,234	1,500
1866	33,000	4,703	16,525	1,003
				18,602

Source: Dorival Teixeira Vieira, "A Evolucão do Sistema Monetário Brasileiro," Revista de Administração, Año 1, #2 (Junho de 1947).

Table 10-9

Independent Banks, 1840–1866
(in millions of reis)

Year (1)	Paid-up Capital (2)	Reserve Fund (3)	Notes in Circulation (4)	Authorized Limit on Circulation (5)	Potential Circulation Increase (6)	(4)÷(5) (7)	(2)÷(4) (8)
1840	2,073	13	54	1,036	− 982	0.1	38.0
1841	2,073	21	296	1,036	− 740	0.3	7.0
1842	2,500	33	325	1,250	− 924	0.3	7.7
1843	2,500	31	233	1,250	− 1,016	0.2	10.7
1844	2,500	44	355	1,250	− 895	0.3	7.0
1845	3,500	62	643	1,750	− 1,107	0.4	5.4
1846	4,126	95	949	2,063	− 1,113	0.5	4.3
1847	4,750	128	1,497	2,375	− 878	0.6	3.2
1848	4,750	163	1,515	2,375	− 860	0.6	3.1
1849	4,850	202	1,147	2,425	− 1,278	0.5	4.2
1850	4,870	239	1,147	2,435	− 1,288	0.5	4.2
1851	9,390	883	1,313	4,695	− 3,382	0.3	7.2
1852	13,837	845	3,631	6,918	− 3,287	0.5	3.8
1853	16,524	948	5,569	8,262	− 2,693	0.7	3.0
1854	23,080	342	5,492	11,540	− 6,048	0.5	4.2
1855	4,380	228	2,175	2,190	− 15	1.0	2.0
1856	2,800	214	1,081	1,400	− 319	0.8	2.6
1857	800	−	41	400	− 359	0.1	19.7
1858	10,530	30	9,068	10,529	− 1,462	0.9	1.2
1859	21,860	1,123	14,231	21,870	− 7,639	0.7	1.5
1860	22,538	1,112	13,039	22,538	− 9,499	0.6	1.7

Table 10-9 (Continued)

Year (1)	Paid-up Capital (2)	Reserve Fund (3)	Notes in Circulation (4)	Authorized Limit on Circulation (5)	Potential Circulation Increase (6)	(4)÷(5) (7)	(2)÷(4) (8)
1861	22,538	1,164	13,514	22,538	- 9,024	0.6	1.7
1862	23,430	1,218	12,383	23,430	-11,047	0.5	1.9
1863	14,750	1,151	4,116	14,750	-10,634	0.3	3.6
1864	14,770	1,171	4,011	14,770	-10,759	0.3	3.7
1865	14,000	1,000	2,854	14,000	-11,146	0.2	4.9
1866	14,000	1,000	2,480	14,000	-11,520	0.2	5.6

Source: Dorival Teixeira Vieira, op. cit., p. 297.

Table 10-10

United Kingdom Investment in Brazil, 1865-1913
(thousands of pounds sterling)

	1865	1875	1885	1895	1905	1913
Government loans	13,036 (64%)	20,355 (66%)	23,242 (49%)	52,410 (56%)	83,319 (68%)	119,608 (47%)
Railways	5,375 (27%)	6,362 (21%)	17,092 (36%)	33,114 (36%)	24,022 (20%)	59,128 (23%)
Public utilities	828 (4%)	2,755 (9%)	3,061 (6%)	3,324 (4%)	6,628 (5%)	55,029 (22%)
Financial	–	–	–	–	1,716 (1%)	9,190 (4%)
Raw materials	589 (3%)	423 (1%)	856 (2%)	1,004 (1%)	3,661 (3%)	3,733 (1%)
Industrial & Misc.	457 (2%)	1,032 (3%)	3,389 (7%)	3,136 (3%)	3,557 (3%)	8,124 (3%)
Total	₤20,284 (100%)	₤30,928 (100%)	₤47,641 (100%)	₤92,988 (100%)	₤122,903 (100%)	₤254,812 (100%)

Source: Irving Stone, The Composition and Distribution of British Investment in Latin America,
p. 153B.

Table 10-11

Length of Brazilian Railroads in Kilometers, 1854-1915

(lines in operation)

Year	Km	Year	Km	Year	Km	Year	Km
1854	15	1870	745	1890	9,973	1910	21,326
1855	15	1871	869	1891	10,590	1911	22,287
1856	16	1872	932	1892	11,316	1912	23,491
1857	16	1873	1,129	1893	11,485	1913	24,614
1858	109	1874	1,284	1894	12,260	1914	26,062
1859	109	1875	1,801	1895	12,967	1915	26,647
		1876	2,122	1896	13,568		
1860	223	1877	2,388	1897	14,015		
1861	251	1878	2,709	1898	14,664		
1862	359	1879	2,911	1899	14,916		
1863	428						
1864	474	1880	3,398	1900	15,316		
1865	498	1881	3,946	1901	15,506		
1866	513	1882	4,464	1902	15,680		
1867	598	1883	5,354	1903	16,010		
1868	718	1884	6,302	1904	16,305		
1869	737	1885	6,930	1905	16,781		
		1886	7,586	1906	17,242		
		1887	8,400	1907	17,613		
		1888	9,321	1908	18,633		
		1889	9,583	1909	19,241		

Source: Anuário Estatístico do Brasil, 1937, p. 850.

Table 10-12

Percentage Distribution of Government Expenditure, 1832-1889

Destination	1832	1833	1834	1835	1836	1837	1838	1839	1840	1841
Ministries:										
Empire	10.6	16.3	7.3	8.6	8.1	8.8	7.7	7.2	7.1	10.3
Justice	6.4	6.5	3.2	4.1	4.5	4.5	3.8	4.3	3.6	4.1
Foreign Affairs	1.4	15.5	1.2	1.8	1.6	1.7	1.9	1.8	1.6	1.6
Navy	13.6	19.5	15.8	14.6	14.4	14.5	14.2	15.0	20.2	14.6
Army	27.5	16.3	25.3	21.9	18.9	20.3	28.2	29.2	35.4	34.0
Treasury	40.6	25.9	47.1	49.1	52.4	50.2	44.2	42.1	32.1	35.4
Total A millions	12,798	15,809	11,478	12,908	14,340	13,980	18,920	18,131	24,969	22,772
Total B millions	12,798	15,809	11,478	12,908	14,340	13,980	18,920	18,131	24,969	22,772

	1842	1843	1844	1845	1846	1847	1848	1849	1850	1851
Empire	9.0	10.2	8.5	11.4	13.1	13.7	13.7	12.7	15.3	12.3
Justice	3.8	4.3	5.4	5.2	5.8	6.2	6.2	6.1	6.3	6.1
Foreign Affairs	1.6	2.4	3.9	2.3	1.9	1.8	1.8	1.8	1.3	3.2
Navy	12.6	13.7	11.6	13.1	14.0	15.7	14.9	13.8	14.6	15.5
Army	36.3	32.3	30.4	28.9	26.4	24.3	23.7	27.8	25.3	27.4
Treasury	36.7	37.0	40.2	39.1	38.8	38.3	39.6	27.7	37.1	35.6
Total A millions	27,483	29,113	25,947	25,635	24,464	25,222	25,373	28,289	28,950	26,276
Total B millions	27,483	29,113	25,947	25,635	24,464	25,222	25,373	28,289	28,950	33,225

Table 10-12 (Continued)

Destination	1852	1853	1854	1855	1856	1857	1858	1859	1860	1861
Ministries:										
Empire	7.9	13.9	13.2	15.5	19.9	16.5	16.1	19.5	19.1	15.4
Justice	4.5	6.9	6.8	7.4	8.3	8.2	7.2	8.3	9.0	7.7
Foreign Affairs	7.1	2.6	3.8	2.9	1.7	1.6	3.1	1.7	1.6	1.6
Navy	11.1	14.1	14.6	15.5	18.1	13.6	20.3	18.1	17.7	15.1
Army	36.7	25.9	25.2	27.5	23.8	26.4	27.5	23.8	24.6	22.0
Treasury	32.9	36.6	36.3	31.1	28.5	33.7	25.9	28.5	28.1	30.9
Agriculture										7.4
Total A millions	42,755	31,654	36,234	38,740	40,243	40,374	51,756	52,719	52,606	52,358
Total B millions	42,755	31,654	36,234	38,680	40,243	40,374	51,756	52,719	52,606	52,358

Destination	1862	1863	1864	1865	1866	1867	1868	1869	1870	1871
Empire	8.2	6.8	7.7	6.1	3.6	3.6	2.7	2.7	3.2	4.7
Justice	5.4	5.1	5.0	3.6	2.5	2.6	1.9	1.9	2.0	3.6
Foreign Affiars	1.5	2.9	1.4	4.9	2.6	1.1	1.3	0.5	0.5	1.1
Navy	14.1	13.9	15.5	16.0	16.4	14.5	14.4	12.0	12.0	12.8
Army	21.4	20.8	21.9	32.8	49.6	45.1	45.2	41.9	42.3	19.2
Treasury	35.0	37.3	34.7	24.1	18.4	23.4	27.1	32.4	30.2	40.2
Agriculture	14.3	13.3	13.7	12.6	7.0	9.5	7.5	8.5	9.7	18.3
Total A millions	53,050	57,000	56,494	83,346	121,856	120,890	165,985	150,895	141,594	100,074
Total B millions	53,050	57,000	56,494	83,346	121,856	120,890	165,985	150,895	141,594	100,074

Table 10-12 (Continued)

Destination	1872	1873	1874	1875	1876	1877	1878	1879	1880	1881
Ministries:										
Empire	4.9	5.9	6.1	6.6	6.3	8.1	14.7	26.9	9.8	6.5
Justice	3.7	3.3	4.0	4.1	4.6	4.4	4.3	3.6	4.4	4.3
Foreign Affairs	0.8	0.9	1.0	1.1	0.9	0.8	0.6	0.5	0.5	0.6
Navy	14.9	14.7	16.4	16.4	14.5	13.1	8.3	5.2	6.6	9.5
Army	15.3	19.8	16.0	15.6	15.6	13.2	10.5	8.0	9.5	9.8
Treasury	38.9	34.6	35.0	35.0	35.0	35.8	33.7	29.6	40.9	43.8
Agriculture	21.5	20.8	21.5	21.1	23.1	24.6	27.8	26.2	27.8	26.6
Total A millions	101,581	121,874	121,481	125,855	126,780	135,801	151,493	181,469	150,134	138,583
Total B millions	101,581	121,874	121,481	125,855	126,780	135,801	151,493	181,469	150,134	138,673

Destination	1882	1883	1884	1885	1886	1887*	1888	1889
Ministries:								
Empire	6.4	6.2	6.0	6.5	6.3	6.1	6.7	14.4
Justice	4.6	4.2	4.3	4.1	4.3	4.2	4.2	3.7
Foreign Affairs	0.7	0.5	0.5	0.5	0.5	0.6	0.6	0.6
Navy	9.2	10.8	9.9	7.3	7.5	7.0	7.8	6.3
Army	11.2	9.8	10.1	9.6	9.9	9.8	9.9	9.8
Treasury	41.2	40.2	38.2	40.3	43.4	42.5	43.9	39.2
Agriculture	26.8	28.3	31.0	31.6	28.1	29.8	26.8	26.0
Total A millions	139,471	153,058	154,257	158,496	153,623	228,186	147,451	186,165
Total B millions	139,471	153,058	154,257	158,496	153,623	228,186	@	@

Table 10-12 (Continued)

Source: Unless otherwise shown, all numbers are from Liberate de Castro Carreira, op. cit.

Interpretive Note: This series is not consistent with that presented in Anuário Estatístico do Brasil.

@Figures for 1888 and 1889 are from Directoria do Servico de Estatística, Finanças do Brasil.

*Previous years fiscal years as shown earlier; 1886/87 also includes the second half of 1887 to place accounts on chronological year. Total A equals sum shown in source. Total B shows total of individual components shown in source. Total B = 100.0.

Table 10-13

Distribution of Expenditure by Brazilian State Governments,
1830/1, 1851/2, 1870/1, 1890/1

Destination	1830/1	1851/2	1870/1	1890/1
Treasury	28.0	22.8	43.4	30.8
Interior	10.3	9.2	6.5	5.9
Justice	3.7	5.2	4.8	4.6
Agriculture	-	-	3.0	26.9
Foreign Relations	4.2	6.2	.7	.3
Navy	18.3	13.7	4.0	7.4
War	35.5	42.8	37.7	15.7
Education	-	-	-	8.3

Source: Diretoria do Servico Estatístico, Finanças do Brasil.

Table 11-1

Incorporation of Firms Through October 1890
(millions of reis)

Category	Capital		
	a	b	c
Banks	118,000	324,000	385,550
Urban transport	24,630	-	-
Sugar works	7,700	1,500	14,250
Railroads	138,921	53,540	316,100
Navigation	26,573	-	29,100
Insurance	52,500	-	2,600
Other manufactures	33,720	3,000	47,540
Agriculture	-	10,500	94,500
Others	8,335	10,070	279,747
Total	410,879	402,610	1,169,387

Source: Report of Finance Minister (1891), cited in Joâo
Pandia Calogeras, La Politique Monetaire du Brésil, p. 233.

[a] Up to May 1888.

[b] May 1888–November 15, 1889.

[c] November 1889–October 1890.

Table 11-2

Percentage Distribution of Brazilian Government Revenue, 1890-1914

Year	Imports	Consumption	Maritime	Exports	Additional	Interior	Extraordinary	Other
1890	51.5	–	0.3	10.2	–	26.8	10.8	0.6
1891	46.4	–	0.3	7.3	–	28.9	17.2	0.6
1892	48.6	0.1	0.3	0.3	23.5	23.6	5.0	0.8
1893	50.8	0.3	0.2	0.1	25.3	17.5	5.8	0.8
1894	51.1	0.3	0.3	0.1	24.9	20.5	2.9	–
1895	51.7	0.3	0.2	0.1	24.9	18.6	4.2	–
1896	76.0	0.5	0.2	–	0.1	18.5	4.8	–
1897	74.4	0.7	0.2	0.1	0.1	19.8	4.8	–
1898	68.0	4.0	0.1	–	0.1	22.1	5.8	–
1899	62.3	7.9	0.1	–	0.1	22.9	6.7	–

Table 11-2 (Continued)

Year	Imports	Consumption	Circulation	Public Services	Earmarked	Income	Other
1900	53.6	11.9	6.2	15.1	5.4	2.1	5.7
1901	53.2	10.4	6.3	15.9	7.7	2.1	4.4
1902	54.0	9.8	5.2	13.6	12.2	2.0	3.2
1903	45.6	8.5	3.9	12.0	25.6	1.6	2.8
1904	44.7	8.0	3.8	11.9	26.1	1.5	4.0
1905	55.9	8.8	4.5	11.6	12.3	1.8	5.1
1906	57.5	10.1	4.1	11.4	11.7	1.8	3.4
1907	53.6	8.9	3.6	9.6	19.3	1.5	3.5
1908	53.7	10.1	4.5	11.1	13.2	1.8	5.6
1909	51.8	10.2	4.5	11.6	14.9	1.1	5.9
1910	55.0	10.4	4.1	9.4	14.7	1.0	5.4
1911	56.4	10.6	4.5	9.7	13.2	1.1	4.5
1912	56.6	10.2	4.5	10.0	13.6	1.2	3.9
1913	52.6	10.0	4.4	11.2	13.4	1.2	9.2
1914	46.1	12.3	5.7	15.7	11.5	1.2	6.9

Table 11-2 (Continued)

Source: Directoria Geral de Estatística, Estatística das Finanças do Brasil, 1926, pp. 6, 7. Rates of conversion from gold to paper milreis for consolidation of accounts used are 1900-1909, 1$800; 1910-1912, 1$687; 1913, 1$692; 1914, 1$842.

Note: The reconciliation of various systems of categorizing the Brazilian tax system was carried out as follows: before 1911, "Interior" is shown, with various subheadings, in the records. From 1911, some - but not all - of the components of "Interior" are listed as separate categories. These are: income tax, circulation tax, lotteries tax, revenue from state property, and revenue from state industries and services. The tax on consumption of water is included in "Interior" before 1910, but in income taxes from 1911 to 1915.

Table 11-3

Percentage Distribution of Expenditures of the Republic, By Ministry

Year	Treasury	Justice	Foreign Relations	Education and Public Health	Agriculture	War	Navy
1890	30.6	9.5[a]	0.7	5.4	31.9[b]	14.3	7.5
1891	28.8	8.9	0.7	6.3	33.2	14.3	7.8
1892	34.9	7.7	0.6	5.6[c]	30.8	9.0	7.7
1893	37.6	5.7	0.6		28.2	18.2	9.7
1894	31.3	5.9	0.5		24.0	31.9	6.5
1895	30.5	6.7	1.0	Roads	29.7	23.3	8.8
1896	34.4	6.1	1.6	and	32.2	15.9	9.8
1897	45.4	5.8	0.5	Public	21.9	16.9	9.5
1898	71.1	3.4	0.4	Works*	12.8	7.5	4.8
1899	42.0	7.3	0.5		25.4	16.2	8.6
1900	55.8	5.3	0.6	21.2		10.7	6.4
1901	46.7	7.0	0.8	24.5		13.4	7.6
1902	42.6	8.6	0.9	24.3		15.4	8.2
1903	48.1	7.4	0.9	21.2		14.0	8.4
1904	55.8	7.7	0.8	17.6		11.6	6.5
1905	46.9	9.3	1.1	21.3		13.9	7.5

Table 11-3 (Continued)

Year	Treasury	Justice	Foreign Relations	Roads and Public Works	Agriculture	War	Navy
1906	42.4	9.7	1.8	21.8		12.3	12.0
1907	43.8	9.4	1.0	23.5		11.1	11.2
1908	36.4	10.4	1.1	26.8		13.8	11.5
1909	36.2	10.1	1.1	25.2	1.7	14.9	10.8
1910	39.5	7.8	0.9	27.8	3.4	11.1	9.7
1911	36.0	7.4	0.9	28.9	4.2	13.2	9.4
1912	30.5	7.2	0.9	35.1	4.8	12.2	9.3
1913	37.0	7.1	2.3	30.5	4.7	10.4	8.0
1914	41.1	6.9	1.0	30.0	2.4	11.0	7.6

Source: Anuário Estatístico do Brasil, 1939-1940, p. 1,412.

[a]Imperio became Interior, combined with Justice appropriation.

[b]Includes agriculture, commerce, public works, roads, and labor until 1900.

[c]Includes postal and telegraph services. After 1892 education was paid for by the states.

*Roads and Public Works took over most of the agriculture functions beginning in 1900.

Table 11-4

Brazilian Railroads, 1889-1914

Government	Ownership in Percent		Operation in Percent	
	1889	1914	1889	1914
Federal	34	53		18
State		8	34	2
Private	66	39	66	80
Total	100	100	100	100

Source: Julian Smith Duncan, Public and Private Operation of Railways in Brazil, p. 66.

Table 11-5

Railroad Freight Charges and Tax Payments as a Percent of Value of Product

Commodity	Average Distance (km.)	Percent of Value of Product		
		Freight Charge	Export Tax	Commission, Insurance, Shipping
Sugar	88	2.40	10.80	5.10
Alcohol	88	4.70	7.98	4.76
Cotton	168	3.40	12.00	7.65
Hides	133	2.50	19.33	3.08

Source: Ademar Benévolo, Introdução á História Ferroviária do Brasil, p. 530.

Table 11-6

Government Real Income, Expenditure, Balance,
1823-1914
(millions of reis)

Year	Receipts	Expenditure	Balance
1823[a]	3,802	4,702	− 900
1824	6,704	10,695	− 3,991
1825	4,872	8,625	− 3,753
1826	3,305	7,113	− 3,808
1827	4,606	7,887	− 3,281
1828	3,816	5,639	− 1,823
1829	4,842	6,816	− 1,975
1830	8,861	9,762	− 902
1831	13,708	16,159	− 2,450
1832	9,460	9,225	+ 236
1832[b]	11,796	11,502	+ 294
1833	15,825	13,992	+ 1,833
1834	12,509	11,512	+ 997
1835	15,250	13,282	+ 1,967
1836	14,276	14,483	− 207
1837	11,234	10,848	+ 286
1838	9,339	13,944	− 4,605
1839	12,426	15,049	− 2,623
1840	12,982	20,325	− 7,343
1841	12,967	18,104	− 5,136
1842	11,489	19,348	− 7,859
1840[c]	15,948	24,969	− 9,021
1841	15,936	22,248	− 6,312
1842	14,116	23,773	− 9,657
1843	15,568	24,236	− 8,697
1844	17,337	21,069	− 3,732
1845	20,340	21,021	− 681
1846	22,767	21,259	+ 1,508
1847	24,948	24,092	+ 856
1848	19,934	21,126	− 1,192
1849	21,820	23,593	− 1,773
1850	26,141	26,837	− 695
1851	30,702	31,198	− 496

Table 11-6 (Continued)

Year	Receipts	Expenditure	Balance
1852	33,376	37,838	− 4,462
1853	35,016	29,090	+ 5,927
1854	30,754	32,284	− 1,531
1855	31,991	34,440	− 2,449
1856	34,346	35,776	− 1,430
1857	42,225	34,681	+ 7,544
1858	40,992	42,647	− 1,655
1859	37,911	42,597	− 4,686
1860	36,447	43,768	− 7,321
1861	41,243	43,143	− 1,900
1862	44,563	45,039	− 476
1863	42,493	50,103	− 7,610
1864	47,293	48,754	− 1,461
1865	45,939	67,176	− 21,238
1866	45,765	95,291	− 49,526
1867	46,834	87,403	− 40,570
1868	39,018	90,960	− 51,942
1869	53,139	91,593	− 38,455
1870	67,436	100,673	− 33,237
1871	74,311	77,557	− 3,246
1872	82,484	81,874	+ 609
1873	93,110	102,496	− 9,386
1874	85,304	100,951	− 15,647
1875	91,933	110,501	− 18,568
1876	82,287	103,579	− 21,293
1877	78,384	107,554	− 29,170
1878	80,824	112,104	− 31,281
1879	77,032	125,032	− 48,001
1880	85,840	107,095	− 21,205
1881	90,625	97,840	− 7,215
1882	89,701	95,259	− 6,157
1883	90,140	106,306	− 16,166
1884	88,440	102,889	− 14,450
1885	73,184	95,098	− 21,913
1886	76,510	92,635	− 16,124
1887	158,166	164,154	− 5,988
1888	122,691	120,025	+ 2,666
1889	137,056	158,613	− 21,577
1890	142,144	160,630	− 18,486

Table 11-6 (Continued)

Year	Receipts	Expenditure	Balance
1891	110,123	106,105	+ 4,018
1892	88,312	108,361	− 20,049
1893	97,184	112,436	− 15,252
1890[d]	195,253	220,646	− 25,393
1891	151,104	145,591	+ 5,513
1892	121,315	148,857	− 27,542
1893	133,533	154,524	− 20,961
1894	118,480	166,620	− 48,139
1895	135,412	151,697	− 16,285
1896	138,831	147,937	− 9,106
1897	137,967	129,733	− 25,966
1898	103,049	212,460	−109,411
1899	105,555	97,174	+ 8,381
1900	101,304	142,640	− 41,336
1901	151,647	166,589	− 14,942
1902	181,190	156,899	+ 24,291
1903	219,733	192,122	+ 27,611
1904	237,767	248,881	− 11,114
1905	280,316	262,033	+ 18,284
1906	306,496	625,360	+ 5,871
1907	362,377	353,015	+ 9,362
1908	293,437	399,824	− 46,386
1909	299,182	373,672	− 45,480
1910	386,987	443,958	− 70,286
1911	398,429	482,112	− 83,683
1912	436,312	559,571	−123,260
1913	462,654	539,402	− 76,748
1914	274,691	497,589	−222,898

Source: Calculated from data in Anuário Estatístico do Brasil, 1956, p. 541.

[a]1821 = 100.

[b]1832 = 100.

[c]1840 = 100.

[d]1890 = 100.

BIBLIOGRAPHY[*]

Alden, Dauril, "Manoel Luis Vieira: An Entrepreneur in Rio de Janeiro During Brazil's Eighteenth Century Agricultural Renaissance," Hispanic American Historical Review, XXXIX, #4 (November, 1959).

------, Royal Government in Colonial Brazil (Berkeley: University of California Press, 1968).

Antonil, André João (pen name for Andreoni), Cultura e Opuléncia do Brasil (Bahia: Libraria Progresso Editora, 1955).

Anuário Estatístico do Brasil, 1936-1966.

Archivo Trece (Impresora Pedantesca, México, no date).

Azevedo, João Lucio, Épocas do Portugal Económica (Lisbon, 1929).

Barbosa, Ruy, Finanças e Politica da República (Capital Federal, 1892).

------, Os bancos emissores--o projecto oficial (January 1892).

------, Relatório do Ministro da Fazenda, em janeiro de 1891. (Obras completas de rui barbosa, vol. XVIII, Tomo III).

Bastos, Humberto, O Pensamiento Industrial no Brasil (Saõ Paulo: Livraria Martins Editora, 1952).

------, Ruy Barbosa, Ministro da Independência Economica do Brasil (Casa de Rui Barbosa, 1949).

Bello, José Maria, A History of Modern Brazil 1889-1964 (Stanford, Calif.: Stanford University Press, 1966).

Benévolo, Ademar, Introdução á História Ferroviária do Brasil (Recife: Edicões Folha da Manha, 1953).

Boxer, C. R., Four Centuries of Portuguese Expansion, 1415-1825. (Johannesburg, Witwatersrand University Press, 1965).

------, The Dutch in Brazil (Oxford: 1957).

------*This is a bibliography of works cited in this book. A more extensive, annotated bibliography on the economic history of Latin America, compiled by several scholars, will be published by the Social Science Research Council.

------, The Golden Age of Brazil, 1695-1750 (Berkeley: University of California Press, 1962).

------, A Great Luso-Brazilian Figure. Padre António Vieira, S. J., 1608-1697 (London: The Hispanic and Luso Brazilian Councils, 1957).

------, Race Relations in the Portuguese Colonial Empire, 1415-1825 (Oxford, 1963).

Braga, Cincinato, Questões Econômico-Financeiras (São Paulo: Duprat, 1915).

Buarque de Holanda, Sérgio, História geral da civilização brasileira (São Paulo, 1960).

Buesco, Mircea, and Vicente Tapajos, História do Desenvolvimento Econômico do Brasil (Edições "A Casa do Livro Ltda"; no date, but probably 1966).

Bulhões, Augusto de, Ministros da Fazenda do Brasil, 1808-1954 (Rio de Janeiro, 1955).

Burns, E. Bradford, A Documentary History of Brazil (New York: Knopf, 1966).

Canabrava, A. P., O Comercio Português no Rio da Prata, 1580-1640 (São Paulo, 1944).

Castro Carreira, Liberate de, História Financeira e Orçamentária do Imperio do Brasil desde a sua fundação (Rio, 1889).

Clough, Shepard, and Charles W. Cole, An Economic History of Europe (Boston: Heath, 1941).

Cohen, Paula, "What, If Not the Jesuits?", unpublished ms., 1965.

Conty, François, L'Independence Financière des Etats Fédérés du Brésil. (Thése Pour le Doctorat) (Paris: Marcel Giard, 1926).

Cruz Costa, João, A History of Ideas in Brazil, trans. Suzette Macedo (Berkeley: University of California Press, 1964).

Dean, Warren, The Industrialization of São Paulo, 1880-1945 (Austin: University of Texas Press, 1969).

Deerr, Noel, The History of Sugar (London: Chapman and Hall, Ltd., 1949).

Diégues Júnior, Manuel, Imigração, Urbanização e Industrialização (Rio de Janeiro: Instituto Nacional de Estudos Pedagogicos, Ministerio de Educacão e Cultura, 1964).

Directoria Geral de Estatística, Balança Geral, 1890-1900.

------, Estatística das Finanças do Brasil, 1926.

Duncan, Julian Smith, Public and Private Operation of Railways in Brazil (New York: Columbia University Press, 1932).

Ferreira Lima, Formação Industrial do Brasil, Período Colonial (Rio de Janeiro: Editôra Fundo de Cultura, 1961).

Finaças do Brasil.

Fite, G. C ., and J. Reese, An Economic History of the United States, end ed. (Boston: Houghton Mifflin, 1959).

Freyre, Gilberto, The Masters and the Slaves (New York: Knopf, 1964).

Furtado, Celso, The Economic Growth of Brazil (Berkeley: University of California Press, 1963).

Goulart, Mauricio, Escravidão Africana No Brasil (São Paulo, 1949).

Haring, Clarence, Empire in Brazil (Cambridge, Mass., 1958).

Herring, Hubert, A History of Latin America from the Beginnings to the Present (New York: Knopf, 1961).

Humphreys, R. A., and John Lynch, The Origins of the Latin American Revolutions, 1808-1826 (New York: Knopf, 1966).

Kirkland, Edward C., A History of American Economic Life (New York: Appleton-Century-Crofts, 1951).

Leite, Serafim, S.J., Suma Histórica da Companhia de Jésus no Brasil (Assistencia de Portugal) 1549-1760 (Lisboa: Junta de Investigacões do Ultramar, 1965).

Livermore, H. V., A New History of Portugal (Cambridge: Cambridge University Press, 1966).

Manchester, Alan K., British Preeminence in Brazil: Its Rise and Decline (New York: Octagon Books, 1964).

Marchant, Alexander, From Barter to Slavery (Baltimore: Johns Hopkins University Press, Studies in Historical and Political Science, #1, 1942).

Martins, Ivan Pedro de, Introdução à Economia Brasileira (Rio de Janeiro: Livraria José Olympio Editôra, 1961).

Mawe, John, Travels in the Interior of Brazil (London, 1821).

Monteiro, Fernando, O Banco do Brasil, Breve Noticia Histórica (Rio de Janeiro: Banco do Brasil, Museu e arquivo histórico, 1967).

Morse, Richard M., ed., The Bandeirantes (New York: Knopf, 1965).

Nascimento Brito, José do, Economia e Finanças do Brasil (Rio de Janeiro, 1945).

Onody, Oliver, A Inflacão Brasileira.

Pandía Calogeras, João, A History of Brazil, trans. and ed. Percy Alvin Martin (Chapel Hill: University of North Carolina Press, 1956).

------, Le Politique Monetaire du Brésil (Rio de Janeiro, 1910).

Pinto de Aguiar, Manoel, Ensaios de História e economía, 1º volume (Libraria Progresso Editora, 1960).

Pires do Rio, J. A Moeda Brasileira e seu perene caráter fiduciário (Livraria José Olympio Editora. No date).

Poppino, Rollie E., Brazil, The Land and People (New York: Oxford University Press, 1968).

Prado Junior, Caio, The Colonial Background of Modern Brazil (Berkeley: University of California Press, 1967).

------, Historia económica do Brasil (Editora Brasilense, 1967).

Rodrigues, José Honório, Brazil and Africa (Berkeley: University of California Press, 1965).

------, Brasil. Período Colonial (México, 1953).

Simonsen, Roberto, Brazil's Industrial Evolution (São Paulo, 1939).

------, Ensaios Sociais, Politicas e Econômicas (Edição da Federação das Indústrias do Estado de São Paulo, Rio de Janeiro, 1943).

------, História Econômica do Brasil, 1500-1820 (São Paulo: Companhia Editora Nacional, 1967).

Stein, Stanley, The Brazilian Cotton Manufacture (Cambridge: Harvard University Press, 1957).

------, Vassouras, A Brazilian Coffee County, 1850-1900 (Cambridge: Harvard University Press, 1957).

Stone, Irving, The Composition and Distribution of British Investment in Latin America (Ph.D. Thesis, Unpublished, Columbia, 1962).

Sturz, J. J., A Review, Financial, Statistical, and Commercial of the Empire of Brazil and Its Resources: Together With a Suggestion of the Expediency and Mode of Admitting Brazilian and Other Foreign Sugars into Great Britain for Refining and Exportation (London, 1837).

Tannenbaum, Frank, Slave and Citizen: The Negro in the Americas (New York: Knopf, 1947).

Taunay, Affonso de E., Pequena História do Café no Brasil, 1727-1937 (Rio de Janeiro, 1945).

Teixeira Vieira, Dorival, "A Evolução do Sistema Monetário Brasileiro," Revista de Administração, Año 1, #2 (Junho de 1947).

United States Historical Statistics (Washington, D.C., 1960).

Viana, Victor, O Banco do Brasil (Rio de Janeiro, 1926).

Vieira de Mello e Teixeira Brandão, A Nova Política Ferroviária do Brasil (Rio de Janeiro: Grafica Olimpica, 1941).

Vilela Luz, Nícia, A Luta Pela Industrialização do Brasil (São Paulo: Difusão Europeía do Livro, 1961).

Wells, James W., Exploring and Travelling Three Thousand Miles Through Brazil. 2 vols. (London, 1886).

Index